The Politics of Intersectionality

The Politics of Intersectionality series u̲ᵤ̲.̲.̲.̲ insights of intersectionality theory from a vast variety of disciplinary perspectives. As a globally utilized analytical framework for understanding issues of social justice, Leslie McCall, Mary Hawkesworth, Michelle Berger, and others argue that intersectionality is arguably the most important theoretical contribution of women's and gender studies to date. Indeed, the imprint of intersectional analysis can be easily found on innovations in equality legislation, human rights, and development discourses.

The history of what is now called "intersectional thinking" is long. In fact, prior to its mainstreaming, intersectionality analysis was carried for many years mainly by black and other racialized women who, from their situated gaze, perceived as absurd, not just misleading, any attempt by feminists and others to homogenize women's situation, particularly in conceptualizing such situations as analogous to that of racialized others. As Brah and Phoenix point out, many black feminists fulfilled significant roles in the development of intersectional analysis, such as the Combahee River Collective, the black lesbian feminist organization from Boston, which pointed out the need of developing an integrated analysis and practice based upon the fact that major systems of oppression interlock rather than operate separately. However, the term "intersectionality" itself emerged nominally from the field of critical legal studies, where critical race feminist Kimberle Williams Crenshaw wrote two pathbreaking articles, "Demarginalizing the Intersection of Race and Sex: A Critique of Antidiscrimination Doctrine, Feminist Theory and Antiracist Politics" and "Mapping the Margins: Intersectionality, Identity Politics, and Violence Against Women of Color." At nearly the same time, social theorist Patricia Hill Collins was preparing her landmark work, "Black Feminist Thought: Knowledge, Consciousness and the Politics of Empowerment," which characterized intersections of race, class, and gender as mutually reinforcing sites of power relations.

Both Crenshaw and Collins gave the name "intersectionality" to a far larger and more ethnically diverse trajectory of work, now global in nature, that speaks truth to power sited differentially rather than centralized in a single locus. What could also be called intersectional analysis was in fact developing at roughly the same time among European and postcolonial feminists, including, for example, Anthias & Yuval-Davis (1983; 1992) ; Brah (1996), Essed (1991), Ifekwunigwe (1999), Lutz (1991), Meekosha, and Min-ha (1989).

Indeed, it seems that, in a manner parallel to that which Sandra Harding characterizes the evolution of standpoint theory, intersectionality was an idea whose time had come precisely because of the plethora of authors working independently across the globe making vastly similar sets of claims. Around the world, those interested in a more comprehensive and transformative approach to social justice—whether sociologists, legal scholars, feminist theorists, policy makers, or human rights advocates—have used the language and tenets of intersectionality to more effectively articulate injustice and advocate for positive social change.

The books in this series represent an interrogation of intersectionality at various levels of analysis. They unabashedly foreground the politics of intersectionality in a way that is designed to both honor the legacy of earlier scholarship and activism, and push the boundaries of intersectionality's value to the academy and most importantly to the world. We interpret the series title, The Politics of Intersectionality, in two general ways:

First, we emphasize the politics of intersectionality, broadly conceived; that is to say, we include debates among scholars regarding the proper conceptualization and application of the term "intersectionality" as part and parcel of the series' intellectual project. Is intersectionality a paradigm? Is intersectionality a normative political (specifically feminist) project? Is it a method or epistemological approach? Is it (merely) a concept with limited applicability beyond multiply marginalized populations? Our own idiosyncratic answers to these questions are far less important than the open dialog we seek by including them within the scholarly discourse generated by the series.

What this means pragmatically is that rather than dictatorially denote an extant definition of intersectionality and impose it on every author's manuscript, as series editors our task has been to meaningfully push each author to grapple with their own conceptualization of intersectionality and facilitate their interaction with an ever-growing body of global scholarship, policy, and advocacy work as they render such a conceptualization transparent to readers, reflexive as befits the best feminist work, and committed to rigorous standards of quality no matter the subject, the method, or the conclusions. As editors, we have taken such an active role precisely because grappling with the politics of intersectionality demands our adherence to the normative standards of transparency, reflexivity, and speaking to multiple sites of power for which intersectionality is not only known but also lauded as the gold standard. It is our honor to build this area of scholarship across false boundaries of theory and praxis; artificially distinct academic disciplines; and the semipermeable line between scholarship and activism.

No less importantly, we emphasize politics to mean, well, *politics*—whether everyday senses of justice; so-called formal politics of social movements, campaigns, elections, policy, and government institutions; or personal politics of identity, community, and activism across a broad swath of the world. While this general conceptualization of politics lends itself to the social sciences, we define social sciences in a broad way that again seeks to unite theoretical concerns (whether normative or positive) with interpretive and empirical approaches across an array of topics far too numerous to list in their entirety.

The second way we interpret the series title—simultaneously, as one might expect of intersectionality scholars—is with an emphasis on the word intersectionality. That is, the books in this series do not depend solely on 20-year-old articulations of intersectionality, neither do they adhere to one particular theoretical or methodological approach to study intersectionality; they are steeped in a rich literature of both substantive and analytical depth that in the twenty-first century reaches around the world. This is not your professor's "women of color" or "race-class-gender" series of the late twentieth century. Indeed, an emphasis on up-to-date engagement with the best and brightest global thinking on intersectionality has been the single most exacting standard we have imposed on the editing process. As series editors, we seek to develop manuscripts that aspire to a level of sophistication about intersectionality as a body of research that is in fact worthy of the intellectual, political, and personal risks taken by so many of its earliest interlocutors in voicing and naming this work.

Currently, intersectionality scholarship lacks a meaningful clearinghouse of work that speaks across (again false) boundaries of a particular identity community under study (e.g., Black lesbians, women of color environmental activists), academic disciplines, or the geographical location from which the author writes (e.g., Europe, North America, or Southeast Asia). For this reason, we expect that the bibliographies of the manuscripts will be almost as helpful as the manuscripts themselves, particularly for senior professors who train graduate students and graduate students seeking to immerse themselves broadly and deeply in contemporary approaches to intersectionality. We are less sanguine, however, about the plethora of modifiers that have emerged to somehow modulate intersectionality—whether it be intersectional stigma, intersectional political consciousness, intersectional praxis, post-intersectionality, paradigm intersectionality, or even Crenshaw's original modes of structural and political intersectionality. Our emphasis has been on building the subfield rather than consciously expanding the lexicon of modes and specialities for intersectionality.

Series Editors:

Ange-Marie Hancock, University of Southern California
Nira Yuval-Davis, University of East London

Also in the series:

Solidarity Politics for Millennials
Ange-Marie Hancock

Social Change and Intersectional Activism: The Spirit of Social Movement
Sharon Doetsch-Kidder

Urban Black Women and the Politics of Resistance
Zenzele Isoke

Urban Black Women and the Politics of Resistance

Zenzele Isoke

URBAN BLACK WOMEN AND THE POLITICS OF RESISTANCE
Copyright © Zenzele Isoke, 2013.
Softcover reprint of the hardcover 1st edition 2013 978-0-230-33903-3

First published in 2013 by
PALGRAVE MACMILLAN®
in the United States—a division of St. Martin's Press LLC,
175 Fifth Avenue, New York, NY 10010.

Where this book is distributed in the UK, Europe and the rest of the world,
this is by Palgrave Macmillan, a division of Macmillan Publishers Limited,
registered in England, company number 785998, of Houndmills,
Basingstoke, Hampshire RG21 6XS.

Palgrave Macmillan is the global academic imprint of the above companies
and has companies and representatives throughout the world.

Palgrave® and Macmillan® are registered trademarks in the United States,
the United Kingdom, Europe and other countries.

ISBN 978-1-349-34208-2   ISBN 978-1-137-04538-6 (eBook)

DOI 10.1057/9781137045386

Library of Congress Cataloging-in-Publication Data is available from the
Library of Congress.

A catalogue record of the book is available from the British Library.

Design by Newgen Imaging Systems (P) Ltd., Chennai, India.

First edition: January 2013

10 9 8 7 6 5 4 3 2 1

Transferred to Digital Printing in 2013

I dedicate this book to black people in the inner cities of Saint Louis, Long Beach, Detroit, North Minneapolis, East Saint Paul, and Newark. Your lives, ideas, and contributions to humanity matter. Own that.

CONTENTS

PREFACE

A WORD ABOUT URBAN BLACK WOMEN AND THE POLITICS OF RESISTANCE

In the third book in this series, *Urban Black Women and the Politics of Resistance*, Zenzele Isoke turns our attention to an urban politics of resistance among Black women activists in Newark, New Jersey. In so doing she builds upon one of the central contributions of Kimberle Crenshaw's explication of structural intersectionality: the need for rendering the invisible visible. Isoke's work reveals the political labor of urban Black women that even in the twenty-first century is too often overlooked or subsumed under the charismatic leadership of Black male political elites. For Isoke, coalitions and community alliances are produced episodically as "assemblages" (Puar 2007) of resistance politics. However, Isoke explicitly locates that visibility through deep engagement with the city of Newark, a site the activists characterize as a "beloved city" that is most commonly viewed by outsiders as an archetype of US urban pathology. In this way her book links Black women's resistance politics to broader questions of long-term sustenance of city life.

Isoke lifts up the "life truths" of 29 activists, women she characterizes as "alchemists of resistance." These women, who "take the harshest realities of urban containment and create wellsprings of possibility for positive social action" offer practices that can expand our abilities to contend with intersecting systems of heteropatriarchy, racism, and spatial marginalization through innovative outlets like the "rant fest," an intimate public space for laughter, tears, nurturance, and catharsis. Seeking to expand our notions of politics as activism that may or may not directly involve interactions with local government, Isoke uses interpretive and qualitative methods to examine "the anatomy of two specific community mobilizations in Newark."

The first three books in the series—*Solidarity Politics for Millennials,
Social Change,* and *Intersectional Activism* and now *Urban Black
Women and Political Resistance*—have each explored various aspects
of the United States as a site ripe for intersectional analysis. We look
forward to a more global focus in the next two installments of the
series, turning first toward Europe and then via an anthology with
chapters exploring intersectional politics from a variety of global locations. As always, we welcome submissions and comments on what is
becoming a very successful contribution to intersectional scholarship
and activism.

Acknowledgments

This book is nothing less than the product of a community of people who had faith in my abilities, faith in this project, and the conviction that social justice can be more than just a socially appealing concept. First and foremost, I wish to thank my mother, Vickie M. Dunlap-Jones, my grandparents Vivian and Charlie Roberts, and my great aunties who have always loved me and encouraged me. I also thank my daughters, Folashade and Thandiwe Wilson, for their unfaltering love and patience with Mommy over the course of their young lives. I also thank Dr. Ruth Nicole Brown for her steadfast support and loving sisterhood since the journey to this book began.

I would like to extend a very humble line of gratitude to the people of the city of Newark, New Jersey. Without people like Baye Adofo-Wilson, Anthony Smith, Hashim Shomari, Monique Baptiste, Fayemi Shakur, Susu Stewart, June Dowell, Angela Garretson, Janyce Jackson, and the staff of the Lincoln Park Coast Culture District, it would have been impossible for me to have access to the range of dynamic voices featured in this book. Anthony Smith, especially, thank you for taking my hand and pressing me onward when I wavered. I also extend a note of deep appreciation to the New Jersey Information Room of the Newark Public Library for keeping such meticulous historical records on the intricacies of New Jersey.

I remember you too, Sakia.

I also thank the Department of Gender, Women, and Sexuality Studies and the College of Liberal Arts at the University of Minnesota for their support of this project through course releases, internal grants, and summer support. The Institute for Diversity, Equity, and Advocacy and the Imagine Fund at the University of Minnesota also deserves a note of thanks for their generous funding of this research. My colleagues in the Department of Gender, Women, and Sexuality Studies, African and African American Studies, American Studies, Communication Studies, the Department of Political Science, and Theatre Studies including Jigna Desai, Richa Nagar, Eden Torres,

Dara Strolovitch, Regina Kunzel, Roderick Ferguson, Catherine Squires, Yuichi Onishiro, Walt Jacobs, and Cindy Garcia are appreciated for their warmth, candid, and insightful feedback, and encouragement of many layers of this work over the years. I also commend Brittany Lewis for her stellar summer research assistance. I also extend a note of thanks to the students in my Black Feminist Geographies classes who have made teaching such a joy: Hana Worku, Anne Wolfe, Tiffany Williams, Shayla Walker, Sherese Taylor, Fazeyeh Rose Augustus, Melody Hoffman, Carra Martinez, Pabalelo Mmila, Barbara St. Pierre, and Bailey Irie Ceesay. I also acknowledge the brilliantly unruly students of my Sex, Politics, and Hip Hop classes, especially Anna and Moira Pirsch, Shareef Omar-Taylor, Erica Deanes, and Parker Benjamin. To Ananya Chatterjea: The book is done. I am ready to dance!

I extend an extra special note of thanks and solidarity to the courageous intellectual leadership of Cathy Cohen, Barbara Smith, bell hooks, Cheryl Clarke, Barbara Ransby, Carole Boyce Davies, Leith Mullings, Beverely Guy-Sheftall, Patricia Hill Collins, Nikol Alexander-Floyd, and Katherine McKittrick. It is upon your shoulders I stand. To Kimala Price, Melynda Price, Aishah Durham, Tracy Fisher, Aimee Cox, Tiffany Willoughby, Nadia Brown, and other young academics who have fought the good fight to produce social knowledge about black women on our own terms, I salute you. I also thank my former graduate adviser, a white, middle class, capital-F, (not so) hegemonic feminist named Mary E. Hawkesworth, who showed, through her applied mentorship, that it was perfectly okay to study black women the way I wanted to study black women without having to apologize for it. Similarly, I thank Rose and Malika Sanders of the Twenty-First Century Youth Leadership Movement in Selma, Alabama, who provided me with the political space to realize and validate my own peculiar role in the protracted struggle for the liberation of people of African descent in the United States.

The organizers of the Malcolm X Grassroots Movement (MXGM) deserve special acknowledgment. It was these highly dedicated, devoted, revolutionary black nationalists who politicized me and kept my skills from being wasted in a law firm or a corporation. Truly, it is their work that keeps black freedom struggle alive in American communities. Akinyele Umoja, Ollimata Taal, Connie Tucker, Senovia Muhammud, Monifa and Lumuumba Bandele, Karl Kamao Franklin, Ijeoma Isoke, Cliff Albright, and April Englund were among my first teachers. MXGM keeps Malcolm's message of human rights, self-determination, and black love alive in communities (rural and urban) that other scholar activist-scholars have abandoned as they have moved on up in the academy. MXGM saves black lives everyday.

Finally, I thank my two best friends since fifth grade, Latasha Pennant and Avys Stevensen, for their loving support over the years. I could not have done it without you. To my next-door neighbors, Saba Teshome, Robel Tedros, and "Maiye," thank you for making me part of the family. An extra special thanks to the new genius in my life, Larry Louisiana. Thanks for reading every single word of this manuscript out loud so that I could hear and consider my own words.

To Mr. Barack Obama: If you get reelected, I expect you to pardon Sundiata Acoli, Assata Shakur, and Sekou Odinga. Let three of our most beloved black freedom fighters come home. They have suffered enough.

1

INTRODUCTION

Urban Black Women and the Politics of Resistance is a sustained examination of how US black women have created political spaces to confront contemporary social marginality in Newark, New Jersey. Political space refers to the physical, symbolic, and relational spaces that black women create to politicize and transform communities plagued by economic disadvantage, social alienation, and highly destructive racial–gender ideologies that routinely constrict the political empowerment of their inhabitants. Using what Nikol Alexander-Floyd (2007) has called "a black feminist frame of reference" that relies upon the political biographies, oral narratives, and political discourse produced by US black women activists, and employing what I call a "black feminist intersectional analysis," this book explores the diverse and divergent ways that black women have resisted structural intersectionality. By linking personal narratives, political histories of place, and the quotidian politics of organizing in a city dominated by black male political elites, I critically examine the possibilities and constraints of African–American women's political leadership in Newark, New Jersey.

Conventional approaches to the study of politics often depict low-income black women as apolitical, and worse as lacking in respectable claims to citizenship and belonging. When judged in accordance with accepted categories of political participation, many black women fare poorly. They seldom vote or engage in partisan political campaigns (Verba et al. 1995). They rarely run for elective offices or lobby elected officials (Burns et al. 2001; Rosenstone & Hansen 1994). Political analysts interpret minimalist participation in mainstream political venues as an index of apathy based on masculinist assumptions about the nature of politics. *Urban Black Women and the Politics of Resistance* challenges this white-washed account of inner-city black women's political engagement. Through an intensive case study of Newark from 2003 to 2007, I document how black women confront contemporary social marginality through political means.[1] By respatializing the mobilization and deployment of social capital, and what I call "the politics of homemaking," black women activists vigorously rework the meaning and significance of urban space and urban politics. By creating and activating disparate communities of political practice in Newark, black women forge new geographies of resistance.

Over the course of this book, I argue that black women activists in Newark function as alchemists of resistance. As school board and city council members, community organizers, executive directors, clergywomen, and underpaid issue-based activists, black women take the harshest realities of urban containment and create wellsprings of possibility for positive social action. Using the wisdom gleaned from dedicating their lives to actively reimagining the social, political, and physical landscape of the city, black women talk back and act against urban despair. Responding to the calls from women of color scholar-activists for academic attention to the specificity of women's oppression, I document how black women combat the intersecting effects of racialized poverty, homophobia, and misogyny (Cohen 1999, James 1999, Collins 1991). I show how everyday black women move beyond the boundaries of any single-identity politics to forge alliances across diverse communities of struggle in order to challenge spatial domination in the inner city. In this book, I outline a theory of black women's resistance politics that describes how black women confront and transform structural intersectionality in everyday life.

Resistance politics are deeply spatialized and rooted in the politics of collective memory. They are realized through the intentional creation of social space in which activists revise and reformulate narratives of black political resistance. Black women make direct linkages between past and current realities of black social deprivation and despair—they unearth, invoke, reenact, and, most importantly, reenvision historic legacies of struggle against injustice. Through testimony, truth-telling, and spontaneous communal storytelling, black women imbue the ailing physical and political infrastructure of the city with meaning, and instigate counter-hegemonic forms of social action. They actively create geographies of resistance by mobilizing disparate pockets of the black community (i.e., black queers, hip hop heads, antiviolence activists, and antipoverty activists) to mitigate the interlocking effects of black heteropatriarchy and white economic hegemony.[2]

Building upon recent theorizations of race and power developed by black feminists who critically engage questions of space, place, identity, and belong in their writings, including Katherine McKittrick (1996), Carole Boyce Davies (1994), and Ruth Wilson Gilmore (2002) and bell hooks (1990, 2009), I argue that black women create geographies of resistance that undermine structural intersectionality—convergent systems of race, class, sexual, and gender violence—in Newark. Illuminating aspects of black female political agency that have been overlooked in research in American politics, urban politics, and in various (inter)disciplinary engagements of women of color activisms in the United States, the book describes modes of urban activism that destabilize stereotypic images of "blackness," "femaleness," and "politics." Through detailed analysis of two community mobilizations in Newark—one following the 2003 murder of 15-year-old Sakia Gunn, and the other preceding the 2004 National Hip Hop Political Convention (NHHPC), I explore how black women use their bodies, identities, and personal histories to subvert urban heteropatriarchy. Developing new forms of social and political action, black women who are young, gender non-conforming, and highly critical of the US racial state and capitalism are active participants in political processes that are often overlooked by traditional scholars.

PLACING RESISTANCE POLITICS IN A DESPISED CITY

I place black women's resistance politics in a despised city that has been brought to its knees by deindustrialization, neoliberalization, the roll back of welfare rights, and efforts to control the effects of racialized poverty through the securitization and privatization of public schools and local prison systems (Arrastia 2007, Gilmore 2007, Harvey 2006, Anyon 1997). Despised cities like Newark, Detroit, Saint Louis, and Gary have unforgiving histories of racial strife, deindustrialization, white flight, and decayed public infrastructure (Wilson 2009, Massey & Denton 1996). These cities undercut the glamour and intrigue of America's global cities—New York, Chicago, Los Angeles, and Seattle. Despised cities are instead marked by extreme levels of poverty concentrated in majority black and Latino neighborhoods, ruthless patterns of gentrification, and political corruption (Cohen & Dawson, 1997). The overrepresentation of racial–ethnic minorities among the poor, combined with virulent practices of media-instigated racism, contributes to the depiction of these cities as "dangerous" blackened spaces (Wilson 2009, Collins 2005, Jackson 2003). The ugly reality of neoliberalism is slammed home in America's central city neighborhoods, too many of which vaguely resemble abandoned war zones.

Newark has barely escaped the bleak desolation of the inner cities of Saint Louis and Detroit, as blacks and Latinos have a marked history of collectively organizing to preserve black and brown political autonomy (Mumford 2007, Woodard 1999). However, racial minorities who succeed in winning public offices must contend with severe social and economic marginality produced by generations of differential racialization.[3] Like other despised cities, Newark has a living history of chronic black male unemployment, the relegation of generations of poor women of color to low wage, service sector jobs and/ or public welfare, excessively large pockets of poverty, and patterns of gentrification that present tempting opportunities for wealthy entrepreneurs while depleting local communities of much needed social capital. African–Americans and Latinos remain at the very bottom of the racial hierarchies that continue to structure the city's economy, despite the emergence of a slowly growing black and Latino middle class (Wilson 2009, Pulido 2006, Massey & Denton 1993). Newark's political landscape is aggravated by patterns of police brutality and law enforcement practices that target African–American men and others who dare to perform black masculinity on inner-city streets. Combined with declining educational and employment opportunities, these conditions have and continue to foster widespread social discontent and various forms of urban insurgency (Mumford 2007, Woodward 1999, Marable 1991, Cunningham 1988, Winters 1978, Parenti 1970, Hayden 1967).

Black women's resistance politics go beyond the usual tenants of racial liberalism, cultural and revolutionary nationalisms, and liberal feminism to address these problems, as black women are not fundamentally concerned with inventing or necessarily even reproducing functionally bankrupt liberal democratic values. Instead black women's resistance politics utilizes a different kind of political subject. Their politics re-imagine the role of the citizen subject in relation to the political system. As opposed to simply aiming to increase participation within the system by marginalized African–Americans, black women's resistance politics expose the sociopathy of the normative political subject (rational, self-interested) by making space for caring, impassioned, affective, volatile, and socially unfettered subjects whose motivations are often otherworldly, and often only articulated dialogically with social spaces that black women either invade or create themselves.[4] Black women's resistance politics involves psychically undoing the harsh material conditions of existence, and envisioning and creating a new terrain of politics that extends from the self outward. These politics are realized time and again by reconfiguring the spatiality of self, home, and community.

To be clear, this is not necessarily a study of radical politics, as radical politics implies active confrontation, opposition, and unveiled hostility toward the political establishment. On the contrary, black women's resistance politics involves demystifying the ways the current systems fails to meet its own stated ideals, while generating collective energy and resources to address the tacitly supported systemic failures of local institutions and elite power structures. Their politics aims not to destroy, but to reclaim, re-envision, vitalize, and transform. This process involves what Grace Hong (2008) has called "bringing out your dead," or invoking the spirits of those who died in their personal struggles for integrity, recognition, and survival. These politics involve the creating of what hooks calls homeplaces: spaces to tell the truth about black and Latino drop out rates in poorly funded and grossly mismanaged public schools; to tell the truth about how politicians have lined their pockets through bribery, racketeering, theft, and fraud; to tell the truth about how government incompetence, indifference, and criminal negligence has led to the premature deaths of countless numbers of young people in Newark; and to tell the truth about how self-interested urban elites wantonly attempt to contain and eliminate legitimate seeds of change within the real and imagined landscapes of the city. Black women's resistance is manifest through an embodied politics of storytelling, truth-telling, and community empowerment.

Spatializing Resistance

This book examines contemporary urban spaces as critical sites in which women are politicized as racialized, classed, and gendered subjects. Rather than construing politics as a means to influence government, I argue that black women interpret politics in relation to the cultivation of social and political consciousness among structurally disadvantaged young people. They foster critical dialogs to spark the possibility of political efficacy of a new generation of activists. Politics of this genre occurs in a large cross-section of nonprofit, voluntary organizations and informal networks that periodically ignite into intense, short-lived coalitions and community alliances—what Jasbir Puar (2007) has recently termed "assemblages" of resistance politics. By tracing the mobilization of these networks, their sustained political work with inner-city youth, and their mobilizations in response to particular crises and opportunities, I make manifest the political labor of urban black women that is too often ignored or mistakenly attributed to the leadership and charisma of politically prominent black men.

In addition to making black women's political work visible, the book links resistance politics to the long-term sustenance of city life. Through "rant fests" organized by hip hop feminists, LGBTQ youth action networks, after-school programs, storytelling, African dance and drumming circles, and the creation of relational spaces in which women can share their personal histories of collective struggle, black women actively reconfigure the landscape of the city. In spite of the most intense forms of social violence imaginable, political black women in Newark march relentlessly and energetically toward a future rooted in justice. Examining the intimate factors that have politicized black women in Newark, this book-length study offers a fresh interpretation of political action in a city in transition, even as it details the personal and political tragedies and triumphs that necessitate oppositional politics on the ground.

By focusing on the spatial dimensions of political resistance, I provide new ways of understanding the complex political dynamics and innovative political practices within major American cities. Activist women devote their lives to creating and sustaining clothing exchanges, sister-circles, rites of passage programs, and other open and progressive spaces of struggle. In so doing, they transform blighted cityscapes into culturally symbolic homeplaces that nurture the life chances, leadership capacity of political efficacy of an emerging generation of activists. By documenting their political commitments and transformative endeavors, I demonstrate how black women challenge, resist, and transform converging systems of domination that circumscribe their lives in Newark.

Black women's political agency and subjectivity are theorized in relation to a nested urban political arena overdetermined by intensifying pressures to adopt and enforce neoliberal social projects that pathologize poor black people who defy middle class norms of respectability (Brown 2008, Arrastia 2007, Alexander-Floyd 2007, Collins 2005, Ferguson 2004). Black women's resistance politics occur within a media-charged global culture that persistently circulates destructive images of black masculinity and black femininity to sell everything from digital media to hamburgers.[5] I describe how new generations of activists use hip hop and queer politics to subvert dehumanizing racist-sexist stereotypes while offering counter-narratives to their presumed apathy and criminality. Whether in public schools, social service agencies, school boards, or even seemingly benign community programs, black women in Newark regularly contend with social, economic, and ideological effects of neoliberalizing policies that have all but destroyed many long-standing public institutions. Ironically, "well intended" employees within these institutions turn around and use morality as a weapon to discipline gender non-conforming youth, blaming black and brown teenagers for systemic failure (Brown 2008, Miller 2008, Arrastia 2007, Anyon 1997).

THE NEW POLITICS OF SLIPPERY IDENTITIES

Black women often negotiate, deploy, and reconfigure identity as they find ways to subvert the negative impact of global neoliberal policies on their communities. As a result, women claiming "blackness" in Newark are not always African–American. Throughout these pages, we will hear from Puerto Rican women who alternatively identify as both black and Latina. As black female political subjectivity gets reconstructed within each mobilization, we learn about politics from black women who are not always black, and black females who are not always "women." The polyvocality of black women's political subjectivity is emphasized by illustrating how black women migrate within and between politicized identity discourses to challenge domination at the local level (Sandoval 2000, Brewer in Busia & James 1993). I show how young black women like Fayemi Shakur, Keisha Simpson, and June Dowell invade discourses like hip hop and black queer activism to "recreate and remove the lines of impossibility" that constrain the possibilities of coalition building to spark the possibility of emancipatory social action (Boyce Davies 1994).

For example, during the NHHPC of 2004, "hip hop" functioned as a strategic signifier to build solidarity within and between African–Americans, Latinos, Asian and Pacific Islanders, and other racialized minorities in the United States and worldwide. Black women activists strategically deployed hip hop as a slippery identity to entice young people of color allured by the culture and aesthetics of hip hop to consider organizing against race, class, and gender-based inequities that impacted the hip hop generation. Within the NHHPC, women alternatively participated in social justice projects rooted in black nationalism and black racial liberalism under the rubric of hip hop. Other activists used hip hop culture to politicize and theorize queerness in the context of black community struggle and empowerment. The Progressive Women's Caucus used the convention to transform the meaning and practice of politics by hosting "rant fests,"

an intimate public space for laughter, tears, nurturance, and catharsis that resulted in building the affective, broad-based support for a
gender-progressive social agenda within the Convention.

Alternatively, in 2003, a 15-year-old named Sakia Gunn was
murdered by a heterosexual black male in the downtown streets of
Newark. The consequences of the double transgression of publicly
acting on same-sex desires and defying socially acceptable scripts of
Black femininity—indeed Sakia's performance of a particular kind
of black masculinity—elicited cat-calls, jeers, and, finally, a deadly
encounter with Newark street violence. Within the resistance politics
framework, Sakia Gunn's death, while tragic, is transformed into an
emblem of defiance to black homophobia and misogyny. Her slain
body and pointed remembrances of her short life are mobilized as a formidable symbol of contemporary black political resistance. Politically
active, but often closeted black gays and lesbians came out to challenge Mayor Sharpe James' refusal to be proactive about protecting
young lesbian and gays whose only refuge from virulent homophobia
were the drug- and gang-infested city streets of the Central Ward. I
argue that the kind of imaginative political work that continues to
take place in Sakia's name, and political spaces that have been subse-
quently created to transform the meaning of her death, constitute the
substance of black women's resistance politics.

METHODOLOGY

By outlining the anatomy of two specific community mobilizations
in Newark, this book delineates the specific conditions under which
some black women become visible and audible—or are rendered
silent and invisible—as they struggle tirelessly to resist structural
intersectionality on the ground. The truth claims made in this book
rely upon the testimonials of *living* activists who have spent much
of their lives devoted to social justice. Within these pages, you are
asked to hear the truths of twenty-nine activists, women aged 23–72
years, who self-consciously maneuver the minefields of Newark's
contemporary political landscape to make a better life for themselves and their communities. Through a close analysis of their life
histories, political biographies, and participant observation, I create
a vivid portrait of black women's contemporary resistance politics.
Through frame analysis and illuminating the spatial stories that are
robust in black women's retellings of their political lives, I present
an interpretivist interdisciplinary portrait of black women politics
and activisms.

My emphasis on personal narrative enables me to more deeply explore and contextualize black women's political agency in living history, existent struggles for social justice, and real communities (Maynes et al. 2008). I use a variety of sources of evidence to create a complex portrait of the social, political, and relational spaces that black women create, navigate, invade, and transform to enact resistance. Using intersectionality as the central frame of analysis and interpretative strategy, I examine how mutually constituting systems of race, gender, class, and sexuality produce marginal experiences, marginal identities, and unique opportunities for political resistance at the local level (Berger & Guidroz 2009, Hancock 2007, Crenshaw 1995). I examine how and when violence directed toward black female bodies gets justified, politicized, and socially castigated (or not). Using a black feminist bottom-up intersectional approach, I explore how and when black women emerge as political subjects in Newark's public sphere.

This project rigorously builds upon recent works that document the existence of "black feminist consciousness" in African–American politics and public opinion (Harris 2009, Alexander-Floyd 2007, Simien 2006). I extend this literature by situating processes of politicization and black feminist subject formation in the context of urban struggle. I go beyond chronicling the biographies of individual African–American women, as I provide nuanced interpretations of motivations, attitudes, and strategic orientations of Newark's grassroots warriors—women who are currently hard at work, challenging injustices in their neighborhoods and communities.

Chapter 2, "Framing Black Women's Resistance: A Black Feminist Intersectional Approach," discusses and critiques conceptions of "the political" that have emerged in studies of American political behavior, feminist studies, history, and political geography. Using the political biography of Fannie Lou Hamer, I interrogate how competing conceptions of politics interact with largely unacknowledged disciplinary presuppositions that determine when and under what conditions black women get constituted as political subjects. Drawing upon ideas developed by feminist geographers, I argue that more fluid conceptions of scale, politics, and resistance are necessary to develop an understanding of black women's politics that is divested from ideological conflicts rooted in academic disciplinarity.

In this chapter, I also clarify, critique, and extend theories of intersectionality that have emerged in the writings of contemporary scholars, including Ange-Marie Hancock, Nira Yuval-Davis, and Rita Kaur Dhamoon. Extending the ideas of Jasbir Puar (2007) and M. Jacqui

Alexander (2005), I incorporate the insights of feminist geographers of color to outline a theory of resistance politics that incorporates the analytics of space, scale, and mobility into accounts of black women's political subjectivity and agency. I argue that thinking critically about space, time, and time–space travel is essential if we are to fully understand how black women make sense of politics and how they practice resistance in urban communities.

In chapter 3, "Making Place in Newark: Neoliberalization and Gendered Racialization in a US City," I present an overview of the political history of Newark's cityscapes, illuminating the gendered processes of racialization that have structured the city's political economy since Newark was established as a British colony in 1694. This chapter examines Newark's contemporary political economy in light of processes of neoliberalism, including deindustrialization, urban revolt, the shrinking of public coffers, and the successful rise of black male political leadership in the city. This chapter combines historical accounts of the city with an ethnography of contemporary black cultural production in the city. It also introduces the voices of three generations of black women activists in the Central Ward, juxtaposing their perceptions of the city against the standard academic assessments. By foregrounding the accounts of women who have witnessed the political and economic transformations of the city over the past 40 years, I contrast the city as home against traditional constructions of urban space. In chapter 4, "(Re)Imagining Home: Black Women and the Cultural Production of Blackness in Newark," I position myself as a political ethnographer. I place special emphasis on the particular insights, biases, and predispositions that I brought to this project as a young black woman born and raised in US inner cities. This chapter remarks upon the gradual transformation of the colonized ethnographer's gaze as I became more familiar with Newark's unique socio-spatial history, my place in it, and the life stories and sentiments of black women who dedicated their lives to the city.

Chapter 5, "The Politics of Homemaking: Black Feminist Transformations of a Cityscape," addresses the complex relationships between space, identity, and black women's political agency. I revitalize the scholarship on black women's activism by infusing the analytics of critical geographers, including Katherine McKittrick (2006), Carole Boyce Davies (1994), and Michel de Certeau (1988). I analyze the spatial stories of these activists to make sense of their politics and political work. Represented as a beloved city that can be transformed, many activists take Newark as their political ground, imagining it as a home that is worth staying and fighting for. Construing Newark as an intimate political space that can be re-appropriated and reclaimed, these black women activists envision and enact the politics of "home-making," the collective production of an oppositional space that nurtures the life-chances of young African–Americans.

I draw upon earlier work on black women's activism, especially Cheryl Townsend Gilkes (2001), Nancy Naples (1998), and Patricia Hill Collins (1991), each of whom theorize black women's political agency as "community work" or "community mothering" to present a new schema of resistance politics: the politics of creating a living history, the politics of reclamation, and the politics of selling-in. Through creative retellings of collective histories of struggle, and by self-consciously situating black women's activism within a larger history of progressive, antiracist struggle, I argue that black women's community work involves reconfiguring the symbolic landscape of the city through the creation of political space. Often these political spaces take the form of what Katherine McKittrick (2006) calls "garrets," or paradoxical spaces that are camouflaged within hostile institutions like public schools, municipal councils, housing authorities, and community organizations financially controlled by political elites. I show how activists use the resources and social capital within these institutions to create opportunities for young people to build meaningful connections with each other, and thereby ignite the process of fostering critical social consciousness.

Chapter 6, "Mobilizing After Murder: Black Women Queering Politics in Newark," investigates the Newark Pride Alliance (NPA), a Newark-based black LGBTQ coalition created after the death of Sakia Gunn to politicize homophobic violence and social marginality directed toward gay, lesbian, and transgender youth in Newark public schools. The chapter analyzes the struggles that occurred during NPA attempts to build coalitions with local antiviolence and civil rights organizations, local black churches, and other predominantly African–American institutions. In the face of robust manifestations of black heteropatriarchy and heterosexism, sex-positive black women, trans-women, and trans-men came together to create a Social Justice Center, a space in which activists could freely confront and challenge black heteropatriarchy and its relationship to various forms of homophobic violence. Contrary to recurrent accounts of universal homophobia in the African–American community, I demonstrate the need for a more nuanced account—an account that can accommodate the politics of black feminist activists who created political spaces to assist young queer people to build a concrete political agenda devoted to raising awareness of the structural interconnectedness of HIV/AIDS, poverty, homelessness, and racialized-gendered street violence.

In "Mobilizing After Murder," I show how black LGBTQ activists were deliberately contained by black political elites driven by heteronormative values. I show how intolerance of gender transgression by school teachers, politicians, and clergymen exacerbated the social vulnerability of young people, increasing the likelihood of high school drop out, homelessness, and general apathy toward the usefulness of public institutions.

Chapter 7, "Keepin' Up the Fight: Young Black Feminists and the Hip Hop Convention Movement," examines how young feminists used the hip hop convention to organize against misogyny, sexism, and homophobia in people of color communities. An initiative devised by ambitious young African–American office-seekers, public intellectuals, and activists, the hip hop convention movement was designed to recruit a new generation of racial minorities into electoral politics. By focusing on the experiences of black women involved with convention-organizing, I illuminate deeply gendered contestations for visibility, access, and public influence within hip hop politics. The chapter provides an in-depth analysis of the struggles of the Progressive Women's Caucus, a renegade group of black feminist intellectuals and activists who succeeded in mobilizing support for a feminist agenda within the context of the NHHPC. Drawing insights from the mobilizations around Sakia Gunn's murder and the NHHPC, this chapter of the book analyzes the forces that continue to constrain black women's political activism and political visibility.

Chapter 8, "The Audacity to Resist: Black Women, Social Capital, and Black Cultural Production," argues forcefully that black women's resistance politics continues to be curtailed by those who cling desperately to conventional masculinist scripts of black political power. Indeed, black women's resistance politics actively undermined local intervening institutions that are unduly influenced by political elites wedded to liberal, bourgeois conceptions of politics. By reinforcing narrowly tailored, masculinist, state-centric approaches to political empowerment through the seemingly benign trope of black cultural production, black male elites continue to silence and tokenize black women. The final chapter discusses black women's contemporary political agency in the context of various manifestations of black cultural production, including black nationalism, black liberalism, and radical black feminisms.

2

FRAMING BLACK WOMEN'S RESISTANCE: A BLACK FEMINIST INTERSECTIONAL APPROACH

For three hundred and more years they have had 'time,' and now it is time for them to listen. We have been listening year after year to them, and what have we got? We are not even allowed to think for ourselves. They tell us, 'I know what is best for you,' but they don't know what is best for us! It is time to let them know what they owe us, and they owe us a great deal.

Fannie Lou Hamer (1965)

The most general statement of our politics at the present time would be that we are actively committed to struggling against racial, sexual, heterosexual and class oppression and see as our particular task the development of an integrated analysis and practices based upon the fact that these major systems of oppression are interlocking. The synthesis of these oppressions creates the conditions of our lives. As Black women we see Black feminism as the logical political movement to combat the manifold and simultaneous oppressions that all women of color face.

Combahee River Collective (1979)

Politics is a commitment to live differently in the present, to think and act against the grain of oppression.

Maria Lugones (2003)

Can I Get a Window Seat?

Erykah Badu (2009)

Thinking about black women's politics mandates that we think about how black women have resisted structural intersectionality. It also requires that we examine their lives using an intersectional analytical framework that privileges the subjective, representational, institutional, and geographic contexts through which their politics emerge. In this book, structural intersectionality refers to the interlocking systems of social violence that circumscribe black people's lives. These include, but are not limited to, racism, sexism, homophobia, heterosexism, neoliberalism, and entrenched poverty. When we situate black women's politics within structural intersectionality, we are better able to see and appreciate the various ways that black women act to resist negative attitudes, practices, and social processes. These violent processes include historic and ongoing discourses and practices of gendering, racialization, and heterosexualization (Dhamoon 2011, Yuval-Davis 2009, Hancock 2007). It is useful to distinguish between "structural intersectionality," "intersectional analysis," and black feminist intersectional approaches to knowledge production and praxis. Furthermore, it is important to make use of a bottom-up intersectional approach to magnify how macro-level ideological processes impact people at the level of the individual, neighborhood, and community. I believe that a close look at the life of Mrs. Fannie Lou Hamer will help define and distinguish between these highly complex terms.

I begin with the story of Fannie Lou Hamer, even though she is not a contemporary "urban" black woman. Mrs. Hamer is largely known for providing organizational support, inspiration, and fierce advocacy for the civil rights of African–Americans during the Jim Crow era. Born in 1917 as the twentieth child of black Mississippi sharecroppers, she began picking cotton at age six. She continued doing various forms of field labor, domestic work, and timekeeping for white plantation owners until well into adulthood. It was not until her late forties that Fannie Lou emerged as an early member of the Mississippi Freedom Democratic Party. Later she became a key member of the Student Non-Violent Coordinating Committee (SNCC) (Brooks & Houck 2011, Lee 1999). Mrs. Hamer was a lifelong fighter for racial and economic justice. Unfortunately, earlier histories of the civil rights movement either neglected to mention Mrs. Hamer because the writers of those histories were more concerned with documenting the lives and politics of civil rights *leaders* or they only discussed her community work in relation to how it bolstered the legitimacy of national civil rights organizations in the rural South. The lack of scholarly and media attention given to Mrs. Hamer's contributions to the civil rights movement prior to the 1990s was a product of the inherent sexism embedded in academic practices that mandated a top-down approach to studying the history and politics of social movements. This approach had the result of producing a metanarrative of the civil rights movement that reified highly visible successes on the *national* level and those identified as "national leaders" who were almost always male. This stood in stark contrast to bottom-up approaches that situated the civil rights movement in a protracted grassroots struggle for rights, recognition, freedom, and social justice (Ransby 2003, Kelley 1990, 1996). A bottom-up approach alternatively focuses on battles waged against local vestiges of state power by countless unnamed actors who worked continuously—tacitly and overtly—to subvert the capitalist white power structure over generations (McDuffie 2011, Gore et al. 2009, Kelley 1999). Thinking about the civil rights movement from the bottom-up provided crucial opportunities to analyze the complex political issues and social contexts that sparked multiple insurgencies across the south, while offering compelling glimpses into the lives and struggles of everyday people who, over time, managed to transform small-scale community organization into large-scale collective action (Payne 1995). Most importantly, bottom-up approaches revealed the radical visions of democracy held by black women like Fannie Lou Hamer who were denied individual rights, group recognition, and personal freedom erroneously associated with US citizenship.

While the conventional narrative acknowledges that Hamer had a "supporting role" in securing black access to basic citizenship rights, it does not adequately illuminate the personal issues—or what we might think of as micro-level forces—that prompted her to get involved in movement building. Nor does it help us understand the distinctive hardships she faced finding her voice as a rural Negro southern woman. Finally, the conventional story of civil rights tells us too little about how or why her vision of inclusion and recognition for African–Americans resonated so loudly, with so many (Bracer 2011, Gore et al. 2009, Collier-Thomas & Franklin 2001). In short, the top-down, masculinist narrative of the civil rights movement denied Fannie Lou Hamer personhood in American history. Ultimately, this narrative divorced how she perceived, experienced, and contested white supremacy with *why* she was such an important political figure. Failing to position Fannie Lou Hamer as an intersectional subject foreclosed answers to questions that had never really been asked. These include: what gave Fannie Lou Hamer the courage and faith to carry on in spite of terroristic threats, drive-by shootings by white citizenry, the loss of her family income, and even her right to bear to children?

A black feminist intersectional approach gives us room to consider how the experience of black womanhood informed her approach to politics and movement-making. A *bottom-up* intersectional analysis of Mrs. Hamer's life reveals that she initially became involved in the civil rights movements to contest the economic exploitation of poor black people in the Mississippi Delta plantation economy. Her early political work consisted of challenging the local injustices inflicted on black sharecroppers by white plantation owners. Mrs. Hamer, herself a sharecropper, was a victim of these injustices. Plantation owners refused to pay black agricultural workers fair wages for their labor. By keeping black people in poverty and denying them the right to vote, southern whites perpetuated a paternalist social, political, and economic system that kept black people virtually enslaved (Lee 1999). This kind of political system defines white supremacy (Lee 1999, Mandel 1978). Before and after Hamer's movement-making efforts spiraled outward and garnered national acclaim, she spent a considerable amount of time organizing food and clothing drives with the not-so-hidden agenda of creating and mobilizing a potentially powerful black political base to challenge white supremacy (Lee 1999). When it came down to it, Fannie Lou believed that access to the liberal ballot would help. She believed that if black people were able to vote, then they *could and would* provide a viable alternative to the racists who socially and economically repressed black Mississippians. Was Fannie Lou wrong?

A bottom-up, intersectional analysis of Mrs. Hamer's political work forces us to ask hard questions about why and how her visions for black self-determination and economic autonomy were never fully realized at the *local* level. Although rarely discussed, Mrs. Hamer *stayed home* in dystopic Mississippi, trying and failing several times to run for public office. She had bone-deep hopes to address the immediate social and economic needs of poor black people in her community through electoral politics and neighborhood-based political organizing. But still after decades of managing and implementing local food and clothing drives, registering tens of thousands of disenfranchised black voters, mobilizing thousands to participate in boycotts, marches, and demonstrations, poignantly articulating the grievances of poor, tired, and beat-down black folks in the halls of Congress, *and* serving as the national embodiment of black people peacefully resisting US apartheid, why was Fannie Lou never considered a viable political candidate in Mississippi? Why was she always so "tired of being sick and tired"?

Many would argue that the legacy of racial terror in the south and the continued economic subjugation of black folks (i.e., white supremacy) made it nearly impossible for Fannie Lou to run an effective statewide campaign for a Congressional seat. She simply did not have enough money, and white people were still too racist. While this argument might be true, such a conclusion occludes the possibility that sexism, heteropatriarchy, and the internalized racism of African–Americans *within* the local political structures could have played some role in her multiple failures to access state power and make transformational change in the Mississippi Delta. On numerous occasions, Fannie Lou was discredited, undermined, and ignored by middle-class African–American men and women because she was not "at the level of development" of more well-known activists who possessed a college education. She was chided as "ignorant" by Roy Wilkins, then the executive secretary of the National Association for the Advancement of Colored People (NAACP) because of her manner of speech (Brooks & Houck 2011). In short, focusing only on macro-level processes misses an important part of why Hamer, like so many women of color today, found it so hard to make political change, in spite of exhaustive, life-long efforts. I raise the story of Fannie Lou Hamer to ask: who are the Fannie Lou Hamer's of today's African–American communities? Who are the black women who struggle tirelessly to positively transform their communities, only to be ignored, disrespected, vilified, or tokenized? Who are the women who challenge urban poverty, social disenfranchisement, and black suffering in America today? Who are the black women who are interested and involved in community decision-making, who participate in diverse and divergent political spaces in their communities, who instigate collective action but still, more often than not, are simply not permitted to make noticeable social change? Finally, I also ask who are the people and powers that *prevent* these women from realizing their own unique visions of social, political, and economic justice.

To answer to these questions, I examine localized practices and normalizing processes that organize and legislate political power in Newark, New Jersey. I use what Irma McClaurin (2000) has called, "a black feminist anthropological lens" by situating "complex intersections of gender, race, and class" while self-consciously positioning myself as a black woman first and as a political ethnographer second (2000, 15). More importantly, my approach, while both theoretical and richly descriptive, is directed toward changing the oppressive conditions that continue to subjugate black people (2000, 16). Building from this perspective, a black feminist intersectional approach requires that we clearly identify and name oppression, as well as identify, name, examine, critique, and contest the multiple forms of subjugation that prevent all people—but especially black people—from being free. A bottom-up intersectional approach to understanding black women's politics requires that we listen to black women, and listen to their answers to these largely unasked questions (Cohen 1997). As Fogg-Davis (2006) instructs in his influential essay on "Same-Race Street Harassment," this process also includes critiquing interpersonal and intraracial black sexist and heterosexist conduct, alongside locating and improving black women's intersectional position within heteropatriarchal racial structures (Fogg-Davis 2006).

A contemporary black feminist intersectional research paradigm must go far beyond simply describing the subjective experiences of a particular marginalized group of people (i.e., black women) (Hancock 2007). Rather, this paradigm, seeks to reveal *how* identities are produced, forged, and then *deployed* to disrupt oppressive vehicles of power (Dhamoon 2011). This means examining the specific conditions through which the category of "black woman" becomes necessary to make sense of how specific localized constellations of race, gender, class, sexuality, and nationality converge to produce an identity that seems all too "real" (Hawkesworth 2003, Collins 1991). This requires that scholars actively identify and analyze which categories of differentiation are produced in contestations around power, recognition, and resources at multiple levels of scale. These include the level of the body, the household, the community, the "local," the national, the translocal, the transnational, and the global. This means thinking very carefully about when and how people make sense and making use of particular identities such as "blackness," "woman," "feminist," or "queer". As importantly, we must also identify and theorize the relevant temporal and geographic contexts in which multiple and intersecting markers of race, culture, gender, sexuality, and class become salient (Townsend Bell 2011). As a result, black feminist intersectional analysis necessarily examines diverse and complex representations and invocations of identity and other categories of difference while at the same time "contextualizing the processes and systems that constitute difference" (Dhamoon 2011). This means taking the time and space to examine how difference is produced by a variety of social actors and social, economic, and political processes. In this book, the processes of neoliberalization, gendered racialization, and hetersexualization are emphasized.

Black feminist intersectional analysis is not just about critique: it also about contestation, resistance, and social transformation. It is about actively speaking against, standing against, and finding meaningful ways to resist oppression. Throughout this book, I frame resistance as the relationships, or social capital, that are built enabling

Mrs. Hamer, and people like her, to be and stay involved in politics in order to resist structural intersectionality over the long haul. Social capital refers to trust, norms of positive reciprocity, and feelings of connectedness that are required to engage in collective action and politics (Putnam 1993). Black women's resistance entails creating spaces to build and foment social capital between black people in the communities they live, work, and go to school in. This means creating physical, symbolic, and ideological spaces for marginalized and minoritized people to come together, express themselves, build a critical perspective, and develop a plan of action to get their voices heard and their ideas acted upon.

For urban black women, resistance entails creating spaces of engagement in which the impetus for radical and transformative political thought and action is sparked. These political spaces make it possible for people who may or may not be consciously interested in the usual means of political participation (i.e., voting, letter-writing, or donating to political campaigns) to form informal coalitions and networks that can help them meet their immediate needs for sustenance, survival, and political support. For Fannie Lou Hamer, the food and clothing shelves were spaces of engagement with issues of poverty, cultural citizenship, and community empowerment. It was within these spaces that poor black Southerners were given the opportunity to consider overtly challenging longstanding injustices and inequality in their communities. It was within these community spaces in the Mississippi Delta that poor black people were provided the information and the means to prepare to take literacy tests, pay poll taxes, and to find the inner strength to publically challenge state-sponsored terrorism by Southern white Americans.

THE WINDOW SEAT: BLACK FEMINIST POLITICAL STORYTELLING

Telling the story of Mrs. Hamer's life is a political act; the telling of her life from an intersectional lens is a black feminist political act. When we consider *how* Mrs. Hamer educated millions of people about the ugly realities of white anti-black racism, we ourselves become educated about how racism was articulated through colonial medical practices designed to regulate, police, and exploit black women's reproductive capacity. In 1964, when Fannie Lou spoke as a delegate of the Mississippi Freedom Democratic Party at the Democratic Convention in Atlantic City, she bore witness to how she had been involuntarily sterilized after she was hospitalized for the removal of a uterine tumor (Nelson 2003, Lee 1999). The telling of this very personal tragedy revealed the extent to which gender domination was intermeshed with racist state and medical establishment practices. Black life was incredibly vulnerable in the South during the old Jim Crow era. Her willingness to make her personal life political by linking racist-sexist-classist state practices to the lived experience of black womanhood is a hallmark of black feminist intersectional politics.

Mrs. Hamer's courageous testimony about the challenges of organizing as a black woman informed community members, media pundits, and politicians about the horrors of being surrounded by police officers with drawn shotguns for simply trying to register to vote in a local election. She testified about the utter powerlessness of having the right to bear children being snatched away from her by a white doctor. Although she was married to a black man, and embraced mothering in both her personal and political life, Hamer can also be read as enacting a queer of color, black feminist critique of the white power structure (Ferguson 2004). She rigorously exposed the violence of heteronormativity that undergirded the political economy of the south. She exposed the hypocrisy of anti-miscegenation laws by commenting on the large and growing number of light-skinned and mixed race people produced by illicit relationships between white men and black women *and* black men and white women both during slavery and during the twentieth century (Brooks & Houck 2011, Lee 1999). She told the truth about the complicity of black men in aiding and abetting white male police officers in a dehumanizing beating that took place in a Mississippi jail cell. Black men held Mrs. Hamer down as white officers punched her in the face, pulled up her dress so as to expose her genitalia, and, yelled vicious racist-sexist insults about her skin color, body shape and size—all because she dared to try to register to vote (Bracer 2011, Brooks & Houck 2011, Lee 1999). Finally, Mrs. Hamer spoke of the sheer hypocrisy of black teachers and black clergymen who encouraged parishioners and students to "trust in the Lord" while excusing racial and sexual injustices perpetuated by local male authority figures, both black and white. Telling the truth about her life, about her pain, about her struggle, and about her resilience gave *others* the courage to do the same. She also impressed upon all Americans the human cost of their denial to stand up and demand racial justice in the United States. Through her political storytelling, Mrs. Hamer transformed the 1964 Democratic Convention into a *political space*—not because black people could vote or participate as so-called rational actors in the then unabashedly anti-democratic American political system, but because she transformed it into a place

where black people could collectively tell the truth about oppression
and be *heard*. It was a place in which they were able to build the
rapport with each other needed to collectively stand against the multiple forms of oppression facing them. Mrs. Hamer, without doubt,
was and continues to be the quintessential intersectional subject who
enacted black feminist resistance.

Resistance and Intersectional Praxis

It is important to underscore that resistance entails more than just arguing, "talking back," or even overtly aggressive acts to subvert power
structures, although these can be understood as important avenues
of resistance. Instead, I want to reframe resistance as the multiple and
complex relationships that were built to enable Mrs. Hamer, and people
like her, to become and stay involved in politics. Resistance transcends
attachment to ideological purity, rather it is a willingness to work through
and across divergent ideological spaces in order to incite diverse forms of
political insurgency (McDuffie 2011, Gore et al. 2009, Sandoval 2000).
Today, an intersectional analysis of black women's resistance requires
that we attempt to understand multiple axes of differentiation that produce black women as political subjects, as well as the multiple oppositional spaces they occupy in order to resist oppression (Brah & Phoenix
2004). I attempt to open a window into structural intersectionality in
order to explain what gives rise to intersectional resistances, and the
intersectional consciousness that precedes intersectional resistance.
Looking from the bottom-up, and across the vast social geography that
is Newark, we are able to see how distinctive nodes of resistance are
constructed and maintained in subcultural spaces that allow diverse
and variable modalities of blackness to flourish (hooks 2009, Johnson
2003). We see how ideology reflects on subjects and their experiences,
and we look at how harmful discourses and practices both inhibit and
instigate the agency of people like Fannie Lou Hamer. Another important aspect of resistance is explaining how structural intersectionality is
intensified through harmful discourses and social practices that inhibit
the agency of vulnerable people.

    In the US political discussions black women are often portrayed as
"welfare queens," "angry bitches," and as "superwomen" who time
and again are rarely understood as fully human (Harris-Perry 2011,
Beauboeuf-Lafontant 2009, Atwater 2009, Wanzo 2009, Hancock
2004).

    A bottom-up intersectional approach to researching black women's
contemporary activism, mandates that we prioritize the perspectives of

those who are most often missing from dominant discussions and analyses of black politics proper (Cohen 1999). For African–Americans, this includes gay, lesbian, bi-sexual, transgender people, and those who otherwise defy heteronormativity (Cohen 1997). This also includes poor black people who cannot or refuse to perform respectability, and gender-race-class radical black people who refuse to adhere to Protestant norms and political values dictated by hegemonic black middle class, Christian culture. Regardless of their sexuality, these non-normative political subjects have special stories to tell about being "othered" or "marginalized" within black communities, as poor folks are often put down because of their manner of dress, hairstyle, and speech patterns. The exercise of power and dominance over black people does not end with racist, sexist white institutions, ideologies, and practices. It also extends to sexist, misogynist, homophobic, and colonial practices internal to the black community. In fact, much of black women's resistance politics today requires creating space to safely acknowledge and heal from wounds that black folks inflict on each other (Miller 2007, Fogg-Davis 2006, hooks 2004, Cohen 1999, 1997).

In the next section, I review the writings of historians, biographers, and political scientists who have written broadly about the politics of black women. I review this scholarship to familiarize readers with new histories of black feminist resistance that have been written in the last decade and to pay homage to earlier studies of black womanhood that have helped me to theorize black women's contemporary activisms.

HISTORICIZING BLACK WOMEN'S ACTIVISM

Feminist historians, including Paula Giddings (1984), Rosalyn Terborg-Penn (1998), Bettye Collier-Thomas (2001), and Deborah Gray White (1999), wrote the earliest book-length accounts of black women's political activism. In particular, their studies of black women's associationalism in the early nineteenth century provide insight into the array of issues that black women's organizations prioritized. Deborah Gray White (1999) developed an impressive study describing a range of black women's "community work" and "racial uplift" programs that mobilized women on behalf of local organizations and associations. Much of this work emphasized education while promoting collective strategies to relieve urban poverty. Gray White's analysis places much of black clubwomen's "race work" within the confines of civil society, following the prominent ideological debates about race between W. E. B. Dubois and Booker T. Washington. These debates led clubwomen to create social programs aimed to improve black people's home and community life by teaching them how to perform and personify middle-class American values, family structures, and lifestyles. Deborah F. Atwater has argued that the rhetorical and political practices of black women who try to uplift their communities using middle-class ethos was an effort to establish their own dignity and personhood in the public sphere (Atwater 2009). However, many feminist scholars have argued that this kind of political agency was often done at the expense of poor African–Americans, causing longstanding cleavages between the haves and the have-nots in the black community (McDuffie 2011, White 2001).

Historical studies of black women's associationalism make the following points: First, black women's organizations prioritized "race" issues like education, poverty-relief, employment and employment training, substance abuse, voting rights, child welfare, and public health. Second, although it was true that many associations limited their membership and outreach to middle-class black women, most of these organizations built coalitions across race and gender lines, especially in their efforts to secure voting rights for blacks and women. Third, throughout the twentieth century, black women's associations were a central component of mass mobilizations in black communities (Hanson 2003, Gilkes 2001, Gray White 1999, Terborg-Penn 1998, Giddings 1984). Finally, black women's early propensity to start and/or join voluntary associations intentionally avoided the divisive partisan politics of the era, widely regarded as corrupt. This is not surprising considering the cutthroat legacy of urban political machines and the use of all-white primaries by political parties to prevent black people from exercising their political voices (Cazenave 2011, Mumford 2007, Woodard 1999, Walton 1985).

Throughout the twentieth century black women enthusiastically took advantage of opportunities to educate, inform, and organize their communities. Even in the midst of their own personal hardship they acted against oppression. Many black women experienced community work as a satisfying necessity. Resisting structural intersectionality was hard but fulfilling because it involved building productive relationships with similarly situated women who were discontent with the status quo. For example, Rhonda William's (2004) study of black women's public housing activism showed how women in Baltimore made use of the opportunity afforded by cheap rent, income subsidies, and living in close proximity to other poor women to organize their communities. They used these circumstances to create a new grassroots movement that prioritized the goal of creating better living and working conditions for themselves, strongly advocating for decent, affordable housing, effective community policing, and urban community empowerment. This political work also had a strong "truth-telling" component that included exposing the actions and agendas of powerful agents within local power structures—including profit-seeking economic developers, local political elites (mayors and city council members), and federal public housing authority officials who colluded to contain and ghettoize poor blacks in the inner city of Baltimore (Williams 2004). Importantly, this kind of political work was not isolated to Baltimore. Tenant and welfare rights organizations sprouted across American inner cities throughout the 1960s and 1970s, including Las Vegas, Philadelphia, New York, and Newark (Mumford 2007, Orleck 2005).

Black women in the United States have an extensive track record for organizing for racial and economic justice. Recent work by Erik McDuffie (2011), Dayo Gore, Jeanne Theoharis, and Komozi Woodard (2009), Ruth Wilson Gilmore (2007), Carol Boyce Davies (2007) and Joy James (1999) doucument black women's participation in multiple sites of radical movement making. These sites include the American Communist Party, revolutionary nationalist organizations, trade unionism, prison abolition, anti-police brutality organizing, and other diverse assemblages of urban insurgency. The radical histories of women like Claudia Jones, Lucy Parsons, Grace Campbell, and Assata Shakur, among others, have recently been excavated and analyzed on their own terms. Refusing to understand these women solely in relation to dominant (i.e., masculinist) ideology, radical historians have unearthed diverse black feminist standpoints. They have illuminated local and national campaigns that black women spearheaded over the last century. The concentrated focus on the political life histories of black women reveal that they eagerly worked within and through multiple ideological sites—including cultural nationalism, Third World Feminism, leftist (socialist/communist) struggle, neighborhood-based single-issue politics, anti-poverty activism, *and* liberal electoral politics to struggle and advocate for black freedom.

IDENTITY POLITICS, INTERSECTIONALITY, AND (NOT SO) HEGEMONIC FEMINIST POLITICS AND PRAXIS

At least seven conceptions of politics have been used in feminist writings since the 1960s to understand women as political subjects. These include: the personal is political, identity politics, community politics,

politics of empowerment, politics of transformation, transnational politics, and, more recently, black left feminist politics. In this section, I analyze a few of these conceptions to assess how well each has facilitated the production of knowledge about women of color in general, and black women's politics specifically. My discussion of politics hinges on the assumption that politics is deeply contextual, situational, and spatial. In the realm of feminist activism, politics begins on the scale of the individual body ("the personal is political"). Next, it extends outward to smaller groups and communities of resistance brought together by perceived commonalities that are devalued, excluded, and/or marginalized from mainstream political movements.

This method of understanding agency had deep roots in the socialist feminist projects of the 1960s, and emerged from feminist dialogues with the New Left (Grant 1993). Socialist feminists' efforts to challenge sexism within the Left, as well as their effort to regard women as a distinctive, more basic form of class in their Marxist critiques, sparked an explosion of feminist theorizing around experiential aspects of women's material lives. Of particular importance, was the development of various formulations of women's and feminist standpoint theories whose most basic premises relied upon the generic category of woman. In practice, "the personal is political" did not require individual or collective acts of resistance or creative rebuilding to transform society, rather the intent was limited to raising white women's awareness of the role of sexism and patriarchy that suppressed their ability to realize their own individual potential (Grant 1993). Among other things, this meant confronting physical, sexual, and emotional abuse within the domestic sphere, interrogating white women's individual decisions to neglect their professional aspirations in order to get married and raise children, and finally examining women's own complicity in their unhappiness, particularly with regard to compliance with compulsory heterosexuality (Rich 1980). White, middle-class liberal feminists appropriated this perspective and built a politics based on the false assumption that all "women" shared *their* experiences, and thereby wrongly and often violently projected their positionality onto all people who shared their genitalia. They also appropriated some of the perspectives of radical feminists to foster liberal social reform (like Title IX) that made it possible for them to compete for jobs with white men and further their ability to exploit and benefit from the unjust treatment of women of color (Glenn 2004). In other words liberal feminists appropriated the gender analysis of power, and dropped the class analyses altogether—leaving intact the racism that produced class inequality.

Women of color, especially radical black feminists, have severely critiqued this narrow practice of feminism while they openly claimed, embraced, and politicized various elements of their identities, including race, ethnicity, class, sexuality, and culture. All of these categories of difference have been used to articulate their experiences and analyses of the social world. Two other closely related, yet distinctive conceptualizations that feminists have used to capture the politics of women are the "politics of empowerment" and the "politics of transformation." I begin with the politics of empowerment. Bookman and Morgen (1988) define the "politics of empowerment" as a "process aimed at consolidating, maintaining or changing the nature and distribution of power in a particular cultural context." Within Bookman and Morgen's edited volume there are extraordinary essays on black women's politics, each stressing the centrality of *process* in black women's grassroots organizing and community work. Karen Sacks (1998) conducted a study of working class black women's union leadership, analyzing the role of kinship and affinity networks in transforming the workplace into a political force to advocate on behalf of women. She found that familial ties (biological and fictive) and language in the workplace created a cultural context that enabled the militant mobilization of black women workers (92). Similarly, Cheryl Townsend Gilke's (1988) essay situates work in community organizations as the premiere political space for black women. She argued that these organizations provided them with the autonomy and flexibility to respond to the articulated and interpreted demands of their respective communities. She writes, "community workers argue, obstruct, organize, teach, lecture, demonstrate, sue and write letters." In other words, they created their own political spaces by forming their own organizations as a strategy of resistance (Gilkes 1994, quoted in Grayson 1999).

The idea of the "politics of transformation" advanced by Cathy Cohen, Kathleen Jones, and Joan Tronto (1997) emerges from an explicitly materialist analysis of social life. For these scholars, "the study of women in politics is the study of changing politics and the politics of change." These function through self-consciously collective social movements that culminate with individual acts of resistance in multiple political arenas. The methods they used to outline the "politics of transformation" intentionally blurred the distinction between the subjects of study and the normative intentions of the researchers. So, the act of investigating these phenomena and assembling accounts of these "politics of transformation" becomes *itself* "an element of these politics." In other words, Cohen et al. did not only embark upon their project for the sake of providing accounts that could have a potentially positive impact on women, they assembled their anthology to transform the study of politics within the discipline of political science. While they held on to conventional understandings of the political, they expanded it to include movement-building, cultural politics, and grassroots organizing. They also introduced the concept of diaspora to link the study and politics of women to both local and global contexts. In many ways, the "politics of transformation" serves as a normative springboard used to tell stories of progressive, oppositional, and constructive political action taken on by women who challenge gender, racial, sexual, age, national, ethnic, and other forms of oppression on multiple levels of scale. Within this broad conceptualization of politics, studies of identity politics, transnational politics, and explicitly "feminist" politics are invoked to encourage engagement with both the study and practice of oppositional politics (Fernandes 2000, Sandoval 2000, Cohen et al. 1997). From this broad perspective, accounts of the activism of women of color become very relevant because the study of black women's activism from a black feminist perspective deeply problematize and even subverts academic institutions that undergird and inadvertently justify contemporary inequalities (Hong 2008, Alexander 2005, Torres 2003).

More recent works by scholar's including Bettye Collier-Thomas (2001), Ruth Wilson Gilmore (2007), Duchess Harris (2009), and Melina Abdullah and Regina Freer (2010) have emphasized the ways that black women have worked within formal and informal organizations and social networks to enact social change. Their leadership within state and local legislative bodies, grassroots coalitions, and public schools, and their willingness to press social justice organizations to engage more directly with the state is gaining more scholarly attention (Gilmore 2007). With this said, the writing of black women's histories of resistance, especially their willingness to work across multiple levels of scale to foment social change, requires that scholars openly value and argue for the production of specialized bodies of knowledge for and about black women (Davies 2007, Collins 2000, 1991). It is in this way that acts of writing and researching new histories, unraveling the layers of power and ideology that constrain and restrict black people's lives, and crafting new understandings of black radicalism and struggle, is an act of identity politics, but more importantly a form of black feminist intersectional praxis.

Academic feminisms' interdisciplinary conceptions of "politics" have been remarkably useful. They have helped us establish a new terrain to study and understand black women's politics. However, only a few of these studies have established clear connections between black women's political practices with the explicit (read local) structural and contextual constraints that have enabled or motivated their activism. In other words, from this review of the literature we have been able to locate black women's politics in community-based organizations and associations; however, a coherent narrative has not emerged on exactly *how* elements of local (formal and informal) social structures have established the parameters of black women's "political" agency.

Identity and Identity-politicking

The "politics of identity" as articulated by black women and women of color feminists differs substantially from the paradigm of "personal is political," which sought to politicize individual aspects of white women's experiences through consciousness-raising. Nira Yuval-Davis defines identity as "the narratives, or stories, that people tell themselves and others about who they are not" (2006). Importantly, when identities get politicized they are more than just personal stories. Rather they emerge over time as carefully constructed narratives about how individuals and collectivities view themselves and society at large. Identities also tell us something about how certain groups perceive how society views and treats people who share certain commonalities. Importantly, identities, especially blackness, function as what anthropologist John L. Jackson theorizes as "real fictions." In this sense, the use of identity is rooted in intersubjective imaginings, performances, social geographies, and discourses that "allow for the possibility of performative ad-libbing and inevitable acceptance of trust amid uncertainty" (2005, 18). This means that our identities are shaped, reinforced, and shift based upon how, when, and where we interact with others. Accordingly, our identities are shaped by the social landscapes that we travel through and inhabit, as well as the people we interact with and do not interact with and the information, stories, and discourses that we are exposed to on a daily basis. In other words, identities are lived, performed, and made real through efforts to survive and make-meaning of lives lived in the context of "white supremacist, patriarchal, capitalist, homophobic society" (Johnson 2003).

What is typically referred to as identity politics enables socially subjugated groups of people to write themselves into dominant histories and narratives that have failed to address specific issues and specialized analyses of power gleaned from surviving oppressive conditions. The politics of identity also examines larger sets of relationships toward the aim of *transforming* existing sociopolitical structures. Identity politics is more than critique, and the politicization of ever more complex victim narratives and insular group politics. It is also about actively working to change oppressive geographies, institutions, and practices. Identity politics often results in the creation of new and sometimes necessarily exclusive social spaces in which innovative itineraries for social action can be established (Blackwell 2011, Torres 2003, Cohen 1997). This process almost always includes the reappropriation, revaluation, and reclamation of what were previously considered as pariah identities—identities that were/are socially despised and positioned abjectly to the idealized norms of dominant culture and society. Self-acclaimed communists, cultural nationalists, feminists of color, and gay and lesbian activists and queer activists have all used identity politics as a tool for social change. Women of color, especially African–American and Chicano feminists who participated in multiple grassroots struggles for self-determination in their respective communities, fight hard to make the case that identities are multiplicative—that is mutually constitutive within, across, and through the boundaries and ideologies of race, gender, sexuality, class, and nation. In this respect, women of color established spaces within identity politicking movements to articulate revised narratives and strategies for movement-making and social change (Blackwell 2011, McDuffie 2011, Ferguson 2004). More importantly, communities of resistance for women of color, especially, were *forged* through reimagining identity by excavating and renarrativizing subjugated, suppressed, silenced, or erased histories (Torres 2003, Sandoval 2000, Perez 1999). Maylie Blackwell refers to this process as retrofitting memory. She writes, "Retrofitted memory is a practice whereby social actors read the interstices gaps, and silences of existing historical narratives in order to retrofit, rework, and refashion older narratives to create new historical openings, political possibilities, and genealogies of resistance" (102).

The politicization of intersectional identities involves linking the macro-level, or structural elements of oppression and domination, to the micro-level of everyday life and praxis. This means making connections between grand and ever more sophisticated analyses of the state and economy to the lived experience of marginality and social practices—that is how it is that people live and make sense of their lives. Identity politics necessarily links ideology to the workings of power in everyday institutions and organizations including interpersonal relationships in family, work, and community life (Weber 2010, Thornton Dill & Zambrana 2009, Yuval-Davis in Berger & Guidroz 2009).

In the last decade, feminists of color have made a point of decolonizing the politics of identity by emphasizing how seemingly transformative identities are rooted in the violent and inherently masculinist geopolitics of nation-states (Moghadam 2009, Yuval-Davis 2009, Yuval-Davis et al. 2006, Alexander 2005, Brah & Phoenix 2004, Mohanty 2003). These insights have forced scholars to think outside of the Americanist intersectional trilogy of "gender-race-class" by considering how the processes of imperialism and so-called nation-building by colonial powers around the globe (i.e., war, genocidal rape, slavery, and the racist-sexist mythologies that legitimized these practices) informed the formation of categories of seemingly "natural" cultural, racial, and ethnic identities (Puar 2007, Stoler 2006, Alexander 2005, Smith 2005). Intersectional politics from this perspective entails revealing transnational processes, practices, and ideologies that have positioned people of color as oppressed.

If we consider Fannie Lou Hamer's life and politics from this standpoint, then we must connect the Southern agrarian economy that relied almost exclusively on cotton, paper mills, tobacco, and a paternalist Protestant system of social control to the exploitation and political subjugation of African–American and native people in the South. Satiating the demand for cotton in other parts of the world, namely the United Kingdom, and the manufacturing and refining of cotton into a useable textile in parts of the global South, especially India and Southeast Asia, hinged upon the wholesale economic and social domination of African–Americans and indigenous peoples in the southern United States. This process occurred through the theft of land from Native Americans, sharecropping, racial terrorism, and the denial of civil and political rights to people of color who lived in this region. Importantly, the owners of plantations and farms, wholesalers, and the ruling white economic elite (in both the North and South) also reaped generous rewards from the poorly paid shop labor of people of color in other parts of the world (Lowe 2006, Chow 2002). This perspective demonstrates that the civil rights movement, spearheaded by activists like Fannie Lou Hamer, not only challenged the local white political structure, but also challenged a global economic system that created the white capitalist ruling class in the United States—including its ability to profit from the exploitation of people of color's labor overseas through processing raw cotton into retail quality textiles to be sold back to the global North. Mrs. Hamer acted against the brutal sexualized and gendered police violence that tried to beat black people into compliance with white supremacy and mid-twentieth-century capitalist exploitation. The politicization of her identity as a black, female sharecropper who challenged American racism, also both directly and indirectly challenged the larger transnational structure of global capitalism that negatively impacted the lives of people of color across at least four continents (Lowe 2006).

BLACK WOMEN, TRANSNATIONAL FEMINISM, AND FEMINIST GEOGRAPHY

In the past few years, many innovative feminist studies centering on politics of women of color have been conducted within the framework of "transnational" or "global" feminist politics. This literature links women's local "politics" with inter- and transnational political and economic institutions that extend their reach globally (Labaten & Martin 2004, Naples & Desai 2002 Sassen 2002, Hernandez & Rehman 2002). These collections have done a remarkable job of identifying how interactions between local women's organizations, transnational NGOs and local and international configurations of power under neo-liberalism enable and constrain women's agency. It is important to note that within this framework, more attention has been given to migrant women and their efforts to extend their activism across nation-states. Only very recently have the politics of *women of color* been identified and carefully described by the local configurations of power that enable and constrain their activism (Caldwell 2006). We are now beginning to connect black women's political agency and subjectivity to transnational circuits of power (Incite! Women of Color Against Violence 2005, Boyce Davies 1997). Similarly, in recent years, more attention has been given to the act of writing resistance. As a result, not enough attention has been given to black women's effort to resist circuits of power collectively, at the grassroots level, especially during contemporary times. It is imperative that these connections be made to have a richer, more complex understanding of black women in "politics" in the United States, particularly if we are to have a more in depth understanding of how raced and gendered dimensions of institutional power shape the activisms of women in different geographic and cultural locales.

Black feminist geographers, especially Carole Boyce Davies and M. Jacqui Alexander, have emphasized the role of diaspora and transnationalism in their writings about black women and black female subjectivity. Carole Boyce Davies, in particular, situates black women's subjectivity in migratory writing practices. Memories of home and "homeplaces" from places both—real and imagined—inform the complex ways in which black women inhabit, conceive of, use, and talk about space and place (hooks 2009, 1990, Boyce Davies 1994). Both urge scholars to more closely consider how the social, physical, and psychic violence created by slavery, colonialism, neocolonialism, and forced migrations have informed black women's writing practices as well as their efforts to challenge global structures of domination in institutions, including neoliberal universities. Memory, understood as a nonlinear process of reassembling forgotten and erased histories, and the writing of memory has enabled the articulation of experiences of black subjugation and resistance that have been deemed "unspeakable" in daily life, but resounding loudly in black women's fiction, autobiographies, autoethnographies, and what Audre Lorde called "biomythology."

Foregrounding the role of space, place, and memory in black female subjectivity requires that we resist framing black women's agency solely in one specific place and time (Alexander 2005, Davies 1994). Rather, according to Davies (1994), we should consider how migrations across time and place inform the complex ways that black women make sense of the world. Katherine McKittrick (2006) insists that "black geographies" go beyond the physicality and materiality of traditional geography. Rather, she argues, black geographies are constituted by ongoing histories of sociospatial denial, confinement, and objectification produced by capitalist value systems that render black geographies invisible. Black geographies are metaphoric as well as material, often subverting and disrupting conventional geographic narratives and mappings of black life that render black people placeless. Slavery, urban containment, and ghettoization, the mass imprisonment of black men, and, more recently, "un-natural" disasters like Hurricane Katrina and the tornadoes that ripped through North Minneapolis have all had the effect of creating complex and often contradictory relationships to traditional understandings of geography and place for people of African descent in North America. The places that black people call "home," and where they are able to find and claim a sense of belonging, are also the same places in which they experience unbelievable violence, trauma, and alienation. Furthermore, the "imaginary spaces" of black social, and political, experience—and the way in which these become material or not—are an important element of black people's subjectivity and, as a corollary, black female political subjectivity. Alexander (2005) argues that memory and what she calls "the sacred" also inform contemporary political itineraries that seek to challenge transnational, capitalist, patriarchy, and neoliberalism within and across the boundaries of race, nation, class, language, and sexual difference. In this way, black women's spiritual practices—especially those that transcend the strictures of religion, as well as narrow, linear understandings of time and space—comprise an important element of black women's political agency, and what I call black women's resistance politics.

Black feminist geographers emphasize the following points: first, black women's agency and subjectivity must be understood as rooted in the real and imagined geographies that black women inhabit. This means that in order to grasp black women's subjectivity we must think about the ways in which black women have imagined space and place. This includes how they move in and travel through physical spaces as well as the way in which knowledge about their political lives and history unfold in space and place. In other words, we must examine the social geographies in which black womanhood unfolds. Second, we must consider what black women's retellings of their lives and personal and familial histories tell us about the nature of the social geographies that they inhabit and seek to transform. It is from these retellings that we learn which structures of domination have constrained their lives and provided the opportunities for political agency. Lastly, this literature urges us to consider how the past has informed black women's spatial politics. This includes confronting controlling images that have their roots in slavery and the old Jim Crow, the hopes, aspirations, and visions of earlier generations of activists, and their imaginings about the possibility of contemporary social change (Harris 2009, Alexander 2005, Collins 2005).

BLACK FEMINIST INTERSECTIONAL PRAXIS AND RESISTANCE POLITICS

Black feminist resistance is popularly and appropriately associated with radical black feminists' activism against the hypothesized interlocking systems of racial, sexual, heterosexual, and class oppression in the now famous manifesto of The Combahee River Collective in 1979. This document articulates the particular struggles of radical black feminist lesbians that concurrently issued a pointed analysis of the politics of the larger, Anglicized women's movement. In many ways, intersectional praxis as articulated by radical black women in the United States and abroad had the effect of expanding white feminists' perception of the "personal is political." Their notions of "personal is political" challenged the stark public/private divide that masked and inhibited white women's political voices. "The personal is political" operated as a single dimension gender analysis of politics that sought to disrupt and challenge white male chauvinism against white women. Black feminists extended this frame of analysis to demand that women challenge the multiple oppressions that faced black feminist lesbians by explicitly politicizing selected aspects of their individual identities. While Fannie Lou Hamer did not identify as "feminist" (black feminist or otherwise) we can see that her political work throughout her life challenged structural intersectionality on multiple fronts. Her political life is an important example of what Carole Boyce Davies has defined as a "radical black female subject." That is, "a resisting black subject...resisting dominating systems organized and enforced by states, organizations, and institutions" (2007, 5).

If we root our understanding of resistance in black women's activism in diverse social movements, then our understanding of identity and identity politics becomes much more complex. Black women's resistance politics is evidenced by their individual and collective efforts to build coalitions with other progressive organizations and movements to challenge multiple structures of power and privilege (McDuffie 2011, Gore et al. 2009, Harris 2009, Collier-Thomas & Franklin 2001, Sandoval 2000). From a black feminist perspective, the politics of identity require a willingness to build a political community around aspects of self-identity that are shared with others, and demands a commitment to use the new elements of identity to critique and transform multiple, overlapping structures of domination, and, importantly, across the borders and boundaries of time, space, and nation (Boyce Davies 2008, McKittrick 2006, Alexander 2005). As Linda Tuhiwai Smith (1999) so eloquently argued, "To resist is to retrench in the margins, retrieve what we were and remake ourselves. The past, our stories, local and global, the present, our communities, cultures, languages and social practices—all may be spaces of marginizalization, but they have also become spaces of resistance and hope" (1999, 2).

We do not need to look all the way back to the civil rights movement to identify black women's resistance politics. In fact, black women resist structural intersectionality every day in various forms of community work in urban areas. Black women in American cities form sister-circles, girls groups, book clubs, create formal and informal networks in their schools and workplaces, and they open their homes, knock on doors, and send emails to form community organizations and unlikely community coalitions. Upon first glance, their work might seem to be very much *apolitical*—meaning that it seems not to have much to do with formal political participation at all. It may seem as if they are creating spaces to hang out, commune with each other, share stories, or commiserate about how hard life is. I argue that in communities that are struggling with racialized poverty, open and hostile misogyny and homophobia, and urban

economic containment—places like the Central Ward of Newark—
they are intimate spaces are that created to build the will to resist
structural intersectionality. These are intimate spaces that make sustained public resistance possible. These are places where young black
people (male, female, transgender, and non-gender identifying) learn
that their voices and perspectives are valid, that their commitment to
social justice is needed, and their sacrifices for political struggle are
appreciated. Most importantly these are spaces where they learn that
they are *not crazy*, but that their feelings of discontent, despair, and
frustration have been produced by an extenuated living history of
black racial subjugation and gendered racialization and *not* by individual deficiencies in mood, temperament, and bad (read pathologi-
cal) behavior (Harris-Perry 2011, Beauboeuf-Lafontant 2009).

Many of the women featured in this book have created multiple
political spaces over the course of their lives. In fact, creating these
spaces is what they *do* politically. They build charter schools, community groups for black queer lesbian and gay teens, movie nights, fashion shows, African balls, hip hop conventions, leadership programs,
needle-exchange programs, homeless shelters, gay churches, etc. to
make it possible for black people to become well enough, confident
enough, and courageous enough to resist structural intersectionality
in multiple sites using diverse strategies. This is not to say that *all*
black women are antisexist, antihomophobic, and/or antiracist. What
I am arguing is that many of the black women who are deemed "political" by *their communities* are involved in this kind of community
work. I call this kind of political work "resistance politics" because
their work provides the emotional, or more precisely, the *affective*
impetus to resist the multiple, convergent, and contradictory forms of
oppression that impact black people. I incorporate spatiality into my
analysis of intersectionality paying very close attention to Newark's
geographic history of black racialization, I place my examination of
black women's resistance in Newark's political imaginary—its political history, its political landscape, and its political geography. I situate
black women's resistance in larger geopolitical configurations including contemporary urban neoliberalization, and increasingly complex
scalar politics that have occurred as a result of globalization.

The next chapter provides a historical sketch of raced and gendered
processes of racialization and deindustrialization that have shaped the
contemporary political geography of Newark. The next chapter provides both the historical, cultural, and geographic backdrop of the
political agency and subjectivity of black women's activism in the city
of Newark. I offer this under-told history to familiarize readers with

the localization of racist-sexist-colonialist ideologies in Newark. In Chapter 3, I also take a place-centered approach to explain how black people became the center of Newark politics proper by the late twentieth century, while simultaneously existing as marginal, oppressed, and socially contained.

3

MAKING PLACE IN NEWARK: NEOLIBERALIZATION AND GENDERED RACIALIZATION IN A US CITY

Being Black in this country, there is very little about it that is mild. The oppression is extreme. Probably the only Black people whose (sic) oppression is somewhat mitigated are those who have class privilege and that is certainly not the majority of Black people here.

> Barbara Smith and Beverly Smith in "Across the Kitchen Table: A Sister to Sister Dialogue" in *This Bridge Called My Back* (1983)

The danger lies in ranking the oppressions. The danger lies in failing to acknowledge the specificity of the oppression. The danger lies in attempting to deal with oppression purely from a theoretical base.

> Cherríe Moraga in "La Guerra" in *This Bridge Called My Back* (1983)

In this chapter, I review the history of Newark, beginning with its inception as a British colony. This historicization of Newark is important because it demonstrates the site-specific ways that processes of colonization, gendered racialization, and neoliberalization produce social geographies in US cities. Too often our discussion of these terms are divorced from the specific geopolitical practices and processes in which they occur. This serves to erase or obscure specific racialized and gendered subjectivities that have been produced by macro-level social processes and their contestations by local political actors.

When we map a cityscape from a black feminist perspective, we capture a view of the city that is shaped by gendered processes of racialization and heterosexualization. From this vantage point we can clearly see the violent economic and political processes that constitute structural intersectionality in Newark. These analytics are a critical first step in illuminating black women's political agency and subjectivity. They help us understand how political identities are spatially constituted within the contours of a city—not only by one's physical location in space, but by the efforts people make to imagine, appropriate, and create new spaces in which to be an activist, a community leader, and a movement-maker. When we situate current racialized and gender identities in historical processes of land theft, genocide, enslavement, racial apartheid, and economic marginality as well as the contestations and community insurgencies to subvert these violent processes we shed new light on urban black people's experiences that are often presumed to be uninteresting, unimportant, and generally invisible within the dominant disciplinary frameworks of geography, political science, and (not so) hegemonic feminist studies.[1]

Understanding black women's resistance in Newark requires that we have a clear understanding of how historical processes of gendered racialization have unfolded during the emergence of Newark as a city. It is imperative to locate the ways in which black heteropatriarchy emerged as a response to the tragedies, disappointments, and failures of a political system that promised but failed to guarantee full citizenship to generations of African–Americans who migrated to Newark in search of opportunity. Black women were a part of this response, but often their political agency was invisible. This chapter sketches the social and political landscape in which blackness and black womanhood have emerged since Newark's formation as a city. I describe the harsh history of racialization in Newark and the ways that gender emerged as a salient marker of power relationships between black women and men, and the white power structure in Newark.

DEFINING CITIES

Cities are not only highly specialized centers of political economy, but are built spaces that are central to communicating meaning. Cities structure meaning as they organize the pattern, flows, and interpretations of both simple and complex human actions and interactions—including political action (Yanow 2006, Grosz 1995). As sites of social and cultural production, cities are constituted not only by the larger historical processes of capitalism (Harvey 2001, Zukin 1995, Lefebvre 1991) but *also* by gendered processes of racialization and race formation (Cazenave 2011, Goldberg 2009, 1997, Wacquant 1997, Mullings 1987, Omi & Winant 1986). Gendered racialization refers to patterns of racialization that produce and legislate hierarchies between people based upon on sex, sexuality, and their ability to conform to dominant gender norms (Hawkesworth 2006, Ferguson 2004, Halberstam 2005). It includes patterns of heterosexualization that are defined as "natural" white, Protestant middle-class family structures and interpersonal relationships (Alexander 2005, Halberstam 2005). In the United States what we regularly think of as "cities" have been constituted by violent social and economic practices designed to eliminate, exploit, and contain people of color, generally, but black people in particular. For this reason, cities are also sites of fierce competition about who belongs, who does not belong, and who should belong. Contestation and competition over belonging are also contestations about power, control, and decision-making about whose vision of the city will ultimately prevail. As a result, conflicts over who has the right to work, live in, vote, and thereby claim the city as their own often take center stage in the histories of US cities. And Newark is no exception.

Recently, scholarship by critical geographers has specified cities as sites of neoliberalization—densely populated locales in which regulatory practices mutate and shift to accommodate and strengthen the ideology of free market capitalism. Neoliberalizing policies and practices typically aim to erode social projects, programs, and policies that place the needs of the collective over and above the imperatives of profit-making and profit-seeking through the imagining and manufacturing of new markets (Mayer & Kunkel 2012, Leitner et al., 2007, Peck & Tickell 2007). Broadly speaking, neoliberalizing practices include privatization, securitization, and the demonizing of policy efforts that would redistribute wealth and resources to poor and vulnerable people through tax increases on rich individuals and corporations, income subsidies, and the provision of free and low-cost social services like public education, health care, and welfare payments (Peck & Tickell 2002, Moghadam 2009, Brenner et al. 2002, Anyon 1997). At the same time, municipalities "contract-out" services previously provided by state bureaucracies under the premise of "efficiency," all the while dedicating increasingly larger portions of budgets to policing black and brown neighborhoods. Financial resources are redirected toward prosecuting and incarcerating mostly black and brown youth for drug related offenses (Alexander 2012, Gilmore 2007, Collins 2005). Interestingly, the municipal resources are frequently earmarked to employ (and provide generous pensions to) predominantly white police officers, prosecutors, judges, court clerks, and correction officers who live outside of the city. Scholars, including Patricia Hill Collins (2005) and Michelle

Alexander (2010), have referred to the racialized effects of neoliberalization in the United States as the "new racism" and the "New Jim Crow" respectively.

For black people in Newark, neoliberalization and its attending patterns of gentrification have had an especially negative impact on public schools and social services programs (Arrastia 2007, Anyon 1997). While state and local governments have consistently decreased the amount of funds spent to support students and narrowly defined educational activities and materials, there has been a systematic increase in the amount of money spent to fund private and charter schools, law enforcement budgets, the expansion and "enhancement" of county jails and youth detention centers, and various surveillance measures in public schools like metal detectors, security officers, and security cameras. Cities and municipalities have often been quintessential sites of neoliberalization, often emerging in time of crisis to aid and abet the ascendancy of the market through "best practices" borrowed from the private sector to solve deeply rooted problems (Leitner et al. 2007, Anyon 1997). Importantly, Newark is also a site of contestation to neoliberalization, as black people have consistently fought to resist, reappropriate, and redefine the racialized neoliberalization of the city. They have done this by initiating social movements and making political space to create opportunities for black political empowerment and socioeconomic advancement.

COLONIAL NEWARK

People of African descent have lived in the area that was to become Newark since before the violent seizure of the Lenape people's land by the British, and the consolidation of their land as a British colony in 1694. From the earliest days of white settlement, the presence of blacks was manipulated to promote the pecuniary interests of white colonizers. The documentation that first established the terms and conditions of British settlement, Sir George Carteret's benevolent "Concessions," granted every colonist coming with the first governor 75 acres of land for every slave held.[2] These generous economic incentives tied the first distribution of wealth in the colony to the enslavement of blacks. These incentives allowed the slave economy of New Jersey to flourish. The exploitation of black people's labor contributed not only to the wealth of individual slave owning colonizers, but to the expansion of the Northeast seaboard's entire agricultural economy. One of the earliest records pertaining to blacks in the Newark area documents the use of enslaved blacks as a form of currency themselves, donated to assist the educational opportunities of white children.[3]

The earliest records of manumission (freeing) of black slaves dates to 1737. As the number of enslaved and free blacks increased, so did efforts to keep black people from belonging in Newark. Documents of black life in New Jersey during this time suggest that anxieties about the presence of blacks began to increase as the status of blacks changed from enslaved to free. By the eve of the Revolutionary War, free blacks were increasingly found among the population of New Jersey.[4] Black men and women were known to vote and take an active role in civil society. In 1804, New Jersey became the last northern state to move toward the emancipation of slaves, when its state assembly granted freedom to all children of slaves born after that year.[5] As enslaved black adults eventually died the slave economy was gradually disintegrated. This precipitated an extenuated history of local efforts by white people to restrict any citizenship claims made by blacks, with efforts going as far as to propose the wholesale removal of free blacks from the state through deportation. After the disintegration of the slave economy, black people were frequently represented through what Patricia Hill Collins (2005) calls "controlling images." In newspapers, black people were commonly depicted as immoral and sexually depraved. These controlling images were used to justify excluding black people from mainstream civil society.

In 1807, the white Governor Pennington was reported to have "gallantly escorted 'a strapping negress' to the polls where he later joined her in the ballot." This highly racialized and sexualized example of a black women exercising her right to vote in Newark mobilized outrage and racial resentment among whites because soon after black women were banned altogether from formal electoral participation, regardless of whether or not they had a wealthy white man at their side.[6] Later that same year, what bell hooks has very aptly called "white supremacist, capitalist, patriarchy" was consolidated when voters passed legislation that barred everyone except free white male citizens the right to vote in state and county elections. The law read: "From and after the passage of this act no person shall vote in any state or county election for officers in the government of the United States, or of this state, unless such a person be a free white male citizen of this state" (McGoldrich & Crocco 1993). This act effectively excluded all blacks, Native people, and women from full participation in New Jersey elections until almost 60 years later.[7] In 1824, white citizens formed "A Society in the State of New Jersey to Cooperate with the American Colonization Society." In its founding meeting, the rationale for the creation of the Society was clearly stated:

> I Rise, Sir, to move, that the Constitution just read be adopted; and I cannot suffer the opportunity to pass without expressing my warmest approbation of the plan embracing in it many manifest and important (sic) to our State and Country. We all agree too, that we owe much to the children of Africa in the way of remuneration or recompense. The adoption of this plan will help us pay what we owe. You already perceive that the view which I take of this subject has regard, as much to our own interest as to the interest of the blacks. What a mass of ignorance, misery and depravity is here mingled with every portion of our population, and threatening the whole with a moral and political pestilence. My answer then to the state of New-Jersey is, that this enormous mass of revolting wretchedness and deadly pollution will, it is believed, be ultimately taken out of her territory, if the plan of the Colonization Society be adopted. This is the special concern—and who will say it is not a most interesting concern—which the state of New-Jersey has in this great national affair.[8]

The language used in the document exemplifies the seething hostility of whites toward blacks, and also speaks to the social acceptability of white people publically disavowing black people's humanity. The thin pretense of gratitude for the "services" of slaves and the suggestion that this action was in the "interests" of blacks is combined with the racist depiction of blacks as a "deadly pollution" and "moral and political pestilence." The presence of free blacks was clearly perceived to threaten the political and economic dominance of whites. Through such rationalizations, white so-called Christians convinced themselves of their own moral rectitude while they advocated for a violent project to forcibly deport black people to another American colony.

Many white New Jersey citizens continued their tradition of stridently arguing that African–Americans did not belong within state boundaries, and did so using juridical-politico mechanisms. This created an especially toxic racial climate. In 1852, the New Jersey legislature appropriated state funds to the New Jersey Colonization Society to transport free people of color to Liberia and "other places on the West Coast of Africa," to build temporary settlement houses or shanties, and to cover other costs associated with transporting blacks to Liberia. Ten years later in 1862, legislation was introduced to criminalize the presence of blacks in New Jersey by declaring all "Negroes or Mulattos" guilty of misdemeanors if they came into the state of New Jersey, and remained there for more than ten days. As penalty for being black in the state of New Jersey, lawmakers argued they should be arrested and detained on sight. Although this legislation was ultimately defeated, it demonstrates the relentless tenacity of white racists' efforts to purge the state of "free" or, probably more aptly termed, un-enslaved black bodies. Rather than recognizing free blacks as citizens, many white New Jersey residents and lawmakers constructed blacks as a political threat, and a hindrance to the so-called natural economic and social progression of the state. When black people's labor was no longer necessary to whites they tried again and again, to deport them.

Clearly anti-black racism was not a uniquely Southern problem in the United States, as is still frequently taught in today's history textbooks in public schools. Deportation may have been an extreme strategy to recreate New Jersey as an Anglicized state, but it was far from the only racist policy considered in mid-nineteenth century. During the Civil War, repeated efforts were made to ban blacks from service in the New Jersey regiments of the Union Army. Legislation was also introduced in the New Jersey Assembly to outlaw miscegenation—the legal right for blacks and whites to marry and cohabitate interracially. In 1865, the New Jersey legislature voted *against* the Thirteenth Amendment, which abolished slavery and involuntary servitude among all free persons, with the exception of prisoners (Alexander 2012, Davis 2003). In 1875, New Jersey became the *last* Northern state to ratify the Fifteenth Amendment, granting black men the right to vote.[9]

White policymakers' explicit efforts to circumscribe the civil rights of African–Americans in New Jersey did not go unchallenged. Black churches, literary societies, associations, and black schools mounted sustained resistance against such racist policies. These relatively autonomous institutions fostered a positive sense of racial identity, and provided spaces to challenge exclusionary practices and racist stereotypes that demonized black people. Importantly, black people chose peaceful and congenial tactics to combat racism. Community leaders urged people to write individual letters and editorials. They also circulated petitions to express outrage at the legislative attempts to restrict their claims to citizenship and belonging. In spite of their efforts, the social progress of free blacks was severely stunted due to highly circulated stereotypes of blacks as "lazy," "uncivilized," "lawless," and "unfit for citizenship." These controlling images gained traction in society as a whole. They were the precursors to the adoption of numerous practices and formal policies to discourage blacks from fully integrating into the social fabric of the state.[10]

NEWARK AND TWENTIETH-CENTURY BLACK MIGRATION

By 1910, blacks from southern states began migrating to Newark in substantial numbers in search of jobs and relief from the economic and social violence of the old Jim Crow in the South. Black migration was encouraged by white businessmen who advertised Newark as a "city of opportunity" in order to satisfy their need for a cheap labor pool. The jobs available to most black migrants were limited to unskilled, menial positions due to job discrimination by white ethnic employers and racially exclusive trade unions (Cunningham 2002, Price 1975). Black men and women were barred from the skilled crafts and trade occupations that flourished during the late nineteenth century, and they usually only managed to secure positions as carpenters, waiters, day laborers, porters, and doormen. Black women were generally confined to undocumented or under the table work as domestic servants and launderers.[11] The Census of 1920 reported that there were no black streetcar or rail transit workers, engineers, sales agents, firemen, or city or county officials. Of the 3,500 black men employed in Newark, only three were policemen, ten were apprentices in the manufacturing sector, eleven were physicians, five were dentists, and three were attorneys. Black male and female workers were barred from the ranks of skilled and semi-skilled craft because white master craftsmen, who controlled access to these positions, refused to accept black people as apprentices. Failure to attain an apprenticeship excluded black workers from union membership, even in those few unions that did not exclude black workers as a matter of policy.[12] In 1930, ten unions within the American Federation of Labor (AFL) and 14 unions outside the AFL barred blacks by "constitutional and ritualist provisions." Employers also utilized collective "closed shop" bargaining agreements to categorically exclude blacks from union jobs.[13]

As a consequence of such pervasive racial discrimination, the most effective way for an African–American to move up the socioeconomic ladder was to try to open an independently owned black business. In Newark, the most typical black entrepreneurs were in the service sector, and most were owned by black men. Thirty-nine hairdressing and beauty shops topped the list of black businesses, followed closely by express trucking enterprises. Nearly half of all black professionals in Newark were full-time or part-time ministers, pointing to the importance of the black church as a creator of the black middle-class in the city. Not surprisingly, black churches were also sites of heterosexualization whereby the virtues of heterosexual marriage, conformity to white middle-class values, and black patriarchy were the most heralded visions of the "good life."[14]

As early as 1920, the Interracial Committee of the New Jersey Conference of Social Work reported that "fifteen Negro women" traveled to Newark from the south to do volunteer relief work in impoverished areas of the Third Ward in cooperation with local black ministers. Though the names of these particular women remain unknown, prominent African–American women like Alma Flagg, Alene Lett, Bessie Lanier Smith, Anna Lee Williams, Pansy Borders, Evelyn Timmons Inge, and Grace Baxter Fenderson were trained social workers or school teachers who exerted considerable leadership within the Newark chapters of the Urban League, and the National Association for the Advancement of Colored People. They went on to create and join organizations like the Negro Women's Republican Club, the Colored Democratic Women's Division, the League of Women's Voters, and smaller community-based antipoverty organizations. While black women were active in a wide variety of organizations and social clubs, they also engaged in social activism aimed directly at confronting racial discrimination and widespread poverty that plagued the Third Ward.[15]

Beginning in 1910, the New Jersey State Federation of Colored Women's Clubs also created programs to promote literacy, and civic education, as well as challenge gendered racial violence against African–Americans (Collier-Thomas & Franklin 2001). The Federation, comprised over 56 clubs with over 2,600 members, explicitly challenged the lynching of black men, police harassment, and the sexual exploitation of young black migrant women who went into domestic work in white homes. Another aim of the Federation was to facilitate the entrance of black people into working class jobs by offering job training programs and job placement services. During this time, the Federation exercised a firm commitment to participate in the formal political process. Active members often introduced and lobbied for legislation to mandate the governor and other state officials to appoint African–Americans to leadership posts in relief agencies and programs (Collier-Thomas & Franklin 2001). They also worked to establish a state commission to document poverty and economic hardship in New Jersey's urban centers. Finally, with the aid of the NAACP, the Federation of Colored Women also successfully lobbied to pass legislation to create the State Commission against Discrimination, which would be responsible for documenting and investigating complaints of race discrimination by employers with state contracts (Collier-Thomas & Franklin 2001).

As the city became more racially and ethnically diverse, rigid patterns of housing segregation developed. White ethnic groups lived in particular neighborhoods and animated the social landscape with businesses that reflected their distinctive ethnic heritages. African–Americans, regardless of class, were confined to specific neighborhoods. Racist housing practices such as redlining and restrictive covenants contained blacks in a few neighborhoods in the Third Ward, where available housing was typically poor and/or substandard. Despite the dilapidated conditions of the housing, African–Americans were forced to pay exorbitant rents to occupy housing owned by whites (Price 1980). Before World War I, there was little racial violence directed toward African–Americans in Newark. Yet during this time of "congenial" race relations, blacks were routinely excluded from services provided at hospitals and clinics. Many African–Americans who came to Newark from far away places like North Carolina, Virginia, Maryland, and Georgia with dreams of gainful employment and the "good life" would more than often not have these dreams deferred.

THE DEPRESSION ERA AND THE CONSOLIDATION OF RACIAL APARTHEID IN NEWARK

Between 1920 and 1930, Newark's black population soared from 16,977 to 38,880, an increase of 129 percent.[16] Media representations of blacks in the city's newspapers shifted from portrayals of comic icons of southern backwardness to almost exclusive portrayals of blacks as criminals (Price 1980). The increased visibility of blacks in the city coincided with a worsening national economic climate. Black residents were the most economically vulnerable population of the city prior to the stock market collapse of 1929. After that point living in Newark became especially hard. As part of Newark's surplus labor force, the overwhelming majority of black citizens continued to be relegated to low-skill and low-wage work. Systematically excluded from trade unions, black workers were the first to lose their jobs when the depression hit, and the last workers to benefit from recovery efforts (Price 1980).

Between 1929 and 1940, the theretofore-bridled racism of the city's white powerbrokers was unleashed. During the depression the best-funded private relief agencies in the city, including the Salvation Army, Goodwill, and the Red Cross, simply refused to assist black families in need. While the public welfare rolls did offer limited temporary assistance to black families, they did so grudgingly, frequently articulating a fear that offering public relief to African–Americans would encourage poor people from the south to travel to Newark in order to get on welfare. In 1932, the Interracial Committee of the New Jersey Conference of Social Work documented widespread racial bias in the provision of relief. Many semi-private hospitals and relief agencies either refused to provide any services to blacks, or only provided services to them on a restricted basis. The few organizations that would provide medical care and relief to blacks did so only on a completely segregated basis. Although the Interracial Committee was relentless in documenting the discriminatory practices of the relief agencies, they provided the information in a way that protected the identities of organizations involved, describing the organizations as "Hospital A" or Agency "B." In 1971, Kenneth and Barbara Jackson (1971) speculated that the Goodwill Mission, the Red Cross, and the Salvation Army were among the major organizations *refusing* to assist impoverished black people during the Depression. This speculation was later confirmed by historian Clement Price through private interviews with William Ashby and Harold Lett of the Negro Welfare League and the New Jersey Urban League, respectively (Price 1975).

At the same time that African–Americans were actually denied access to many forms of relief, they were blamed for imposing costs upon local taxpayers. Essex county commissioners, yet again, developed a scheme to relocate recent black migrants back to southern states in order to cut costs. In spite of the fact that 75 percent of the public relief cases comprised white families, and less than 2 percent of black families receiving assistance had migrated to Newark within two years of the depression, many white politicians believed that the out-migration and displacement of blacks would be an appropriate policy response to these hard economic times (Price 1975). In reaction to the blatantly racist policies enacted by both the city of Newark and so-called philanthropic organizations during the Depression years, there also emerged leadership, organization, and strategic resistance led by black people.

Black institutions included storefront churches, new independent news journals, black business associations, and civic organizations. Blacks with working class consciousness organized Newark's first rent strike in 1939. Small black nationalist resistance groups emerged, including the House of Israel and the Allah Temple of Islam, which rejected the ideological tenets of integration. On September 28, 1936, the *Newark Evening News* reported that 5,000 followers of Father Divine demonstrated in Newark, and speculated that this organization had at least 10,000 followers in Newark alone. Like other nationalist organizations, Father Divine's group favored a strategy of building independent black businesses, schools, and apartment communities. In keeping with this black nationalist agenda, his organization went on to purchase one of Newark leading hotels, The Rivera.[17]

Most of the organized opposition to unfair public policies was initiated by Newark's small, yet burgeoning black middle class. This resistance was fueled by complex motivations, including a desire for opportunities to enhance its own visibility, establish rapport with the larger white political community, and ensure a better quality of life for their offspring. However, fissures between the interests and priorities of black middle-class professionals and impoverished blacks were emerging. The more affluent sectors of the black community operated small business such as barbershops, small professional practices, and salons that catered to and depended upon African–Americans. But impoverished blacks, struggling to establish an economic base for themselves, were too poor to regularly patronize black businesses. They were not in a position to instantly benefit from the priorities of middle-class black leadership. This class separation continued to grow throughout Newark's history in the latter part of the twentieth century.

The economic crisis of the 1930s created an overwhelming demand for public housing, which stands as a case in point. The Newark Housing Authority began to construct public housing, building large high-rise, low-income apartment buildings in what would become the Central Ward. Nearly all (95%) of public housing residents in the Central Ward were of black and/or Spanish speaking origins (Curvin 1975), while housing projects in other wards were more than 95 percent white.[18] Massive white middle-class exodus from Newark began during World War II and continued through the 1960s. Wartime prosperity provided economic incentives for businesses and their customers to relocate into the suburbs, and provided temporary manufacturing jobs for otherwise underemployed black men and women. The end of the war also ushered in widespread layoffs of black workers, and renewed attention to the unresolved economic and racial tensions that racked the city.

In 1946, Curtis Lucas published a grisly novel set in the Third Ward during the denouement of World War II.[19] The story's protagonist, a 21-year-old black woman named Wonnie Smith, is tormented by the memories of witnessing the murder of her best friend, Mildred, for refusing two white men sex. Lucas' fictional account attests to limited employment opportunities of impoverished black girls, and how white men's sense of entitlement to black female bodies during the 1940s was enough to incite them to terrible fits of murderous rage, particularly if they were denied full enjoyment of black women's sexual charms. The storyline unfolds against the familiar backdrop of poverty, rampant housing discrimination, and the devaluation of black life by Newark police who failed to thoroughly investigate the circumstances surrounding Mildred's death. One of the story's killers, Ernie Mihie, a white Third Ward nightclub owner who relied on prostitution as a major source of business revenue, became disgruntled by dwindling profits due to the absence of black female sex workers, who, during the war years left for the temporarily available manufacturing jobs. Ernie became crazed with anxiety when Wonnie directly confronted him in the *Gin Mill* when she recognized him as the murderer. Ultimately, Wonnie's refusal to have a drink with a newly returning white soldier results in a brawl—the perfect distraction Ernie needs to take Wonnie's life in a chaotic public place and thereby avoid arrest and prosecution for the black girl's life he had taken five years earlier. Lucas's novel elucidates black women's vulnerability to sexual violence by white men in Newark, and the failure of both white and black men to protect them in a city plagued with social inequalities driven by white racism and decades of racialized poverty.

POST WORLD WAR II NEWARK

Post World War II Newark ushered in the final processes of deindustrialization that started earlier in the twentieth century. Between 1950 and 1960, 250 manufacturers left Newark, opting to relocate plants and factories to oversees locations. By 1970, more than 1,300 had either closed their doors or relocated, dramatically increasing unemployment (Curvin 1975). While the concentration of blacks in the Central Ward became the basis of its enhanced political power, it was also consolidated into a ghetto characterized by poverty, strict racial apartheid, physical blight, and various forms of social, political, and economic violence (Curvin 1975). White ethnic groups, particularly Italians from other parts of the city, maintained overwhelming political control over the Mayor's office seat and the city council. Italian politicians regularly resorted to covert decision-making practices that excluded blacks from knowledge of and participation in issues of specific relevance to their communities (Mumford 2007, Woodard 1999, Cunningham 1988, Curvin 1975, Hayden 1967).

Concentrated poverty, chronic black male unemployment, and overcrowding in segregated Third Ward housing projects such as Stella

Wright and Hayes Homes, exposed black families to loitering, crime, and unexplained and unaccounted-for acts of violence.[20] Central Ward public housing projects became premier sites of racial apartheid and social despotism. The Newark Housing Authority routinely dispatched housing officials and maintenance staff into the homes of residents without advance notice, violating their privacy. The elevators frequently broke down, and the stairways were unsanitary and often unlit. The Executive Director of the Housing Authority, Louis Danzig, routinely denied charges of intentionally segregating black residents, arguing that tenants were placed in apartments where they wanted to live. He did, however, publicly admit that he did not offer white people apartments in the Central Ward unless they requested them: "To the extent that suitable vacancies permit, the applicant is assigned to the project of his choice." He explained that it was "natural" for immigrants to live among the same racial or nationality group. He explained, "The Germans and the Jews preceded the Negroes in the Central Ward and did the same thing." It just so happened that the most of the housing projects in the Central Ward were dangerous, over-populated, and more than 90 percent black.[21]

The failure of the Newark police department to patrol these communities and the disinterest in thoroughly investigating criminal activity left most public housing residents feeling unsafe. Scudder Homes resident, Mrs. Patricia Dessau, remarked: "the police don't seem to care what happens in the projects."[22] The president of the Scudder Homes Tenant Association charged: "The locks on the doors are very inadequate. The average [number of] break-in[s] is eight per month." While the police refused to protect families from criminal activity, they were also widely known to brutalize and harass young black men for doing nothing more than standing on street corners. The climate of fear, anger, resentment, and hopelessness pervaded the Central Ward.

Animosity among blacks toward the city's governance structure was fueled by white politicians' persistent refusals to appoint qualified blacks to leadership positions within Newark's city administration. This, added on to the proposed displacement of 40,000 Third Ward residents to construct the University of Medicine and Dentistry of New Jersey, drove black people over the edge. When cabdriver John Smith suffered "caved ribs, a busted hernia and a hole in the head" at the hands of seven white officers while in police custody, the building tension finally exploded into the 1967 Newark Rebellion.[23]

The week-long insurrection ravaged the city of Newark. Thousands of disaffected youth, protesters, and Central Ward community members took to the streets. The revolt took the form of looting, massive destruction of private property (especially white-owned retail stores), non-violent civil disobedience, and vivid expressions of contempt for whites traveling through the riot-impacted areas. The police department retaliated with targeted beatings and assassinations of young black men, *all* of whom were suspected of looting. The Newark Police Department, together with the New Jersey National Guard and the New Jersey State Troopers made aggressive displays of force—including vengeance attacks on black-owned businesses that transformed the area into an enemy-occupied battle zone. More than 3,000 National Guard troops were activated from surrounding suburbs and nearly 500 New Jersey State Troopers were called in to patrol the streets.

At least 22 African–Americans were killed by police gunfire during the week of riots. Six were killed inside their homes or on their front porches. Hundreds more were brutalized, arrested, and/or charged with petty crimes (Cunningham 1988, Winters 1978, Hayden 1967). The Newark rebellion magnified the hostile conditions that many blacks had to withstand in other American cities during that time. The rebellion also came to express and symbolize the widespread social discontent produced by generations of anti-black racism and racial apartheid. White people left the city in droves as levels of fear and intolerance intensified. White flight also came to symbolize white people's base indifference to black suffering. They chose to abandon the city instead of changing it (Sugrue 1996, Jackson 1985).

The intensifying militancy of both the Newark police department and socially ostracized people of color created an environment in which black nationalism would seed and flourish. In 1970, Amiri Baraka's cultural nationalist organization, Committee for a United Newark (CFUN), rose to prominence by helping to politically mobilize blacks and Puerto Ricans to elect Newark's first black mayor, Kenneth Gibson. CFUN organized under the tenets of cultural nationalism, which required a commitment to black nation-building through the cultivation of a distinct "Black African" identity. This meant the cultivation of autonomous black, community-based businesses, organizations, and institutions and through a concerted effort to elect black elected officials in majority black political districts (Woodard 1999, Curvin 1978).

While CFUN clung to many heteropatriarchal attitudes held by black nationalists at the time, they also provided fruitful opportunities for black women to lead and to organize. The Women's Division of CFUN created exclusively female study groups, established independent schools that taught basic reading, writing, and arithmetic using black cultural nationalist symbols. These schools incorporated Swahili dance, drumming, and rhythmic storytelling techniques into their community programming efforts. The Women's Division of CFUN became the largest section of the organization, and assumed responsibility for many of the day-to-day organization operations (Mumford 2007, Woodard 1999).

The rise of cultural nationalism in the Newark in the late 1960s provided a unique opportunity for young women to become involved in community-based efforts to organize the poor black and brown communities of Newark. Initially CFUN attempted to promote its male membership to prominent leadership positions within the organization, but for most of it existence, the majority of CFUN's members were black women (Mumford 2007, Woodard 1999). These women were presented with a unique opportunity to build working relationships with other women. Lead by Amina Baraka, many also viewed CFUN as a fertile space in which to expand their politics to include consideration of the impact of sexism on their communities. This also included a specialized analysis of how imperialism, colonialism, and racism effected the lives of black and Puerto Rican women (Woodard 1999). While CFUN maintained a cadre of highly visible black male leadership who regularly engaged in electoral politics, the "nation-building" that provided much of the ideological meat that constituted black cultural nationalism was both designed and implemented by CFUN's highly committed, multi-talented female activists within the organization (Woodard 1999).

Black women's organizing efforts within CFUN simultaneously bridged several communities. Their creative community-based programming attracted young visual and performing artists and teachers. The women's division needed to secure the financial resources to implement these initiatives, so they reached out to middle-class black professionals and college students from the cities surrounding Newark. This outreach was accomplished despite CFUN's ideological commitment to enhance the formation of black political consciousness in Newark. Their need to mobilize resources from the black middle class superceded CFUN's pledge that the organization would focus its energy on a population that was predominantly poor and uneducated. CFUN successfully forged relationships and established much-needed rapport with Newark families, including many of the teachers who taught in the public schools. These relationships budded into a new organization, the Black Women's United Front (BWUF), which eventually merged into a national network of black women activists, artists, and educators who had close community ties, helping to boost the legitimacy of CFUN, as well as the soon to be created Newark Black Convention Movement.

NEOLIBERALIZED NEWARK

Newark became one of the ten cities with the largest increase in the number of the "ghetto poor" from 1970 to 1980 (Jencks & Peterson 1991). By the time Ronald Reagan took office in 1981, the United States faced its worst economic crisis since the Great Depression. During the 1980s, Newark lost more than 81,000 manufacturing jobs (Anyon 1997). The remaining blue-collar manufacturing jobs, which public school students in urban areas were being trained to fill, eventually disappeared (Harris 1998, Anyon 1997). The condemned industrial fortresses of factories, workshops, and warehouses were abandoned in the wake of the job losses, and worse, were shielded from demolition. The massive buildings became untouchable due to the likelihood of dioxin and other toxic emissions into the air and groundwater, and the prohibitive costs of clean-up. Most whites moved away from Newark's inner city, settling in suburban areas, escaping with the municipal budget's tax base. As conservatism swept the nation, social programs and social investments dwindled (Sugrue 1996, Jackson 1985). The remaining whites, including Italians and white Hispanics (Spanish and Portuguese American immigrants and citizens) settled into the North and East Wards of Newark. By the end of the 1980s, there were an estimated 8,000–11,000 homeless people in Newark (Mumford 2007).

In 1990, New Jersey public schools were among the most segregated in the nation. Newark's public school system exemplified this trend, with over 70 percent of its students identifying as black and 27 percent as Hispanic (Anyon 1997). In a state that regularly boasted being one of the five best educational systems in the United States, Newark public schools performed dismally on standardized testing. Similarly, high school retention rates and other empirical measures of school performance continued to suffer. In the fall of 2010 Facebook founder and CEO, Mark Zuckerberg donated $100 million dollars to the Newark Public School System. When asked "Why Newark?" in an interview with Oprah Winfrey, Zuckerberg responded, "It's because I believe in these guys," referring to New Jersey Governor Chris Christy and Newark Mayor Cory Booker.[24] No mention was made of the generations of deprivation and poverty that produced the "failing school system." Zuckerberg's generous and well-intentioned donation was largely administered by the Republican controlled, state-run school system. Even so, some progress has been made. Two new high schools for "troubled" students were built to increase graduate rates as well as to disrupt the school to prison pipeline for many African–American males in the city.[25] With this said, many, including Sheilia Oliver, an African–American woman who represents Newark in the New Jersey State legislature, immediately expressed concern about such large sums of privately held funds being infused into the public school without proper accountability measures.[26] In September of 2011, many community leaders complained about large portions of money being spent to pay the salaries for executives for various private educational companies.[27] In any case, change continues to be slow.

The prevalence of HIV/AIDS in New Jersey compounded the pernicious social conditions that faced generations of black people in Newark. In 2005, Newark ranked fifth in the nation for new cases of HIV/AIDS. Over half (55%) of all people known to be living with HIV/AIDS in the state of New Jersey are non-Hispanic blacks. Sixty-four percent of women in the state of New Jersey living with the illness are black women, comprising 41 percent of all African–Americans living with the virus. In the city of Newark, 1 out of 31 (4,634) blacks are known to be infected with HIV, with Newark topping the list of ten identified "Impacted Cities" in the state of New Jersey.[28]

In June 2006, Newark voters bid farewell to five-term incumbent Mayor Sharpe James, electing ambitious, young, African–American, Ivy League attorney Cory Booker to this critical leadership post. Other favored contenders for highly coveted seats in the municipal halls of power include the well-known native sons of Newark such as Ras Baraka (son of renowned poet, black cultural nationalist and political agitator Amiri Baraka), Ron Rice Jr. (son of Senator Ron Rice, representing Newark in the New Jersey State Legislature), Donald Payne, Jr. (son of nine-term incumbent US Congressman from New Jersey, Donald Payne), and Oscar James Jr. Enthusiasts are hopeful that Newark is finally experiencing its long anticipated renaissance from the ashes of the riots in the summer of 1967. This *New*-Ark symbolizes the rise of the phoenix from over 60 years of blight, deindustrialization, and neoliberalization.

Emblematic of this rising Newark are newly formed institutions that implement neoliberal solutions to economic blight without much consideration for racial justice or the end to racialized poverty in the city. Expensive structures like New Jersey Performing Arts Center, the new hockey arena for the New Jersey "Devils" and more than 10,000 new housing units for "middle and low income" families were constructed between 2006 and 2008. These attractions were designed to foster urban homesteading by the tens of thousands of mostly white suburban administrators and managers who have for several decades enjoyed secure salaried positions in the downtown corporate offices of IDT, Prudential, Wachovia (now Wells Fargo), Rutgers University, University of Medicine and Dentistry of New Jersey, and The New Jersey Institute of Technology. The new sites of cultural consumption are also meant to attract those millions of New Jersey commuters who use Newark Penn Station and Newark "Liberty" (since 9/11) International Airport, encouraging them to stop, spend, and consume within the political boundaries of the city.

These optimistic imaginings of Newark's so-called renaissance must be considered in contrast to the lives of 28.4 percent of the city's residents who currently live at or below the poverty level. Poverty is not evenly distributed across Newark. On the contrary, it is concentrated in areas adjacent to the spaces in which "urban renewal" is being constructed. In the predominantly African–American sections of the city like the Central Ward, for example, poverty levels and unemployment rates have soared to more than 40 percent. These somber empirical facts give pause, even to the most animated young office-seekers. They also provide the impetus for much the political activism of the black women who are the focus of the remainder of this book. The processes of racialization and social alienation that has accompanied deindustrialization in Newark have mired the lives of so many African–Americans in despair. But these dire circumstances have also provided opportunities and impetus for political agency.

The Central Ward of Newark reflects racial dynamics central to "American" culture, and account for the neoliberal processes that have transformed black majority spaces into both real and imagined sites of danger and decay. Yet, Newark has a long and vibrant black urban culture. Although Newark lacks the caché of the "Black Meccas" such as Harlem or Atlanta, it has a long history of black political activism, cultural work, and cultural expression, despite a history that has been elided by images of "racial-ethnic wars" and political corruption. In marked contrast to a Black Mecca, John L. Jackson (2001) has suggested that cities like Newark exist as "blackened" spaces, due in part to the residual effects of urban insurgency on the white public imagination. The Central Ward, previously known as the Third Ward, played a critical role in this blackening. Against the backdrop of "urban blight"—poverty, overcrowding, deteriorated landscapes, and public housing scandals, and police beatdowns—in 1967 riots ignited the Central Ward. Several other factors contribute to the image of Newark as an axiomatic "blackened space." Three consecutive electoral victories of African–American mayors who have held Newark's mayoral seat for the past 38 years, and the well-established history of the black nationalist organization and agitation within the city further consolidate negative images of Newark in mainstream white media outlets.

Newark continues to be marked as a despised city in national public imagination. On August 12, 2010, AOL's Wallet Pop, a daily blog that is circulated to ten million plus users named Newark as one of America's "Ten Worst Places to Live." On January 27, 2012, the Center for Disease Control released a report that found that Newark had one of the five highest levels of gang-related murders in the United States, alongside Los Angeles, Oakland, Long Beach (California), and Oklahoma City. Given the severity of these social indicators, it is difficult to overstate the social and economic crisis facing African–Americans as a distinctly racialized group of people in Newark.[29]

THE CENTRAL WARD IN THE
TWENTY-FIRST CENTURY

Formally known as the historic "Third Ward," The Central Ward was the poorest section of Newark. Poverty and rates of unemployment had topped 60 percent in some census tracts. In 2000, 71 percent of the 56,738 people living in the Central Ward identified as African–Americans. Among the 36,931 African–American residents in the Central Ward, 41.6 percent lived at or below the poverty level. The average per capita income of all adults living in the Central Ward was only $11,610 dollars. According to the US Census Bureau, of the 12,712 African–American males over 16, only 5,919 (46.5 percent) were in the labor force, while 29 percent (1, 719) were unemployed. Of the 16,732 African–American women over age 16, only 7,843 (47.6%) were in the labor force; 23 percent (1823) were unemployed. Although African–Americans constituted just over 70 percent of the Central Ward's population, they owned only 1,882 (10.5%) of the 19,685 occupied housing units. The remaining 12,793 African–American-headed households occupied rental units.[30]

The consequences of poverty and unemployment in this "blackened" enclave are vividly depicted in the mystery novels by acclaimed African–American female novelist Valerie Wilson Wesley. Her not-so-fictional accounts map a cityscape in which intersecting histories and institutions—black and white—constrain and enable black women's agency.[31] Gang violence, drug trafficking, political corruption, and police misconduct provide the context for African–American private detective Tamara Hayle's investigations of Newark's unsolved murders. Born and raised in Newark, protagonist Tamara Hayle uses her local contacts to solve murder cases that the Newark police department never bothers to investigate. Hayle's clients are financially strained, but they are unwilling to resign themselves to the view that the murders of their loved ones are unworthy of investigation. Instead of resignation, they turn to Tamara Hayle, whose hard-nosed personality enables her to overcome the difficulties of being single, black, and female in Newark, and to succeed in navigating the streets and bureaucracies of Newark to solve her mysteries. Attention to the intersecting histories of black and white residents and institutions in Newark helps contextualize the creation and current condition of the Central Ward.

The next chapter offers a contemporary sketch of Newark's political landscape from women with long familial histories in Newark, and who have made a commitment to *stay home* and sell-*in* to Newark by dedicating a good portion of their lives to envisioning and enacting an alternative living history of the city. I situate their voices within discourses of black cultural production that saturate the Central Ward. In this way, I participate in the writing of a new history that centers the perspectives of those whose families have experienced, survived, and made the best of the social, economic, and political conditions presented in this chapter.

4

(RE)IMAGINING HOME: BLACK WOMEN AND THE CULTURAL PRODUCTION OF BLACKNESS IN NEWARK

A big part of our work is helping to overcome the problem of perception. People make jokes about living in Newark. But we have to find and make people stakeholders in our city, people who believe that some good can come out of Newark. Rebuilding Newark isn't just building bricks and mortar. It's about rebuilding our people and the neighborhoods we live in. It will take a while, but I'm going to stay here and do the work.

Gayle Chaneyfiled-Jenkins,
former Newark At-Large Councilwoman

My father always told me that you didn't have to move to become what you wanted to become, that you could actually create what you wanted to create where you were.

Dana Rone,
former Newark Central Ward Councilwoman

NOT MY HOOD: THE COLONIZED GAZE OF THE BLACK FEMINIST ETHNOGRAPHER

It was impossible for me to get the full sense of the kind of black urban containment that existed in Newark until I actually had a chance to visit the home of someone who lived in one of the housing projects. Actually, it was quite accidental. While shopping for diapers and formula at the local Pathmark grocery store, I asked the cashier where she got her hair braided. During that time thick cornrows were the style and I had been itching to get my hair braided without what I then considered "overpaying" at the African braiding shops on Broad Street. The cashier, a young African–American woman who appeared to be in her early twenties, told me that she braided it herself. She asked me if I wanted to get my hair done. Of course, I said yes, thinking that I could save some money. After changing numbers quickly and settling on a time and day (the next afternoon), I paid for my groceries and left.

The next day, after picking up my hair extensions from the beauty supply superstore, I drove to the young women's home. Upon approaching the entrance to her apartment complex, I felt out of place: the consummate outsider. Although I grew up in a neighborhood in which gangs and drug dealing were prevalent, and because as an adolescent I had close relationships with black folks who hustled in front of their apartment homes, I was on edge. I had slipped. I had gone into a strange neighborhood that was territorialized by young men hanging out and showing colors. Furthermore, I had traveled alone and I did not tell anyone exactly where I was going. A long time ago, I learned that one of the best ways to avoid drama (i.e., unnecessary, avoidable, and potentially dangerous bullshit) was to never travel through anyone else's hood by myself. After I parked my car, I realized that I was foolishly inviting drama.

During the previous six years of my life, I had spent most of my time as a student on painstakingly choreographed college campuses. As a result of my educational privilege, I assumed that I was going into one of the artsy, feminized and/or "conscious" or "progressive" black spaces that I had become accustomed to as a college student. I did not tell anyone where I was going, because I generally experienced Newark as safe, albeit infuriating at times. My privileges, including my research-activist itineraries, left me unprepared for uncertainty. As I pulled up in my black Nissan Altima, people stopped what they were doing to size me up. I imagined that some of the brothers were checking me out. I found this worrisome because I figured that any one of the men may have been the love interests or baby daddies of the women who were sitting on the stairs in front of the buildings. In any case, I ignored the stare-downs, grabbed my bag of synthetic hair and purse, then went upstairs and rang the doorbell. Shaterra, the grocery store clerk, opened the door and let me in. "I'm surprised you came," she said, "You ready?" I lied and said I was ready, although I was fighting the urge to turn around and get back into my car before someone stole it.[1]

There was no furniture in the house except for a grey card table that functioned as a kitchen table, two folding chairs, and a box fan. In the other room of the one-bedroom apartment was a mattress covered with a sheet sitting in the middle of the floor with a toddler napping peacefully. I sat in Shaterra's makeshift dining area and stayed put for two hours while she braided my hair. She parted my hair with a black rat-toothed comb, picked out my curly black naps, and slathered "Blue Magic" grease on my scalp after scratching dry areas on top of my head that she said had dandruff. Over the course of the afternoon, I found out that Shaterra was 17 years old and had dropped out of high school in the tenth grade. She was on welfare, and worked at Pathmark to keep her income subsidies and health benefits. She wanted to go to back school but did not feel "like the time is right and, plus, I don't want to take out loans." She said she was always worrying about not working too many hours so that she could keep her check coming. It was for this reason that she braided hair on the side. In fact, she told me, a lot of women from the grocery store said they wanted her to braid their hair, but they would make appointments, then not show up. That was why she was surprised when I actually came. "You didn't look like the type," she said. I did not formally interview Shaterra, but we talked a lot about being young and having kids. At the time, my first daughter was about seven months old. I felt guilty when I talked about being a graduate student and living with my children's father. I complained that he did not want to get married. Shaterra's son's father was locked up. Trying to build with her, I told her I was struggling too, because I could not afford to pay someone $85 dollars to do my hair at one of the hair shops on Broad Street. I complained about student loans that I was not even paying back yet. Even though I could not see her, I'm sure she rolled her eyes. Shaterra cut me a deal, and only charged me $35 for the cornrows. I was grateful, but I was also complicit.

"This *has* to be *the* worst place on the face of the earth," was a thought I frequently vocalized when arguing with my partner or whining to my best friend who lived in Florida. Newark was too dirty, too crowded, too old, and too grey. Newark somehow managed to defy all of my 24-year-old, wannabe middle-class expectations of what life should be. The real problem, I surmised, was having completed college (one of only two people of my family to have done so) *and* my first year of doctoral course work, and living in what I deemed "the hood." Especially one that I could not claim as my own. Newark was foreign to me in every way imaginable. Black people themselves were very different from the ones who had inspired me while growing up in St. Louis and even those who failed to inspire me during my adolescence in Long Beach, California. Even worse, black Newarkers seemed completely different from African–Americans I regularly interacted with while completing my undergraduate degree

in political science in Atlanta, Georgia. In Atlanta, blackness functioned as social currency. It provided a sense of belonging and pride
even among strangers. There, everyone seemed proud to be black and
most of us seemed eager to connect with other black folks. I found
the mannerisms of Newarkers curt, aggressive, unfriendly, and by
and large wholly uninterested in strangers. Since, I had no family,
no friends, and did not know my way around, I often felt extremely
isolated. Somehow my presence in the Central Ward of Newark just
did not make sense.

Living in downtown Newark, while offering an easy and relatively
cheap commute into New York city vis a vis the World Trade Center
Station (before it was caved in by the aircraft attacks on 9/11) and a
12 minute drive to Newark Airport was a headache, to say the least.
I often felt trapped. In my first several months, there was no aspect
of the city that I did not slowly come to despise. I resented the fact
that the police officers and city transit workers seemed to make streets
more dangerous with their seemingly reckless disregard for the traffic signals. I resented the fact that the Newark sanitation department
could never seem to get all or even most of the trash up off the street,
resulting in an accumulation of used paper products near the street
curbs and in the gutters. Above all, I resented that, among African–
Americans, there seemed to be little or no commonality across different social classes. You either had it (or pretended to have it) or you
clearly did not. Finally, I came to resent the fact that there seemed to
be so little solidarity expressed by first and second-generation African
and Caribbean immigrants and African–Americans. In addition to all
of these gripes I had about this city Newark, in spite of all of its problems, seemed to be a relatively expensive city to live in for a person
with aspiring middle-class sensibilities to live in.

The initial gaze I leveled against Newark was colored by media
accounts of "inner city crime" statistics presented on local evening
news channels in the late 1980s in the Midwest. It was during this
time that "Newark" as a place took shape in my adolescent imagination. At the age of 12, during the summer of 1989 while visiting
cousins in St. Paul, Minnesota, I remember watching local news
accounts of the "most dangerous cities in America." White news
reporters eagerly listed these by incidences of violent crimes including per capita rates of homicide, carjackings, and drive-by shootings.
These were portrayed as symptomatic of the larger problem of drug
trafficking in American cities. Surprisingly Newark—a place I had
theretofore never heard of—surpassed my birthplace of St. Louis,
my neighboring "hood" of South Central Los Angeles, and even

Detroit. Newark topped the list in nearly all of the categories that marked a city as "dangerous." Without doubt, I was deeply biased against Newark—even though I had never been there and did not know anyone from there. The frequent barrage of local news coverage about carjacking, gang violence, and drug wars over the selling and distribution of crack cocaine made me never want to go to Newark. After falling in love and becoming pregnant with my first child, I moved to Newark to build a life with my then partner. However it took me several years to begin to appreciate the history and the culture of the city, and to truly get a good understanding of how black Newarkers experienced the physical and social space of the city.

I became more familiar with the history of Newark through scholarly accounts, everyday talk, interviews with activists, helping to organize a hip hop convention, and months spent studying at the Newark Library. The imagery of "New-Ark" from the eyes of those who live and work in the city is one of a Newark that is resilient, hopeful, and even triumphant in the face of the cold statistical accounts of social and economic decay and hardship. While most would agree that Newark defies that canonized image of a "Black Mecca," like a Harlem or Atlanta, Newark's history is rooted in African–American arts, culture, and political transformation. Women like Sarah Vaughn, Whitney Houston, Tisha Campbell-Martin, Sista Souljah, Queen Latifah, and Lauryn Hill have origins in and around the city of Newark—women who have all breathtakingly transformed African–American music by offering an alternative vision of the relevance to art, culture, and political consciousness by exposing the painful, empirically grounded sketches of African–American women. These sketches seem inspired by a unique manifestation of black feminist sensibilities in their art yet are haunted with aching, familiar struggles that are heaped on black women in urban areas including drug abuse, emotional abuse and abandonment, and a sense of being "fed-up" with the extremities of misogyny as reflected and perpetuated through hip hop culture.

In Newark there are blocks that preserve a pre-1960s landscape of lush elms lining narrow streets, sprawling porches, and the more modest well-kept multi-family flats and neat one-family homes. These rare blocks, while attractive, remain vulnerable to the drugs, gang violence, and high unemployment rates among both black women and men. It is precisely within these small oases of black working-class urban culture one finds women who are determined to change the conditions, and create venues in which young men and women are given the opportunities to learn, grow, and assert their own leadership. It is within these neighborhoods that black "political" women exert their agency to improve their communities by creating and utilizing their own stores of social capital. These neighborhoods are the birthplaces of resistance politics. Black women make it their home, and make it a political point to keep it their home in spite of the overwhelming social forces that tempt them or force them to leave.

Over several years of living in Newark, then studying Newark, and once again, as an affectionate outsider analyzing Newark as a social justice scholar interested in questions of space and identity, I now understand that the most important part of my political work is describing and theorizing the processes through which Newark becomes a beloved community, rather than a "despised city." Most of the work that we did during our interviews was ensuring that *I* understood and could adequately articulate the ways that we could love *through* the pain, frustration, disappointment, and trauma produced by structural intersectionality. Envisioning Newark as an emotionally significant place of belonging makes Newark a "home" worth staying close to and fighting for, in spite of its many problems. This loving sentiment for Newark's cityscapes transforms Newark into a fierce site of resistance rather than merely a blighted city marred by poverty, inequality, racism, and various forms of social despair. This sentiment marks Newark as place where black female political agency can and has thrived. The cultural production of blackness is one of the more powerful visual markers of the Central Ward.

Newark cityscapes immediately convey the historical processes of racialization that have shaped Newark's political economy as well as the contemporary divides that exist between working and middle-class blacks, and the thousands of unemployed and impoverished blacks who reside in the city. Central to the negotiation of economic inequality that exists between residents and patrons of the Central Ward are manifold black and African-owned businesses that mark the affection for blackness in the city. On one block west of Broad Street, Newark's major thoroughfare, one encounters a multitude of businesses that display black/African cultural signifiers. One immediately senses the presence of a strong, intact, and culturally vibrant black community (See Appendix A, Figure A.2). A walk down the historic corridor of Halsey Street immediately eclipses the impersonal crowds of students, commuters, street people, and suites that crowd Broad Street. Whether it is a bold mural for "Afrique Hall" a rental hall for weddings and other social events, Sahara International Trading, "Mecca Café," a small red, black, and green lunch truck catering to street vendors selling oils, and incense of frankincense, "Egyptian Musk", and sandal-wood, incenses, and "Nature's Blessings" hair oil (see Appendix A.2). Black Muslim retailers along Branford Street play the invaluable role of showcasing the potential longevity of independently-owned black businesses, providing a longstanding cultural alternative to models of black prosperity and respectability represented by the black politicians, bureaucrats, and municipal and corporate officers who work on and travel through Broad Street (see Appendix A.1). Hamidah's Café and Body Shop sells homemade and small batch-produced "Nubian Heritage" lotions, soaps, and a variety of bath and body products, handmade imported West African jewelry and fabrics, vegan juices, smoothies, sandwiches, and bean pies. The black Muslim mother and daughter team who own and operate Hamidah's are a living embodiment of a diasporic past and present when black women owned and controlled local markets on the coast of West Africa and well-defined gender roles, though certainly not Western, contribute to a bustling, relatively autonomous black economy.

In the Central Ward competing stories of black people tethered to American inner cities is told: one story is indicated by the visual markers of black poverty and social alienation, the other is over-determined by symbols of black cultural agency and resistance. In the center of downtown, one becomes immediately aware of how larger economic forces of neoliberalization including gentrification, cultural commodification, and globalization shape the city. It is commonplace to see young women, sometimes even pregnant women, panhandling in front of the esteemed New Jersey Performing Arts Center. Busses wheeze in and between lanes to avoid double parked cars and curiously brave pedestrians jay-walk to avoid a 45 second wait at the busy traffic light. Walking along Market Street one passes countless young black men standing in front of Army/Navy surplus stores, electronic repair shops, discount clothiers, hat shops, and music retail stores. These mostly black men sell a variety of small products including skull caps, sun glasses, t-shirts, tank tops, belts, purses, and sometimes items like colored contact lenses, bootleg CDs and DVDs, and other sub-legal products that happen to be in demand.

In contrast, on the other end of Broad street corridor, the Starbuck's Coffee Shop is built to accommodate the conspicuous (and mostly white) white-collar professionals of Prudential, IDT, and Wachovia (before the bank collapsed, and was bought out by Wells Fargo in the Great Recession), and (mostly black and Latino) Newark city bureaucrats. Seven blocks east, west, or southwest of downtown, one suddenly confronts the inherent truth of social analyst's jargon, "social alienation" and "marginality." Middle-aged, and seemingly unemployed black men stand in front of food pantries and shelters. They sit on broken porches on streets strewn with garbage. Young black women walk to the corner grocers with young children in tow to pick up bread, milk, and a quick meal from a fried chicken and fish joint (see Appendix A.4). The streets are sparsely populated on city blocks that on first sight seem abandoned. It only takes a few seconds for one to notice that in between the boarded up flats and the vacant overgrown lots and liquor stores that people actually *live* here. These are communities. In the public housing projects the scene was even worse. At the then Baxton Terrace Homes school-aged children played in filthy parking lots surrounded by apartments that were either boarded up with plywood, or had unscreened windows gaping open in an effort to find minimal relief from the summer heat. As they played, the children deftly ignored the shattered glass, the food wrappers, the bare chicken bones, and the cars that pulled up to exchange cash for drugs with the young men who seemed to covertly patrol the entire scene.

The extenuated history of racialization of African–Americans in Newark forms the existing conditions that shape the everyday experiences of black folks. In fact, one strategy of resisting the negative effects of gentrification and neoliberalization for African–Americans is to claim blackness as a rich and desirable cultural commodity. This includes a robust effort to situate one's life within a history of black political, cultural, and economic resistance to white (and increasingly non-black) economic domination. Claiming blackness as an identity in Newark requires much more than the voluntary enactment of any unidimensional politics of black identity. Rather, claiming blackness involves intentionally creating spaces of nostalgia, belonging, and hope. For young black people whose life chances and opportunity structures are constrained by persistent social, political, and economic violence, including gang and drug violence, black on black street violence, police violence, and increasing homophobic violence directed toward queer teens, this kind of spatial work is considered dire.

Politically, gentrification in Newark depends on efforts to attract young African–American professional families and consumers from the surrounding suburbs of Montclair, Bloomfield, Hillside, and Maplewood. This requires city administrators and interested developers to lure upwardly mobile professionals away from the sprawling malls and shopping centers in the towns of Wayne, Clark, and Union and the mass appeal of highway retail strips on Routes, 3, 10, 22, and 46, as well as from New York City itself. However, political efforts to further solidify and expand the majority of the black political base are often frustrated by the rapidly increasing Spanish-speaking and Latino populations in the city. While many of the retailers featured in this section of Newark's cityscapes have managed to survive and even capitalize on efforts to gentrify Newark, the inner city is becoming increasingly non-black. The increasing Latino population of the East and North Wards of Newark and the corresponding concentration of political power among Latinos problematizes any effort to envision Newark as a "Black Mecca." Indeed, the current political climate requires adjusting black political rhetoric from "the community" to "black and Latino communities" and "people of color communities" to signify inclusion and the hope for some kind of solidarity.

Home, rather than just being a mere site, locale, or physical infrastructure, is a place in which specific racialized and gendered histories shape people's longstanding affective ties and shifting relationships to the city's physical, symbolic, and cultural landscape. For black people in Newark's Central Ward, it is a place where the question "of who we can be and still be black can be politically re-imagined and practiced" (Soja 1996). Rather than a source of frustration, indignation, or disappointment, Newark is a place of belonging and nostalgia. It is a place where struggles are waged, families are nurtured, history is lived, and hopeful tomorrows are embraced. Black people, through their daily activities as vendors, commuters, shoppers, small business owners, parents, students, hustlers, old people, sex workers, street people, homeless people, and activists breathe life into Newark by actively and often aggressively reclaiming its cityscapes as their own. As a place, Newark is a locale where black people's sense of what political scientist Michael Dawson (1992) called "linked fate" is translated into a form of deeply rooted social and political consciousness whereby black people understand their futures to be deeply interconnected. Black linked fate is often co-produced by tragedy and resistance, and within each blackness itself is a category that gets remade. In other words, blackness, and black linked fate, is always in flux in the social geography of the city.

Conceptions of blackness are deeply contested in Newark, making it a dynamic and constantly shifting landscape constituted by diverse and often contradictory discourses of blackness. For example, across from "Mecca Café" a colorful mural invokes a more contemporary representation of urban "blackness." In an effort to attract male consumers, Dr. Jay's, a retailer specializing in sneakers, denim jeans, and sportswear, depicts scenes of young black men in the act of laying down tracks on a keyboard, playing basketball, and gawking at two hypersexualized images of two light-skinned women of color (see Appendix A.3). Alongside the numerous African hair braiding salons in which stylists routinely braid synthetic hair into the heads of black women and queer black men, are wig shops, exotic leather retailers, tattoo parlors, and even "All Brothers Liquors" (see Appendix A.5).

While the cultural production of blackness is a resonant element of Newark's visual economy, gentrification has permeated Newark's streets and neighborhoods. During the period from 2001 to 2008, gentrification brought huge retailers like Old Navy, Home Depot, and Starbucks to the Central Ward. Countless numbers of single level parking lots are sprawled across Newark's downtown district, evidencing the availability of cheap downtown space—easily sold to mediocre bidders. Current patterns of gentrification illustrate that the vast majority of financial beneficiaries of Newark's inner-city employment opportunities are not local. By six o'clock in the evening tens of thousands of white commuters leave the streets mostly empty, the exception being weeknights when one of the city's professional baseball or basketball teams is playing and/or when there are weekend performances at the New Jersey Performing Arts Center on Broad Street. Well connected, local black and Latino politicians and businessmen use the Robert Treat Hotel and the Ironbound's satellite restaurants and lounges as exclusive retreats from the hustle of late afternoon downtown traffic.

Today, Newark exists as a racially and ethnically segregated space shaped by deindustrialization and a longstanding hope for revitalization. Newark's urban landscape is not only shaped by its physical structures but also by the movement of its people within and between those structures. This includes the amorphous spaces created to fulfill the specific everyday needs of the people who occupy them comprising the need to eat, to work, to get an education, to get from point A to point B and back, and also to just simply belong. The satisfaction of these needs are simultaneously economic, social, cultural, and political and, therefore, also spatial (Harvey 2001, Lefebvre 1991, de Certeau 1984, Foucault 1967). People who claim Newark as home are reluctant to claim it as a space of black suffering and oppression. Instead they claim it as a place of black political resistance and self-determination. Black political women claim it as home because it is a place that they are willing to stay in, cling to, and go back to physically, emotionally, socially, and politically. As a home, Newark nourishes one's capacity to *resist* both feelings and practices of marginality, displacement, dispossession, and alienation from structural intersectionality (hooks 1990).

Newark as Home: Decolonizing the Gaze

The portrait of Newark painted by local black women, the political subjects of this book, resists the dismal caricature drawn by the dominant social science discourse focusing solely on urban social, economic, and political decay (Cunningham 2002, Winters 1977, Hayden 1967) and my own initial reactions. Black political women's narratives of Newark complicate discourses that focus exclusively on stories of racial marginality; even so the social and economic marginality of African–American youth remain significantly central. The history of black resistance to white racism was the most powerful theme that emerged from our dialogues about Newark. In fact, one of the most prominent themes that emerged from our discussions were the women's insistence that a counter-narrative be created, one that is rooted in transforming the entrenched social problems produced by decades of racial exclusion and economic marginality. The women I interviewed, educated me about Newark's history of survival and how the city enabled them to embrace Newark as a desirable, and much beloved "home." Their optimistic commitment to "home improvement" emphasizes Newark's history of black cultural resistance to racial marginality, and serves as one of the most important elements of their "political" lives. In Gayatri Spivak's (1990) words, black women in Newark taught me how to "unlearn my privilege as a loss." This means that they taught me how to "trace the other in myself" and to locate that otherness within complex webs of power and knowledge that granted me the privilege to tell the story of black women's resistance. I had to understand that I was also telling my own story through the metaphor of Newark. They taught me how to tell it with dignity.

When I first interviewed her, Gayle Chaneyfield-Jenkins was a 44-year-old Newark city councilwoman who was born and raised in the Hayes Home housing projects. She explained during our interview, "Folks here are very protective of Newark, almost to a fault. Like when a mother protects her child." Gayle, whose family had an extensive history of political organizing and office-seeking in Newark after migrating from South Carolina in the 1940s, was broadly identified as "very political" in my many discussions with various community members. While her mother graduated from college later in life, Gayle's father only got to the fourth grade. While growing up Gayle's father did factory work, often working two or three jobs to keep food on the table. Her father eventually became a union organizer in Newark. Her mother worked for several years as an administrative assistant for University of Medicine and Dentistry of New Jersey (UMDNJ), and then went on to start "Babyland," Newark's first center offering child care and domestic violence services to poor and socially vulnerable mothers.

As early as 2005, the councilwoman argued that we need to "change the debate," foreshadowing the concerns of the contemporary "Occupy" Movement. She argued that, we need to "take on the banking industry" who, in her opinion, were "making millions of dollars collecting interest on loans, but "never investing in our communities." Throughout our three-hour interview she frequently criticized the strategy of state and local politicians to "fix the economy" by building sports stadiums and the new performing arts center (NJPAC). She explained, "It just don't work. It doesn't. What it does is create an almost servile class where black Newarkers serve white suburbanites for peanut wages. The workers don't make enough to pay the tickets to see the games. Most black people don't benefit from the 'trickle down' method."

However, when discussing Newark's history, Gayle praised it a space that has a unique history of African–American leadership. She explained, "Newark has been a place where movements happen. You know, the N.O.I. [National of Islam], which I belonged to. The Masons and Eastern Stars. We have music, gospel, soul, R&B, hip hop. Black art originated here. As a matter of fact, Newark has [had an] impact worldwide! But still, it's a small town, you know. Everybody knows everybody. There are always less than six degrees of separation. You know what I mean? And so in some ways it's kind of conservative."

When asked why she has stayed in Newark, even after having a somewhat tumultuous political career and eventually losing her council seat in a race that she lost because of her close ties with then Mayor Sharpe James, she told me, "Because I love my city. Newark is the vanguard of all urban cities. I am committed to being like my family. I want to help Newark make a comeback. And for that reason, I will always be involved in politics, in some form."

Staying home in Newark and appropriating its cityscapes as a beloved home was often articulated as sense of responsibility, almost as a form of care. Care, Joan Tronto argues, embraces the ideals of community engagement, acceptance of the burden of meeting an identified need, and demonstrating a sustained effort to "maintain, continue and repair our world so that we can live in it as well as possible" (1993, 103). Dana Rone, a 40-year-old school board member who lost her seat after trying to help a family member avoid being arrested, said that at one time she felt like she could do "better than Newark." During her early twenties when she saw the opportunities of her friends who finished high school and college and then, "moved on," she felt that she could have done the same. Dana was conflicted because she still felt she had more in common with those who were not afforded the opportunities and resources to leave than those who did. The story of how she came to run for public office for the first time is testimony to her feeling of being torn between pursuing her narrowly defined interests and public service.

> The safety that you wanted, the culture that you wanted. You could bring that to your neighborhood, you didn't have to go outside to find that place, but that you could create things that you [want]. So that's what I guess helped me to stay home. I guess everything that he gave me as a kid, and how hard it seemed my parents worked to change Newark, and the change that they brought to Newark that was essential.

For Dana, surviving public housing, one of the most politically maligned institutions in the city, was viewed as a source of strength and pride. She understood her own life to be a living testimony to the resilience taught by the city. She expressed an inherent need to be part of the "fight" to improve the conditions in the city.

> I was a young person who saw the fight. It was at the end of the riots when I was born. So it was that whole Black Power Movement that changed our economy, and our social services. So I had to see us fight, and I got to see the results of the fight. It was very different for me. I'm one who understands that no matter what you endure, the good times will come, because I benefited from that. There was a time when we didn't have anything, but after fighting we had something. Dad always encouraged me that it can get better, no matter how hard it gets. That's what helped me to stay.

For Dana, Newark represented a home that was worth staying and fighting for. But she also saw the many more people who were left behind and not able to afford the opportunities, nor did they have the resources to leave. Her sentiment was intensified when she noticed the inadequate leadership of the people serving in public office.

> I was running out [of my house] on my way to Virginia, and a neighbor of mine who was an alcoholic came to my door and knocked on my door, and he asked me to sign this petition for school board. I

sort of laughed...because I was looking at this individual...and, he was telling me who was supporting him and everything. And I'm saying...this is incredible that this individual would be able to run for the most important seat. The school board is the most important local election that you can participate in. And I was telling my friends on my way down to Virginia. And they said, 'Dana, we're so sick of you talking about all this, why don't you do something about it?' So when I got back, I picked up my petitions. That was on a Tuesday, they [the petitions] were due that Thursday. And only ten names [were] required to get on the ballot, ten registered voters.

When confronted with the reality of who *might* be representing her neighborhood on the school board, Dana felt that she was also confronted with her own complicity in perpetuating the problem of poor leadership if she did not put her own education, oratory, and organizing skills to work. Even though she had very little experience in public service as an adult, she was certain that she could offer much more to Newark families than the inebriated wannabe candidate. She felt a sense of responsibility to put action behind the vividly articulated arguments that she usually reserved for family and close friends. Her "political" life was initiated when she realized her own leadership potential.

Dana went on to win the school board seat and, in spring of 2006, became the new councilwoman for the Central Ward. While Dana came from a civically involved family, and was outspoken on a variety of political issues among her peers, she was essentially politicized after she became an elected official. Although she grew up in a household that advocated for "poor people," she now became intimate with the severity of the problems facing Newarkers through her service on the school board. Dana, who had only completed two years of community college, was shocked to learn that most students currently graduating from Newark public schools could not pass the New Jersey State Exit Exam. She was outraged when she realized that many recent high school "graduates could not read or write at the eighth grade level," and that school board administrators felt that this was acceptable because it boosted the graduation rates. What was most frustrating to Dana during her work on the school board was that most of the parents with whom she interacted were single mothers and were either too intimidated or lacked necessary information to publicly challenge these conditions and the underlying attitudes that supported them. Inundated with statistics that revealed the vulnerability of black students and severity of the institutionalized problems that faced them in her home town, Dana felt as if she had no choice but to try to offer them something better through public service.

Candidly, she "told them the truth" about how she perceived the school district was failing students, and explained how school and district level administrators were complicit in this failure. This then became the brunt of the political work that Dana did as a Newark school board member.

Education was one of the most frequently invoked issues linking contemporary social ills to the long history of racial domination. Although formal education was viewed as one of the most pressing problems the city faced, "education" by formal means was *not* viewed as a panacea by the women I interviewed. Children were viewed as lacking an education about the structural forces that drive the city, especially in terms of race, political economy, and the black cultural resources contained within Newark's borders. As dismal as Newark public schools were perceived to be, the lack of knowledge about Newark's rich cultural history of black resistance was seen as much more problematic by local activists. To combat the hopelessness and despair engulfing Newark's school system, this form of education was perceived to be crucial for the city's collective social and economic revitalization. In the words of Frederica Bey, Executive Director of Women in Support of the Million Man March:

> You know, the state took over ten or fifteen years ago, the state took over the education and its gotten worse. Naturally because New Jersey is the last state that abolished slavery, and so they are in charge of the education of our children. This is why we strive. Three times— twice we were denied for charter school, and the third time we were approved. I think that we as African people are the only ones who can remedy our plight. We must educate our own children. This country banned us from reading, banned us from an education, legally. Banned us from marriage. So we have to educate our own people and our own selves. And from that education will come the economics that we need and the self-sufficiency that we need. We have to do it our selves. Black folks doing for black folks, that's how it going to look when it happens. It's happening [now]. Creating the first African American cultural center in the history of this state . . . this is how you begin to make it happen.

For activists like Frederica, collective opportunities to learn and value the role that African–Americans had played in shaping Newark's history were understood to be just as important a factor in creating individual opportunities for young African–Americans within the borders of the city to prosper socially and economically. Formal education itself was not viewed as simply a means for individual advancement, but rather as a way to increase awareness of the history of black racialization in order to confront contemporary state-sponsored efforts to curtail the social, political, and economic empowerment of African–Americans.

Frederica was a 62-year-old Muslim mother, grandmother, and real estate agent. To her, Newark symbolized a unique black urban culture of endurance, tenacity, and a resilience with roots in the south. For other lifelong residents, Newark symbolized a "home" away from the imagined home of "down South" that presented a unique set of opportunities for black female political agency. This is an agency that emphasizes the creation and maintenance of community-based organizations and institutions that address Newark's mostly deeply entrenched social problems including poverty, poor housing, and manifold strategies of resistance to racial domination. Like the other women I interviewed, Frederica exemplified loyalty to both activism and residency within the Central Ward of Newark, which were tied to their basic sense of self, community, and place. Black women activists boldly connected the temporal dimensions of Newark's cityscape by linking the personal intimacy with the "old Newark" of their parents to the "enduring Newark" of the present and to a vision of "Newark" for the future. This form of agency fueled decisions to remain in Newark and live as well as possible in the city. This process called for courageously articulating an alternative narrative of transcendence and resurrection about a city that was left for dead in the larger American public imagination.

In the mind's eye of black women activists, the image of an enduring, symbolic Newark coexists with keen awareness of the crisis that black people face in the city. Black women activists mobilize against powerful forces: the multigeneration failure of Newark's public institutions to provide a quality education to African–American youth, and refusal of public service organizations, including social welfare and law enforcement agencies, to support the growth and development of black families.

POWER, KNOWLEDGE, AND NARRATING NEWARK'S CITYSCAPES

The plight of African–Americans, like that of all black and brown people who spend a substantial portion of their daily lives in Newark, is tied to a living political history that is plagued with stark economic, racial, and ethnic inequalities, as well as some of the most pernicious and socially detrimental political practices known to scholars of American politics. These practices include the corporate looting of public coffers, white flight, gentrification, and a corrupt, incompetent, and patronage-based municipal governance structure. These practices fed two successive, entrenched, potent, toxic, and powerful mayoral machines that controlled Newark for 36 years. This form of heteropatriarchy over local black community politics has played a critical role in shaping black women activists' conceptions of politics and their current exercise of political agency.

In order to accurately reflect these alternative understandings of politics, the next chapter captures the oral narratives of black women activists who continue to engage and transform social problems facing Newark's black residents. Oral narratives reveal the political and personal histories of black female subjects, illuminating the subjugated knowledge of black women's political lives, as well as their strategies of resistance (Beauboeuf-Lafontant 2009, Vaz 1997, Etter-Lewis & Foster 1996, Etter-Lewis 1993, Collins 1991). These personal testimonies explore local black women's reflections on the significance of their own "political" strategies to resist various forms of social, political, and economic marginality. Narratives are drawn from women who are not well-known poets, scholars, activists, or artists. Indeed, they are not well-known outside of the city of Newark. Their lives would not have been likely subjects for scholarly or journalistic scrutiny. Yet the significance and impact of their political work is far too important to be neglected. For these reasons, I have undertaken systematic excavation and analysis of the political voices of Newark's black women activists. As mothers, aunties, and othermothers raising children and grandchildren in Newark, as social activists concerned with diverse issues, and as elected officials who are enthusiastic about the exciting possibilities that Newark has to offer, these women radiate strength, vulnerability, and courage. In this next chapter, I examine the "politics of homemaking," a unique and important form of black feminist intersectional praxis in Newark.

5

THE POLITICS OF HOMEMAKING: BLACK FEMINIST TRANSFORMATIONS OF A CITYSCAPE

I didn't chose it [Newark], my parents did. As an adult, I chose to stay because I like Newark. To this day, if I'm gone two weeks, I'm coming back home. I don't stay away too long. It's a part of me.

Amina Baraka

I love this town. I love the people in this town, even the rawness of it. I love the...ahh...energy! The survival...the will of the people to survive and thrive, and to keep on keeping on...regardless. I love that energy here. Seeing it from the sixties, and the fifties, and seeing it now in 2006 is amazing. It's amazing to be able to see it from say...forty, fifty years of transition.

Frederica Bey, 61-year-old community organizer,
black Muslim and founder of Women in
Support of the Million Man March

You can't really understand Newark, if you don't understand how this city was burnt to the ground. You can't understand Newark, if you don't understand how black folks organized to take power back in the city, and how they had to fight for their own independence and self-determination. We had to fight. We had to rebuild from the ashes, from the bottom up. And we still haven't finished. We still have a lot of work to do.

Fayemi Shakur, 26-year-old freelance journalist,
community organizer, political prisoner activist,
and single mother of two boys

INTRODUCTION

For black women activists Amina Baraka, like Frederica Bey and Fayemi Shakur, the Central Ward of Newark represents a home that

is worth staying and fighting for.[1] In spite of generations of deindustrialization, social upheaval, chronic African–American underemployment, and the troublesome impact of gentrification, Newark
represents a symbolic space that *can* be transformed. Newark is a
beloved intimate space to be reclaimed, reworked, and reimagined
as a homeplace—a symbolic space that nurtures the life-chances of
young black people. In this chapter, I develop a political theory of
homemaking that attempts to make sense of how space, place, and
identity shape black women's political activism. I examine and retell
the spatial stories that black women shared with me in order to clarify
how gendered racialization impact black women's conceptions and
practice of contemporary grassroots politics.[2]

Homemaking is a central mode of black women's political resistance in Newark. Homemaking stretches beyond individual wom-
en's work in households and the sphere of domesticity. Instead,
homemaking involves creating homeplaces to affirm African–
American life, history, culture, and politics.[3] Homeplaces are
political spaces that black women create to express care for each
other and their communities, and to remember, revise, and revive
scripts of black political resistance.[4] For women like Fayemi and
Frederica, homemaking involves creating and preserving autonomous spaces for relationship building between black people that
foster hope, leadership capacity, and a strong, stable, and positive
sense of self-identity.

Homemaking is a critical form of intersectional spatial praxis.
It involves reconfiguring a hostile and deeply racialized landscape.
Homemaking requires respatializing social capital, that is, recon-
structing and reconfiguring relationships of trust, positive reciprocity,
cooperation, and care within and between black people and Newark's
political imaginary. It means finding ways to creatively confront and
transform multiple structures of domination. In this chapter, three
distinctive modes of political homemaking are identified. They are:
(1) creating a living history of resistance, (2) the politics of reclamation, and finally, (3) the politics of selling-in. The first mode of homemaking, creating a living history of resistance, entails making space in
the community for folks to remember and reenvision earlier modes of
black freedom struggle. These include contemporary cultural nationalist spaces and community coalitions that insist that white supremacy,
anti-black racism, and neoliberalization run amuck *still* have an overde-
termining negative impact on black people's lives. Within these community spaces activists reinvigorate and politicize the importance of
black love, black solidarity, and the development of autonomous black

community leadership. The second mode of resistance encompasses the politics of reclamation. These politics involve telling the story of black political and cultural resistance in order to transform the use, symbolism, and cultural potential of abandoned and neglected public spaces. Black women revive and retell counter-narratives of black resistance in order combat feelings of disconnectedness, alienation, and hopelessness in urban space. The final mode of political resistance is "selling-in." This is comprised of dedicating one's professional and community life to uplift, revitalize, and transform the city. All three modes of resistance are based upon a deep-rooted attachment to African–American's marked history of struggle for racial and economic justice.

While the concept of homemaking is a designator of black women "contemporary" political agency, the histories that black women mobilize in order to transform the present emerge from attempts to re-ascribe new meanings to a past that has shaped the present conditions of black people in Newark. In other words, through homemaking black women resist linear narratives which insist upon a clean break between past, present, and future. Their efforts to "tell the truth" about histories of domination *and* resistance are folded into contemporary imaginings and practices of black hardship and suffering; and, as a corollary black/urban political transformation. M. Jacqui Alexander has theorized the temporal aspect of black feminist praxis as "palimpsestic time" which she describes as a rescrambling of "the 'here and now' and the 'then and there' to a 'here and there' and a 'then and now' (page 190)." Within this framework, the three elements of the politics of homemaking—creating a living history of resistance, the politics of reclamation, and the politics of selling in—function as critiques of modernist fictions that confine white supremacy and black suffering as a thing of the past.

THEORY AND METHODS: A STRUGGLE AGAINST FORGETTING

Our struggle is also a struggle against forgetting: a politicization of memory that distinguishes nostalgia, that longing for something to be as it once was, a kind of useless act, from that remembering that serves to illuminate and transform the present.

bell hooks,
Yearning: Race, Gender and Cultural Politics (1990)

Black women activists in Newark transform their communities by reimagining and reconfiguring people's relationships to the physical, symbolic, and relational spaces of the communities that they live in (Harvey 2001). Following Pratibha Parmar (1991), I argue that the use and appropriation of space is a political act. This kind of political agency can be understood as "resistance politics." Black women's resistance politics do not just function through efforts to spark collective action, but through the *bodily* sacrifices they make in order to create, nurture, and reproduce political space. Black women's resistance is often articulated affectively through discourses of care, belonging, affect, and *relationality* rather than through logic, objectivity, and rationality. Affect is more than just individual feelings or emotionality. Seigworth and Gregg (2011), argues that affect is the *force that drives us toward movement, toward thought and extension*. Homemaking, as an affective form of resistance, involves more than just being attentive to and providing care to individuals. It also requires building an enduring affective relationship to the physical environment. It is the imaginative political work that transforms the built environment of the city into a home: a place of belonging, a place of remembrance, and a place of resistance. Homemaking, then encompasses black women's efforts to *build the will to resist* the alienating and dehumanizing practices and ideologies that continue to ghettoize and minoritize black people in Newark's Central Ward. It involves making people—or bodies—*care* about space.

From a political perspective, homemaking goes far beyond voting or deciding who gets what, when, and how, and at what cost. Instead, as Barbara Ransby wrote in her biography of Ella Baker's social activism, "Politics [are] immediate and measured in flesh and blood realities. You have to love the people around you, and those struggling right next to you, as much as the anonymous and amorphous mass of humanity" (2003). Care, Tronto argues, embraces the ideals of community engagement, acceptance of the burden of meeting an identified need, and demonstrating a sustained effort to "maintain, continue and repair our world so that we can live in it as well as possible" (1993, 103). From this perspective, black women's affective politics is not rooted in a mere psychological attachment to the city of Newark, but an active and *collective working toward* physical, symbolic, and relational transformations of Newark's landscape and political imaginary.

Scholars, including Patricia Hill Collins (2006, 1991), Nancy Naples (1998), Leith Mullings (1997), Cheryl Townsend Gilkes (1998), Kimberly Springer (1999), and, more recently, works by Sheila Radford-Hill (2000), Evelyn M. Simien (2006), Annelise Orleck (2005), and Duchess Harris (2011) began the work of documenting the history of black women's politics in the United States. They, in various ways, have argued that black women express their political agency through "community mothering." Community mothering, like homemaking, involves pursuing activist politics that attend to current structural inequalities and injustices that impact colored people's lives. Further, this scholarship documents black women's historical role in mobilizing around issues like poverty, affordable housing, welfare reform, prison abolition, police brutality, and gender violence (Gilmore 2007, Orleck 2005, Springer 2005, Williams 2004, Naples 1997).

I explore how memory and affect shape black women's political work by considering how their unique relationship to space and place inform how they define and deploy discourses of identity and community. The politics of homemaking is an attempt to sketch a response, not a definitive answer, to these questions: What are the meanings that black women attribute to space and place? How do identity and affect impact the range of politics that black women pursue in urban spaces? How do black women enact political resistance in contemporary urban spaces?

This chapter centers the narratives of four out of 29 Newark-based black women activists I interviewed. These women were selected because the theme of homemaking was resonant in our conversations. Each woman carefully linked her politicization to highly personal events in her own life, and each suggested that the conscious decision to mark Newark as "home" was an intentional sacrifice motivated by a deep-seated desire to transform the city. The women featured in this article represent three generations, ranging in age from 26 to 70. Their stories were solicited through one-on-one talk sessions that took place in various locations including activists' workplaces, community centers, my home, their homes, and/or local eateries.[5] Limiting this analysis to just four women enables a meaningful exploration of their experiences and motivations. This move should be received as a pointed attempt to offer a counter-narrative to the widely analyzed racist–sexist discourses of black women as lazy, hypersexual, baby-making "hoodrats," "welfare queens" or "nappy headed ho's" who are more concerned with private consumption than contributing to the public good (see, for instance, Harris-Perry 2011, Sharpley Whiting 2008, Collins 2005, Hancock 2004). Using what Beauboeuf-Lafontant (2009) has described as a "voice-centered framework," this project is centered on *listening* to black women in Newark had to say about politics and their political lives. Oral narratives and political biographies are theorized as spatial stories to illuminate the distinctive ways that black women imagine politics that, I argue, are realized through a distinctive way of imagining social space.[6] In this chapter, "Newark" emerges symbolically through embodied, collective histories gleaned from the recollections and dialogues between black women activists, including myself. I honor the trust that was developed over the years by featuring the activists' agency in own words, as much as possible. After all, it is their work in the city, and the personal sacrifices that they make in order to do their work that makes this article both possible and relevant. In the next section, I discuss my own relationship to Newark and reveal how my personal background, predispositions, politics, and social endeavors frame the politics of homemaking.

NEWARK THROUGH THE REAR VIEW MIRROR

On my way home from class, I come to a stoplight after exiting 280-East. A slender young woman with permanently straightened hair gelled back into a tight ponytail approaches my car. Her black stretch pants and faded black t-shirt pull taut across her unusually large stomach. I roll the window down. "Can I have dollar?" she asks, "I'm eight months pregnant and need to buy some food for me and my baby." I look into the young woman's face and see all the telltale signs of drug addiction: the dark crusted lips, the ashen brown skin, the anxious, unapologetic desperation…I pull out all the change in my car door—probably a dollar, maybe a little bit more—and dump it into her can. I maneuver my six-year old black Nissan through the McCarter Highway construction traffic. From the rear-view mirror, I see the young woman solicit the car behind me. I speed past the famed New Jersey Performing Arts Center dodging pedestrians, and turn into the parking lot of my downtown apartment building. I'm stunned, I'm pissed, and I'm speechless. What can I say? What is there to say? Excerpt from field-notes

As a "part Mexican," brown-skinned, dreadlocked, African–American identified female activist and researcher in Newark, admittedly, my experiences, field-notes, records, relationships, and social interactions with these women were assembled and analyzed to reproduce the milieu through which the politics of homemaking comes into focus. The brief interaction with the pregnant woman soliciting change on the highway exit is not coincidental and cannot be understood outside the macro-level processes that make the mundane interaction between us the subject of scholarly reflection. As racialized and gendered subjects, we are both products and agents of history and politics (Bourdieu 1980). Within a social space marked by racialized poverty and class inequality, the politics of homemaking requires that I imagine her as a sister and comrade in our mutual struggles for a better life for both of our unborn children. The experience of being solicited for money on the streets by young African–American women of childbearing age became almost commonplace. This "everyday" experience underscores how privilege coincides with domination, and illuminates the complicity that all scholar-activists face when trying to speak with and on behalf of people who live in or are confined to communities racked with deprivation. I resolved to make legible the ways that black women activists combat the conditions that produce the desperation, vulnerability, and distress that we *both* experienced in the city. The politics of homemaking requires naming psychological violence produced by the class distance that made her beg and me give with guilt and repressed rage. It also challenged me to consider and articulate a counter-narrative to this instance of geographic domination.

This embodied account placed *me*—a three-month pregnant, 27-year-old, unmarried black female from Long Beach, California— right smack in the middle of Newark's social and political milieu. The initial enthusiasm I had about doing socially relevant black feminist scholarship was dampened by the real limitations that such a project is likely to have on the everyday experiences of the young woman I encountered off the 280 interstate exit. As a graduate student mother bringing home less than 12,000 dollars a year, I could empathize with feeling compelled to request financial assistance in hostile places from potentially hostile people. However, the obstacles she faced were more ominous. Unlike myself, she was exposed to the harshest, most bodily forms of violence imaginable in Newark's streets. Over time, it became obvious that what I could do for this woman and her child, and myself and my children, was produce an account of her community and its politics that invoked a sense of empathy and hope that we all could have a life worth living in Newark. In the next section, my analysis of homemaking continues with the story of Fayemi Shakur, a courageous, hardworking, and uniquely effective political homemaker in Newark.

FAYEMI SHAKUR: CREATING A LIVING HISTORY OF RESISTANCE

I understand the quest for a better life for your children, but why deny a part of your history, a part of your past that is a part of you? I always

looked at Newark as a place that had a really rich cultural history—a
history that I could be a part of. Fayemi Shakur, office manager for
community economic development corporation, free-lance journalist,
political prisoner activist, and single mother of two.

Fayemi's words boldly refute the dismal caricature that emerges in
dominant social science discourse and popular media accounts about
Newark that focus squarely on Newark's economic decay and fraught
political landscape. National media attention on the city is typically
confined to reports on high unemployment, persistent poverty, and
the dramas associated with winning or losing the coveted office of
mayor. White flight, the overrepresentation of racial-ethnic minorities among the poor, high, urban riots, and the widely publicized high
rates of auto theft and violent crime in national media throughout the
1980s and 1990s contributes to the routine depiction of Newark, as
a dangerous, "blackened" space (Wilson 2009, Collins 2005, Jackson
2003). Scholars who "study" places like Newark typically focus their
investigations on failing inner city schools, unemployed black men,
or political "saviors" like Cory Booker who manage to accumulate
massive stores of political power but fail to deliver electoral prom-
ises due to "structural forces" that inhibit the realization of "vision-
ary" political leadership.[7] Fayemi, however, encourages us to consider
an alternative narrative. She experiences Newark as a deep source of
inspiration and belonging. Newark's history of black political resistance through grassroots organizing is central to her positive affect
toward the city. Acquiring personal knowledge about this history,
and the skills and confidence to share it with others, allows Fayemi to
embrace the city as a desirable and a beloved home.

Fayemi was raised in a suburban, middle-class New Jersey family.
Ironically, she did not experience her relatively privileged childhood as
a source of pride. Instead she willfully shunned many of the benefits
that her upbringing could have afforded her. For Fayemi, her parents'
desire for a "middle class lifestyle" symbolized a conscious choice to
turn away from Newark's predominantly black cityscapes and toward
what she considered an "ahistorical" existence. In her view, the suburban environment in which she was raised in minimized the historical
significance of black culture in Newark in exchange for a "better life."
She interpreted her parents' decision to move away from Newark as a
moving away from her extended family and childhood friends as well as
a conscious turning away from contemporary black freedom struggle.

As a young mother, Fayemi's decision to make Newark a physical
home for herself and her two sons signified an important return to a

"place that had a really rich cultural history." For her, black culture itself was an attractive commodity that outweighed other quality of life issues that might have logically made suburban New Jersey a better place to raise her children. She explains,

> My extended family is here [Newark]. My grandmother lived here. My sister is here. My cousins are here. A part of me felt like we were trying to be middle class, but we were really from another environment that we didn't acknowledge any more, and tried to suppress. I really didn't understand why.

As a college student, Fayemi strongly identified with Newark's oppositional political history. Her initial interest in politics was sparked when she joined the Black Student Union during her second year at a local community college. This popular campus organization had recently taken on a more nationalistic identity, renaming itself "The Black Freedom Society." As a member, Fayemi was exposed to nationalist and Pan-Africanist readings of African–American history. She attended community meetings, Kwanzaa ceremonies, and participated in study groups where she, "met a lot of elders. They shared information with me that I had never really been exposed to before, but I felt like I knew it. And once I heard it I wanted to learn more."

From this point on, Fayemi became an active member of several local organizations including the People's Organization for Progress, the New Black Panther Party, and the Malcolm X Grassroots Movement—all of which she felt had a "positive impact" in the city. She went on to spearhead the New Jersey chapter of the "Hands Off Assata" Campaign—a national coalition that aggressively linked contemporary injustice against people of color to state-sponsored efforts to criminalize radical activists like Assata Shakur who participated in local movements for self-determination and racial justice in the late 1960s and 1970s.

Fayemi, like several other women interviewed in this study, made reference to the Newark "rebellion" (not riots) of 1967, and the subsequent community mobilizations of Newark's minority voters. Although the riots took place years before she was born, she insisted,

> You can't really understand Newark, if you don't understand how this city was burnt to the ground. You can't understand Newark, if you don't understand how black folks organized to take power back in the city, and how they had to fight for their own independence and

self-determination. We had to fight. We had to rebuild from the ashes, from the bottom up. And we still haven't finished. We still have a lot of work to do.

When the streets cooled, resistance to racial injustice materialized as a blend of cultural and political nationalism that was geared toward seizing electoral power using Newark's increasing number of African–American and Puerto Rican voters.[8] This history of political organizing inspired a personal commitment to participate in and *make* struggle for racial justice in Newark today.

At the onset of the new millennium, in spite of having lost one of her children's father to gang violence, Fayemi played a central role in three local youth mobilizing efforts in Newark: the Million Woman March (1997), the Million Youth March (1998), and the National Hip Hop Political Convention (2004). As an organizer, Fayemi made sure that young black bodies from local community colleges and public high schools had the opportunity to participate in black freedom struggle. For Fayemi, mobilizing black people to participate in demonstrations and marches was a way for her to personally extend and re-envision black radicalism in Newark. Her willingness to publicly articulate a message that reflected the sociopolitical needs of what she sarcastically called the "undesirables" of Newark in national venues provided a special meaning to her political work. Taking an active role in the living history of political resistance in Newark far outweighed other quality of life issues that could have made suburban New Jersey a "better place" to raise her two young sons, each of whom were enrolled in Newark's troubled public school system. She explains,

> When I found out who I was, by learning about my history from the elders in my community, I was able to see that my life could have purpose. I could do more than just work for myself. Instead, I could work to leave a legacy that my kids and other young people could appreciate. That's what my political works provides. An example. It provides an example that you can be more and do more, and not be satisfied with the status quo.

Fayemi's work with predominantly black grassroots organizations that openly challenged contemporary white supremacy, police brutality, and poverty was testimony to the fact that there *were* people in Newark who were *working toward* something better than the status quo. Through her work, Fayemi aggressively debunked the idea that black people in Newark are apathetic and did not want anything better. She explained,

> People blame those who suffer, but how can you blame a whole generation for their suffering? Who can you blame when an entire generation fails? Look at how young people are being raised. They don't really have that many [positive] examples. But for me, when I come around, they are going to see an example of someone struggling to make a difference. They're going to hear about an opportunity for them to do something better, to be something better. That's why I organize. I organize because Newark is our home, and it's up to us to make it better.

"Better" was more than green manicured lawns, shiny new two-story homes and strip malls. For Fayemi, better constituted justice. Better constituted freedom. Organizing a national campaign for the amnesty of the exiled Black Panther Assata Shakur was one way that she could be more than just another single "baby momma," but also be a community homemaker.

THE POLITICS OF RECLAMATION: AMINA BARAKA AND FREDERICA BEY

Claiming blackness in Newark entails the loving cultivation of spaces of nostalgia, belonging, and reclamation. Sixty-two year old poet, singer, and activist Amina Baraka, who was born and raised in Newark, was quick to remind me that black artistic expression in the form of jazz, R&B, and blues found a home in Newark's numerous nightclubs and bars. This, combined with the heavy inflow of southern African–American culture, made Newark a home away from the imaginary home of "down south." Amina's mother and grandfather were two of the first African–American union organizers in Newark during the 1940s. As a child, Amina's three-bedroom flat became a homeplace for the neighborhood because of her grandmother's willingness to mother other people's children. She wanted to make certain that her grandmother's legacy of community mothering was channeled into her own political work. She reminisced,

> She made clothes for the community. She made clothes, chair covers, darlies. She was a kind person, my grandmother. People in the community called her "ma" because she was always cooking, she would take kids off the street and tell them they need to come and take a bath. She would give them a bath and wash their hair.

Amina's family was also musically gifted. Her grandfather and grand-mother played the guitar and the harmonica, and her grandmother played blues tunes on the piano. These musical talents were often put on display in their many house parties and at local Newark night-clubs. She understood this cultural production as "work."

> The work they did was in culture. Cultural work. Actually, it was their second job when they came home from work on the weekends. We would have these parties. We had these pokers parties, and they would sell dinners and little shots of liquor (which was illegal). But they had their means of doing so. I was supposed to be in bed, but it was too much fun to miss!

Amina's remembrances invoked more than the individualized nos-talgia of childhood, they also served as social commentary on the importance of artistic production for her understanding of family and community. These gatherings showcased the deep respect and admi-ration that community members had for her family as activists and artists who were deeply committed to providing venues for Newark's black social life—a life molded by her family's attachment to southern African–American cultural mores. Newark was the closest thing to the "Carolina" that her grandmother reminisced about. A life-long resident of Newark, Amina considered herself a self-educated and a self-acclaimed "cultural worker." As the daughter and granddaughter of union organizers, she continued her family tradition of mobilizing the black working class. Throughout adulthood Amina wove her fam-ily history of labor organizing into her own cultural work. As the part-ner of an early founder of the Black Arts Movement, Amiri Baraka, she continued to forge bonds between her biological family and what she called the larger "black working-class." Newark was the place where her political work was rooted, as it was essential to the preservation and maintenance of familial cultural and political bonds.

In 2004, Amina's daughter, Shani, and her partner, were mur-dered by a black man. Shani, a Newark high school girls' basket-ball coach, and a lesbian, was shot to death while helping her sister leave her abusive husband. Even as tragedy "struck the core of her existence," Amina did not retreat to grief and despair, instead she extended her personal heartbreak outward toward the transforma-tion of poor people of communities. Less than a year after her death, Amina cofounded the Newark chapter of Parents and Families of Lesbian and Gays (PFLAG). Politicizing and taking a stand against the intersecting effects of gender violence and homophobia in the black community became a new focus for her local organizing, communal storytelling, and artwork. Perhaps not so ironically, even after surviving the untimely death of her child to violence, Amina viewed Newark as a "place to be cherished, not condemned."

Over her lifetime, Amina's political work included cofounding the African Free School, the Black Women's United Front, Community For a United Newark, and other progressive community coalitions. Today, the most important component of all of her political work was "telling the story" of black cultural and political resistance. At age 68, Amina continued to speak out, playing the revered role of neighborhood griot. She makes political space by telling stories about Newark's black cultural history through poetry and spoken-word, volunteering in after-school programs in her neighborhood, and participating in community meetings. She helps young people imagine and reclaim Newark as a sacred space that gave birth to musical legends like Sarah Vaughn and Gloria Gaynor. For Amina, the old bars that are now viewed as isolated, potentially dangerous eyesores are abandoned repositories of black cultural productivity. She helps young people who are otherwise ignorant of Newark's history see its neighborhoods as sites of creative possibility and resistance.

Born in Newark in October of 1944, Frederica Bey was raised by her mother and stepfather, a Chinese laundry owner. After marrying at age 23, separating at age 31, and delivering two healthy children, Frederica removed herself from her five year stay on Essex County's welfare roll, and her family from a Section 8 housing unit by earning a real-estate license and starting her own business. In 1974, after divorcing, and enrolling in at Kean College to work toward her bachelor's degree, Frederica decided to take out a loan to purchase a devalued piece of property, renovate it, and move her family into it. Frederica confessed,

> I took a part of my loan and put it on a house because I couldn't have my children graduating from the projects, and stepping over drugs in their little prom gowns going downstairs. I had to get out of that place. It had become a real slum.
>
> When I was at Kean, I applied for all of the grants and loans and put a down payment on a $23,000 house. I bid on it. It was boarded up [at the time] and I got the bid. That house is now valued at $300,000.

Frederica never finished her undergraduate degree, but in 1965 joined the Nation of Islam and began an extensive career in community organizing in Newark through the 1970s and 1980s. In early 1995 she was asked to chair the fundraising effort for the Million Man March called by Louis Farrakhan, and eventually incorporated this fundraising arm into an independent non-profit organization called "WISOMMM" (Women in Support of the Million Man March). In 1995 WISOMMM, under Frederica's leadership, purchased a dilapidated mansion in the Central Ward, renovated the building, and used it to host a variety of community programs including: African dance, an African ball, after-school care, health and wellness education classes, and a variety of town hall meetings. In October 2004, WISOMMM purchased the Second Presbyterian Church, a 65,000 sq. ft. facility consisting of three buildings, which currently houses the African–American Education, Cultural and Resource Center. All three facilities host ongoing community events and programs. Some of the programs now sponsored by WISOMMM include the Boycott Crime Campaign, and the "American Prisons...Second Coming of Slavery"—a series of open forums and town hall meetings held to raise awareness about racially motivated human rights violations in US prisons.

Education was one of the most frequently mentioned social issues linking contemporary social ills to Newark's extended history of racial domination. Although poorly administered public schools were frequently acknowledged to be one of the most pressing problems facing African–Americans, education through formal means was not viewed as the panacea. More pressing was the fact that many children lacked a basic understanding of Newark's political history of racial injustice. The inability of students and teachers alike to connect overcrowded, poorly funded, dangerous, and crumbling schools with Newark's history of systematically ghettoizing African–Americans was seen as a roadblock to student success. Frederica Bey insists,

> We must educate our own children. This country banned us from reading, banned us from a legal education. So we have to educate our own people and our own selves. And from that education will come the economics we need and the self-sufficiency we need. Black folks doing for black folks—that's how it's going to look when it happens. Creating the first African American cultural center in the history of this state...this is how you begin to make it happen.

Frederica's lifetime goal was realized with the founding of the Adelaide L. Stanford Charter School, an independent, African–American majority school designed to enhance the education of Newark's youth. By incorporating the principles of Kwanzaa, and enhancing the standard

New Jersey K-12 curriculum with a rich and varied assortment of black diasporic histories and African-centered pedagogies, Frederica made good on her promise to,

> Have our children enjoy the best education that we can possibly give them, and have all the self-esteem that they need to excel, and do whatever it is they want to do. Yes, we are teaching our children African values and a strong sense of self, of who they are, and who and where they are in relation to this society. And, yes, it's highly political.

Frederica's political work in the Central Ward should be understood as black feminist spatial praxis and not simply black nationalist rhetoric. Frederica's political work spiralled out from wanting to provide a home for her biological children to reimagining to ultimately transforming the Central Ward into a communal home for people of African descent. Her raw materials were her formidable organizing skills, her ability to excavate and promote a living history of resistance to racial domination in the city, and to create sustainable spaces of cultural resistance.

Frederica's and Amina's political homemaking established a new geographic relationship between the past and present, and, created new spatial possibilities in a blighted geographic area. While much of Amina's work was reviving lost histories and transforming hardship and loss into a *will to live* gracefully within Newark's space, Frederica's work was about physically building spaces of solidarity, knowledge production and sharing, and consciousness for the uplift and prosperity of new generations of Newarkers. Both women had life-long ties to the city and stand steadfast with the city through its many transitions.

THE POLITICS OF SELLING IN: KIM GADDY

Not all of the women identified as "very political" in the Central Ward resided within Newark's geopolitical boundaries. Kim Gaddy, a 42-year-old environmental activist was born and raised in Newark, graduated from a local high school and from Rutgers University's Newark Campus. Two years prior to our interview, Kim moved to the bordering town of Irvington. Her decision to move her children outside of Newark illuminates how much is at stake for people who live in the Central Ward. Her desire to provide a safe, functional public education for her children outweighed her desire to stay close to the place where she did most of her work around environmental racism.

Kim visibly grappled with her fairly recent decision to "move away" from her family. With an expression of poorly disguised guilt she justified her decision,

> I moved here [to Irvington] two years ago. The reason I stayed in Newark so long was not only because of my political activism, but also because it was a safe place. I was a widow at twenty-nine. My husband had cancer. I just had to get away.
>
> When I was out of high school, instead of uprooting myself and moving out. I lived in the community where my family was. I realized a lot of my friends who went to college decided, "I'm not coming back to Newark."
>
> That was not me. I put a lot of energy into this city. And it was good for me. But it is not a place where I can raise a family now, and have my children be successful.
>
> The educational system is very, very bad. You have more kids who drop out than [who] are in school. Instead of creating the future leaders and making education a priority, they're [school administrators and public officials] allowing our children to be functional illiterates, and putting them in the streets to survive…knowing they won't survive. So it is not a place that I think my kids can make it. Definitely not.

What makes Kim's commentary so poignant is that she previously served two terms on the Newark Board of Education, and served as campaign manager for the first African–American woman ever elected to serve on Newark's City Council, Mildred Crump. Remarkably, Kim was one of the first local activists who organized against HIV/AIDS in Newark in the early 1990s. She recounted,

> Two of my brothers and my sister died of AIDS. One [brother] got it heterosexually. My older brother was gay, and he caught it from one of his friends. My sister was on drugs. That had a tremendous impact on me, and I had to support my mother. And that just led to the activism, and trying to educate the community about…you know…there are just so many ills in our society. AIDS just ran through our community. At that particular time they just wanted us to die. Folks didn't want to talk about AIDS and how it was destroying our community.

Kim transformed her family's tragic encounter with the disease into a strong motivation to do political work around HIV/AIDS in Newark's inner city. After the loss of her school board seat, and the untimely death of her husband, Kim accepted a position as executive director of a Montclair, New Jersey-based environmental justice organization. Now, her political work links the prevalence of cancer and cancer-related deaths in Newark to the proliferation of air and water pollutants in the inner city, the excessive use of pesticides in urban grocery stores, and other taken-for-granted, yet dangerous materials contained in discounted household cleaning products heavily marketed in poor urban communities. Her political work took new forms as she became exposed to new information, and new ways to expose and critique severe imbalances of power, health, and opportunity that produced Newark's uneven geographic development. She proudly embraced her reputation as a fighter. She declared,

> It's my responsibility to engage the African American community. There's a disconnect among African Americans. We tend to think the environment is going to last forever. If we don't become better stakeholders, and better providers of this earth we won't have a planet—and we black people [will] be the first one's to go. I have the credibility of being a fighter. I collaborate with organizations, churches, and elected officials to get them to see the importance of the environment. When I come to the door and I'm talking about environmental issues, they listen.

In addition to her environmental activism Kim also served as head of the local chapter of the National Black Women's Congress, an organization that actively recruits and trains African–American women to be community leaders in both electoral and non-electoral politics. Kim's extensive portfolio of community organizing is awe inspiring, considering that within four years of our first interview she had lost both her grandmother and husband to cancer and a niece she parented to street violence in Newark. Still she insisted,

> The strength of Newark is that regardless of the lack of support that we are getting, there is a group of us who is standing up, who, no matter what, we are bucking that system. We are standing up and speaking out.

Kim's story teaches us that black women's political work in Newark takes multiple forms in different stages of life. Kim spent her formative years as an activist living and working in Newark. After years of withstanding multiple instances of family tragedy, Kim chose to move her physical home out of Newark's inner city to neighboring town of Irvington to give herself and her children reprieve from everyday struggles that might have very well resulted in more hardship. However, from nine to five, Kim put her heart, skills, knowledge, and *know-how* into educating people and mobilizing resources to combat different forms of geographic racism in Newark. In the end, Kim created a niche that enabled her to give back, make a living, and make a difference. Her effort to politicize connections between issues like public health, poverty, education, and the environment were echoed by many of the women I interviewed. The interconnectedness of these social issues, and the complicity of local black politicians in exacerbating these issues were emphasized.

Although Newark's city council has been dominated by African–American males for over 40 years, it was not viewed as an institution that recruited or otherwise nurtured black people's community leadership. In most of the conversations I had with black women, "City Hall" emerged as an oppressive institution that frequently shirked its responsibility of addressing the complexity of racialized poverty in Newark. According to many of the activists I spoke with, elected officials often settled for easy, oversimplified policy solutions that left intersecting structures of domination intact and fully operative. Many women suggested that the city's heteropatriarchal governance structure was "non-democratic," "hostile," "despotic," and, even more shocking, "a contemporary vestige of slavery."

In spite of this, Kim *sold-in* to Newark by transforming the neo-slave narrative of escape from urban poverty, despair, heartbreak, and powerlessness into a story of *staying home* to create spaces to redefine politics as commitment, care, sacrifice, and a hard-won resolve to do and be something better.

RECONSTRUCTING HOMEMAKING
THROUGH SPATIAL STORIES

Acts of expressing and saying place are central to understanding what kinds of geographies are available to black women.

Katherine McKittrick
in *Demonic Grounds: Black Women and
Cartographies of Struggle* (2006)

And it is here that I think African American culture is instructive as a way of rethinking, of reshaping our thinking processes, our understandings of history and politics themselves.

Elsa Barkely Brown, "What has Happened Here?"
in *The Feminist History Reader* edited by Sue Morgan (2006)

The spatial stories that black political women told reveal that Newark was a "home" that was worth the individual sacrifices of extraordinary stores of time, energy, and resources. The painful history of racial discrimination and violence was not as important as reviving and creating myriad forms of resistance. This is the essence of the politics of homemaking in Newark. Whether through selling in, reclaiming space, and forgotten histories, or through creating a living history of resistance, black women's politics involved creating spaces to build healthy and nourishing relationships to the city. Their political work was imaginative, as it involved spatially reworking symbolic representations of the inner city and making oppositional discourses readily available to the city's inhabitants. Political homemaking serves as a pointed reality check to politicians who try to publicly dwell on Newark's strengths while programmatically ignoring the city's inability to provide some of the basic amenities of a "free" society (a decent education and opportunities for social and economic advancement). Through homemaking, black women activists created political spaces to tell and to actualize counter-narratives to the harsh material realities of the city. Their counter-narratives linked time, space, and place toward the conscious aim of fostering what bell hooks has aptly called radical black subjectivity—an identity/standpoint that enables creative, expansive self-actualization (hooks 1990). Their political agency transformed Newark's urban landscape into a geography of resistance.

With this said, the complexity of these women's lives is inspiring and deeply disturbing. Their stories were inspiring in the sense that they provided with living, breathing, real-time examples of women who had come from humble backgrounds and managed to create fulfilling lives for themselves doing the political work they loved. However, they were disquieting in the sense that stories provided such an intensely personal portrayal of the dire and often deadly social and economic circumstances that constitute so much of Newark's geography. Case in point: after I conducted a gender violence awareness workshop at a local community college organized by one of the women I interviewed, a tenth-grade girl from the workshop came up and told me that in the past two years at Central High School, about ten of her "friends or friends of friends" had been killed in street and/or gang-related violence. This chilling account makes eerily real the "fatalities of power" theorized by Ruth Wilson Gilmore (Gilmore 2002) over a decade earlier, and underscores the gravity of the political work that activists in Newark engage in daily. The "hierarchies of difference" that Gilmore argues render black life ungeographic operate through premature death, imprisonment, addiction, and, most importantly, by *forgetting* a legacy of black political resistance.

The politics of homemaking is a politics of *not* forgetting, of *not* looking away, and, most importantly, creating *new* spaces to affirm black life, black struggle, and black survival. Even as the contours and boundaries of identity, place, and community shift and are contested with increasing number of non-blacks living in the Central Ward, these women still seek to build a homeplace for, in Amina's word's, "my grandchild, or my neighbor's child, or my cousin's child, or that child standing over there on that corner."

The next chapter, "Mobilizing after Murder" connects identity and identity politics to the politics of scale by focusing on black queer activism in Newark. While Newark is still understood as a "home" it emerges as a home that has abused and mistreated members of the lesbian, gay, bisexual, transgender, and queer community in Newark. In chapter 6, we remember Sakia Gunn.

6

MOBILIZING AFTER MURDER: BLACK WOMEN QUEERING POLITICS AND BLACK FEMINISM IN NEWARK

> The whole issue of gays and lesbians is...number one; people just think it's wrong. How do you fix it? Don't be gay or lesbian. Even though those people are in office and don't say these things out loud, they bring all those feelings with them.
>
> Janyce Jackson, Pastor of Liberation
> in Truth Unity Fellowship Church in Newark, New Jersey

> Taking apart the story, revealing underlying texts, and giving voice to things that are often known intuitively does not help people to improve their current conditions. It provides words, perhaps, and insight that explains certain experiences—but it does not prevent someone from dying.
>
> Linda Tuhiwai Smith
> in *Decolonizing Methodology* (1999)

On May 11, 2003 a 29-year-old African–American man named Richard McCullough stabbed an African–American female named Sakia Gunn in the chest. At age fifteen she was already out. Her preference for baggy jeans, double XL white t-shirts, and a closely cropped afro stood in stark contrast to the conservative aesthetics of Newark's black middle-class leadership. In fact, the "ag" (aggressive) presentation of her sexual identity marked her as a product of Newark's inner city gang culture. Sakia defied the sexual and gender norms of Newark's predominantly black community. The outward appearance of bravado, however, did not diminish Sakia and her three girlfriends' vulnerability as they traveled home from Greenwich Village after a night of partying. Shortly after 3:00 am, the unmanned "24-hour" police kiosk located at the corner of Broad Street and Market Avenue left the four teenagers unprotected. They were accosted by two adult men in a passing car as they walked from Newark Penn Station to the Broad Street bus stop. The girls' flat out rejection of the drunken advances of the men resulted in a brawl. In the midst of the conflict, Richard McCullough pulled a knife and stabbed Sakia in the chest. She bled to death on the way to the hospital.

How do queer black women politically navigate urban spaces? How are their bodies read, their politics enacted, and their agency understood and interpreted? How do queer black women use their bodies and identities to challenge structural intersectionality in American cities? The community mobilizations that took place in Newark after Sakia's death provide a rare opportunity to sketch a few answers to these questions. After her death, queer black women destabilized conventional notions of blackness and politics and incited new forms of political resistance in Newark's Central Ward.[1] By linking the politics of respectability to homophobic violence and building unlikely coalitions within and between local and national organizations, queer women challenged bigotry in local black vernacular institutions. They made it possible for queer black people to be seen and heard as political actors in Newark.

In this chapter, I explore how black women embraced a set of oppositional spatial practices to resist the intersectional effects of misogyny, homo/transphobia, racism, and poverty. Exploring migrations between "black women," "black queer," and "black feminist," I examine how black women respatialized social capital, and enacted resistance.[2] I describe how black women remapped public spaces by forging new relationships between queer youth and black vernacular institutions, and made political space for honest engagements with sex, gender, poverty, and power to take place. This process involved dissolving rigid scalar structures produced by narrow, single-issue identity politicking in order to create much-needed opportunities for black queer youth to articulate their needs and make demands on local and national political structures and organizations that had theretofore denied their very existence. In too many ways, Sakia's death was the "perfect murder." It brought to light many of the subtle ways in which civil society punishes gender dissidence in the African–American community.

In "The Scaling of Bodies and the Politics of Identity," Iris Marion Young (1990) argues that ideologies of racism, sexism, homophobia, and ageism construct certain bodies as abject and undesirable. Later research by Cathy Cohen (1997) and Ange-Marie Hancock (2004) revealed the explicit ways that black women have been rendered abject in American political discourse—in many ways situating them as essentially "queer" subjects unworthy of empathy, consideration, and appreciation as human beings. In her classic essay, "Punks, Bulldaggers, and Welfare Queens," Cohen (1997) argued that poor women of color, regardless of whether or not they fell into the category of homosexual or heterosexual are rarely perceived as normal, moral, and worthy of community support. Consistently framed as unworthy and routinely denied cultural citizenship, Hancock (2004) demonstrated hands-down that poor black women have routinely been the target of perverse democratic attention in the American public sphere. Following Hancock, In chapter 3, I argued that the manipulation and mobilization of racial resentment against poor black people is in many ways, constitutive of Newark's political history and political culture up until this very day. But as I have argued in chapters 4 and 5, black women have and continue to resist.

Back to Sakia Gunn. Sakia's subjectivity was communally valued only *after* her physical body was slain and queer black women rallied to make sense of and respond to her death. Sakia's death exposed the limits of single identity politics that either ignore or marginalize queer blackness, and underscores the severe social consequences of occupying both subject positions at the same time. As antiviolence activists, gay rights activists, and conventional civil rights organizations tried to figure out what "really" happened, narrative and interpretative battles ensued. This chapter examines how racial and gender ideologies were framed, manipulated, and subverted through spatial agency to challenge race, gender, sexual, and class subjugation in Newark, New Jersey.

Stories about Street Life: Where Black Feminism Meets Political Geography

Black feminist geographers argue that social and political domination produces uneven geographies that alienate black people, often rendering them invisible, or worse, vulnerable to premature death (McKittrick 2006, Gilmore 1998). Through the production and reproduction of intersecting hierarchies of difference, black feminist geographers insist that the lived experience of blackness is physically and symbolically tied to space and place (McKittrick & Woods 2007, McKittrick 2000). However, few studies of urban politics or "black" politics examine how multiple identities intersect with blackness, or how this impacts the meaning and practice of politics. This omission makes it difficult to ascertain the political agency of

women of color in cities—who organize from multiple and intersecting social locations (see for instance, Judd & Kantor 2008 and
Ross & Levine 2006). As a result, much of what social scientists
know about black women specifically is divorced from the physical and social geographies that shape their subjectivities. However,
black women *are* active participants in emancipatory practices that
are rooted in particular locales. Much of their political agency takes
place on the ground—or more aptly in the streets. In this chapter, I
unearth how black women enacted political agency through storytelling and metaphor, as well as materially through spatial acts that
reshaped and redefined power relationships in Newark. By bringing the concerns of the most vulnerable, most despised, and much
maligned to the forefront of contemporary Newark, black women
enacted black feminist resistance. By fighting for places for queer
people to tell and make meaning out of their life stories and making political space for queer subjectivities to be articulated, heard,
and acted upon, black queer women, using intersectional praxis,
remapped the symbolic landscapes of the city.

In this chapter, black women's resistance politics are revealed
through spatial stories. Spatial stories, it is argued, transform spaces
into places by mapping meaning onto histories, norms, values, and
practices that occur in everyday urban spaces (de Certeau 1980).
I consider and retell the stories that activists told me about their
efforts to stand against the recalcitrance of Newark's political establishment, and I reassemble the community mobilizations that queer
women organized to force people to see, acknowledge, and affirm
the humanity of queer black people. Central to my retelling of their
politics are the multiple contestations around space, place, and identity—especially their efforts to appropriate spaces within Newark's
hostile political geographies. The spaces activists claimed for social
justice work became libratory places where queer youth could forge
new relationships with others and map alternative histories to city
streets, community centers, and neighborhoods. The symbolic
remapping of public spaces, including the destabilization of rigid scalar discourses (local/national) that often rendered their bodies and
politics illegible, comprised a major part of political work of queer
women in Newark. Prior to Sakia's death, queer people were written
out of dominant histories of black struggle and resistance, and generally excluded from the city's larger political imagery. Queer women
in the Newark Pride Alliance (NPA) also rescued Sakia's story from
political actors who effigied Sakia in order to legitimate the political

projects of national and predominantly white LGBT organizations. Ironically, both national lesbian and gay activists local grassroots antiviolence politicized her death by *forgetting* the complex aspects of her life that resulted in her death. However, through NPA's activisms, and the personal stories and experiences that prompted it, black women made it possible for Sakia and other queer young people, to recognized as worthy and socially meaningful members of Newark's black community.

Spatial stories reveal the ways that black women experience, make meaning of, and resist geographic domination. The stories that queer black women tell about their politics in Newark are imbued with anecdotes that vividly describe how social trauma, alienation, and displacement structure their subjective relationships to the city. These horror stories—as Carole Boyce Davies once called them—are not meant to shock, outrage, depress, or disappoint. Rather, they are intended to illuminate how black women transform heartbreak into resistance—providing meaning and affect to those whose lives, dreams, and innocences may have ended prematurely. Likewise, my retelling of the Sakia Gunn's tragic death should not merely invoke feelings of anger, loss, and frustration, as the primary intent is to *elucidate and make possible* affective, place-based strategies of political, social, and thereby *geographic resistance.* For black women in Newark, this entailed creating spaces to build resistance to the heteronormative black status quo in order that they might *move toward* social transformation. By transforming the symbolic function of local community centers, creating afterschool programs, organizing a sustained grassroots mobilization campaign, and insisting on keeping the complexity of Sakia's life and death in our hearts and minds, queer black women effectively resisted the intersecting effects of sex, race, gender, and economic subjugation on the lives of all young black people in Newark.

Using a bottom-up intersectional approach, I triangulate (1) personal narratives of queer black women who have dedicated a good part of their lives organizing against homophobia in Newark, (2) the public statements made by local activists who galvanized community support to protest Sakia's untimely death, and (3) the perspectives of black and queer feminist theorists who have taken extraordinary pains to situate sexuality as a core element of intersectional analysis and praxis. I move back and forth between these three spheres of evidence and argumentation to create an unflinching account of how heteropatriarchy saturates black political culture, while showcasing the role of space, place, and scale in black women's political activism.[3]

DEFINING QUEER IN A BLACK FEMINIST CONTEXT

What does it mean to be a queer black woman? In homonormative queer studies, the most frequently analyzed tropes of black queerness are the male "homothug," "black drag queen," and the transient black male gay intellectual (see for instance, Walcott 2007, Ferguson 2006, and Johnson 2006, 2001). Less understood and analyzed are representations of black female queerness that builds from the experience of black lesbians, "aggressives," and transwomen who are active and engaged members of black civil society, those whose voices, politics, activisms, and theoretical interventions are simply ignored.[4] Queerness in the context of black feminism must be thought of as more than rejecting the performance and embrace of heteronormativity (i.e., "being straight"). Rather, queerness should be viewed as an unwillingness or, perhaps even a glorious failure to conform to both the dictates of white normativity (skin color, body shape, phenotype) and the politics of respectability rooted in contemporary black Protestantism (White 1999). This means rejecting codes of dress, social mannerisms, and gender performances deemed "respectable" in heteronormative black working and middle-class culture (Collins 2005, Johnson 2005, White 1999).

I argue that queerness signifies an embrace of an oppositional *praxis* that specifies sexuality as a core site of black female subjugation. Black feminists have long argued that the subjugation of black women under white supremacy operates through the historical exploitation of black women's sexuality, especially through the global proliferation of controlling images that mark black women (especially poor black women) as abject and unworthy of love, caring, respect, and sympathy (Wanzo 2009, Collins 2005, Hancock 2004). Black feminists have linked the global circulation of images of black women portrayed as "mammies," "jezebels," "sapphires," and today, "bitches," "ho's," "welfare queens," "gold-diggers," and "dykes" with the legacy of slavery, the confinement of generations black women to low-wage work, and the global appropriation and commodification of black American culture (Perry 2005). As a result, the dehumanizing images of black womanhood popular in America almost always overshadows the important role that black women, especially queer black women, have played in American civic life (see for instance Sharpley-Whiting 2007, Collins 2005, Ferguson 2004, White 1999, Davis 1981). This chapter aims to displace this tendency by centering the ways that black women actively challenge ideologies and practices that position them as abject in the communities they live in. This move immediately requires us to attend to how the dynamics of space and place inform their political agency.

In some cases, we might consider staying home and place-making in cities (in cities as a uniquely black working class female strategy of *queer* resistance. This process entails claiming Newark as "home" and actively making places to resist the alienating effects of neoliberalism, homo/transphobia, racism, poverty, and misogyny. Motherhood is not tethered to domesticity and subservience, but rather is understood as an opportunity to care for community. Homemaking, from a queer perspective, goes further to collapse the artificial boundaries of political identity rooted in heteronormative scalar politics (raced-gendered body/home/local/national/transnational/global) in order to make space to create the trust and positive reciprocity necessary to build coalitions and alliances within and between diverse social actors in Newark's political imaginary (Sandoval 2000, Davis 1997).

I reconstruct queerness in my retelling of black women's politics by assembling a bricologe of stories, media accounts, and personal interviews. Using feminist queer of color epistemic interventions outlined by Roderick Ferguson (2004), I expose how dominant frames of community and identity make it difficult for black gender transgressive people to be construed as viable political subjects.[5] As an ummarried African–American single mother and an ally of queer feminists in Newark, I examine the multiple and conflicting identifications between "black women" and "queer," unhinging accounts of black women's political subjectivity that are fixed to a presumed and unquestioned heterosexuality. Taking a cue from Rinaldo Walcott (2007), I argue that black women organizing and mobilizing in Newark forged an "intimate geography and space of black queer identities" that effectively traversed class, gender, sexual, and age formations that permeated Newark's landscapes. Through respatializing social capital—creating and redefining relationships within and between black vernacular institutions and local and national lesbian and gay organizations—black women queered black political space in Newark. As a verb, here "queering" signifies the insistence that the politics of difference—a politics that emphasizes multiplicity and heterogeneity of identities—insists upon a strident disinvestment in *both* black heteronormativity and white homonormativity in order to build an alternative culture of political empowerment for all black people (Ferguson 2004). Finally, queering signifies the disruption of unitary identity politics that are rooted in predetermined levels of scale. This point will be further elaborated upon in the second half of this chapter.

PLACING BLACK HETEROPATRIARCHY

Before theorizing black women's agency, we must first place it within a specifically raced and gendered geopolitical context. I argue that heteropatriarchy is an adequate descriptor of Newark's geopolitical climate. Heteropatriarchy is constituted by convergence of processes of black racialization, heterosexualization, neoliberalism, and patriarchy (Smith 2007, Alexander 2005, Hart 1992). As I have described in early chapters, heterosexual black men have dominated Newark politics since the election of Newark's first African–American mayor in 1970 (Mumford 2008, Woodward 1999). Sharpe James, who succeeded Kenneth Gibson in 1986, served five four-year terms, declining a bid for a sixth term after being indicted on 25 federal charges of fraud, corruption, and racketeering in 2007.[6] In 2006, the son of the disgraced mayor, John Sharpe James, contemplated a bid for mayor. After coming home with a purple heart from Afghanistan, James Jr. made a point of visiting "two churches every Sunday" to build community support for his unsuccessful effort to oust the current Mayor Cory Booker. In 2006, Booker, an Ivy-League educated Rhodes Scholar, dismantled the Sharpe James machine by aggressively courting wealthy liberal campaign financiers vis a vis cable news outlets, multiple appearances on the Oprah Winfrey Show, and two broadly claimed documentaries about Newark, *Street Fight* (2004) and *Brick City* (2008).

Heteropatriarchal political practices and racial ideology are tightly bound in Newark. Black civil society continues to be patrolled and regulated by a relatively small circle of influential and well-connected black men who are oriented toward deeply masculinist and liberal understandings of political and economic empowerment that have origins in the civil rights and black power movements (Mumford 2007, Woodward 1999). In 2009, the city council was comprised of Ras Baraka (son of the esteemed activist poet Amiri Baraka aka LeRoi Jones), Donald Payne Jr. (son of US Representative Donald Payne, representing New Jersey's 10th Congressional District), and Ron Rice Jr. (son of New Jersey Congressman Ron Rice). These men's ties with African–American churches and community organizations including the Urban League, NAACP, state and national Congressional Black Caucuses, and the Democratic Party are notorious. They wield considerable influence in the identification and selection of candidates

for the Board of Education, the Zoning Board, and municipal council seats. All of these men are heterosexual, monotheistic, and generally mute on issues of gender and sexuality in their basic orientation
and practice of politics.

Like all politicians in Newark, these black men actively contend with
the social aftereffects of deindustrialization, which includes chronic
black male unemployment and high poverty rates among African–
Americans and Latinos. As a testimony to their commitment to racial
uplift, most of these men have admirable track records of employing
black people in the local public sector, creating much-needed opportunities for black entrepreneurship, and recruiting black male *and*
female civic leaders to rail against black on black violence, racial profiling, police brutality, and lack of quality of education for poor people
in Newark. However, this political framework has largely restricted
the development gender progressive political outlook that challenges
the combined effects of race, gender, class, and sexual oppression on
the lives of women of color and gays, lesbians, bisexual, transsexual,
and/or transgendered people in the city.

In Newark it is not difficult to find support for Wahneema Lubiano's
(1997) observation that "there is no way of being outside of the state,
we encounter it in our public imaginings about the nature of our
world." As an enormously productive site of heterosexualization, M.
Jacqui Alexander (2005) theorizes the state as a set of "contradictory
and uneven locations, institutions, personnel, managerial practices,
and imperatives; and as a gendered, classed, racialized, and sexualized ensemble" (195). I further argue that Newark functions like
a "city-state," serving as the central locale for the production and
circulation of raced and heterosexualized political power for black
people in North New Jersey (Grosz 1995). In this sense, the "city"
of Newark becomes a place that is both imagined, constructed, and
reproduced through New Jersey's urban racial state (see Chapter 3).
Black heteropatriarchy, and the gender ideologies that undergird it,
saturates local community institutions, governing bodies, the public
education system, and, not surprisingly, most of Newark's majority
black churches. However, after Sakia's death, the city's heteronormative black power structure was challenged by a loosely affiliated
network of black queer activists and socially ostracized teens. Cathy
Cohen (1997) defines heteronormativity as "those localized practices
and centralized institutions which legitimize and privilege heterosexuality and heterosexual relationships as fundamental and 'natural'
within society" (440). Black queer women exposed the violent consequences of unchecked black heteropatriarchy and brought attention

to the invisible fault lines of Newark's black community. Through their efforts to remember Sakia Gunn by creating spaces for black queer people to be in the city, the NPA demonstrated, through their hard won *failures*, that heteropatriarchy and heteronormativity can be effectively challenged in American political and civic life. I begin my analysis of how black queer women enacted resistance with the story of Newark activist, Laquetta Nelson.

LAQUETTA NELSON AND THE NEWARK PRIDE ALLIANCE

She was murdered early Sunday morning. I found out about it on Tuesday. That day I sent an email that went out all around the country and overseas. We got condolences from all around the country and the world, but we didn't get condolences from right here in this city, from our community. Our community was in crisis then. We suffered and nobody cared. There were some people who cared, but it just wasn't enough.

Laquetta Nelson, 50-year-old retired bus driver,
Army veteran, and community organizer.

The story of black queer activism in Newark begins with Laquetta Nelson. Immediately following Sakia's murder Laquetta, a long-time activist with the New Jersey Stonewall Democrats, took note of the marked differences between the reactions to the murder. She expressed dismay that local black leadership seemed oblivious to the political significance of Sakia's death. While Sakia's death received attention from national gay rights organizations as the "murdered black lesbian," in Newark she was just another example of black on black violence. Ironically, while the facts surrounding her death exploded in the majority white lesbian and gay blogosphere, it was not yet important enough to feature in mainstream printed news media. It was the widespread disorientation and inept response by Newark's black community that lead Laquetta to spearhead the creation of the Newark Pride Alliance (NPA).

Laquetta Nelson and James Quedle founded the NPA in June 2003, only a month after Sakia's murder. Their original mission was straightforward: "NPA seeks to make Newark a city to be proud of and a city to be proud in, a city safe for all its people: gay, straight, bisexual, lesbian and trans-gendered."[7] One major objective of NPA was to build a community center that catered to the needs of lesbian, gay, bisexual, and transgendered youth through the creation of an Ags and Femmes Sakia Gunn Memorial Fund. Laquetta reached out to closeted gays and lesbians active in Newark politics, and offered personal support to Sakia's family and friends. Laquetta and James mobilized a close-knit, yet invisible network of black lesbians and gays who worked or volunteered for a variety of community programs. Shortly thereafter, activists began pressuring state and local officials for antiviolence/antibullying measures to protect queer students and to provide the resources to build a community center to address their needs.

This was a difficult task to say the least. The longstanding relationships that Laquetta Nelson had with local Democratic political operatives did not make them willing to publically entertain questions of queer identity and violence. In 1992, Laquetta was elected leader of the twenty-eighth Congressional District in the Central Ward. She quickly became known as a "workhorse." For over a decade, Laquetta registered hundreds of voters and coordinated to get out the vote campaigns during state, local, and national elections. She also organized petitions to get local leaders on the ballot. In spite of such extensive political work in Newark Laquetta developed a "real passion for politics" after joining the Stonewall Democrats. With the support of a Newark-based gay mentor, and a newfound community of supporters, Laquetta came out to her family, friends, and colleagues and spent the next four years working with Stonewall. Coming out was an important turning point in her political life, as it enabled her to advocate on behalf of a constituency that was largely ignored by the local political machinery—black gays and lesbians. Proving to be an ambitious, hardworking, and charismatic leader, Laquetta went on to establish the New Jersey chapter of Stonewall. After four years of sustained LGBT activism with Stonewall, Laquetta resigned her post. What she called the "troubling gap" between the Stonewall's rhetoric of multiculturalism and their refusal to fund local LGBT programming initiatives in Newark was inexcusable. Stonewall's verbal pledges of LGBT solidarity did nothing to alleviate the chronic problems facing the black gay and lesbian population in Newark—the community Laquetta ultimately identified as "her own."

When Laquetta read about Sakia's murder in the *New Jersey Star-Ledger*, she sent mass emails to her regional and national contacts. She used her national stature with Stonewall to politicize Sakia's death among national lesbian and gay organizations. Her appeal to these organizations proved effective. Several regional organizations sent their respective representatives to Newark to cover the story, and immediately began publishing information about the circumstances surrounding Sakia's death on their websites. Laquetta was grateful for the early show of support, however, she surmised that the only reason Sakia's death mattered to these was because she was lesbian.

The other circumstances surrounding her murder—poverty, poor policing, and the social violence that was openly directed at queer youth were ignored by the gay news media that covered her story. While Sakia's death was politically useful as a symbol of homophobia, it seemed disingenuous to ignore the other elements of her identity that played a role in her death. For Laquetta, focusing solely on Sakia's sexual preference was a dangerous tendency that unwittingly colluded with conservative efforts to criminalize black men. In her view, demonizing McCollough did little to help establish an anti-homophobic and culturally inclusive community of people of color in Newark. Laquetta wanted to build a local, grassroots similar to the ones that made many national organizations so effective. She recalled,

> When I went among white gays and lesbians I saw what they had, I saw how they did things. I wanted what they had here in Newark for my people. But I couldn't get them to bring that here. It wasn't until the murder of Sakia Gunn, that they began to say, "Oh there is a problem in Newark." Had they come when I first asked them to come, Sakia may not have been murdered. That's one of my issues with them.

Laquetta's prominence in lesbian and gay rights circles did not translate into the social capital needed to politicize Sakia's death in a way that made sense to Newarkers. So she and a handful of her friends and associates singlehandedly mobilized scores of queer people, especially young queer people, in Newark. With their help, over 2,500 people attended Sakia's funeral. Over the next few months, several demonstrations and vigils were organized in conjunction with Sakia's family and friends and an increasingly visible and outspoken black queer community.

QUEER BLACK FEMINISM IN
THE STREETS OF NEWARK

> We were the peacekeepers. We actually formed a human line between the young people who attended the funeral and the police.
> Janyce Jackson, 49-year-old retired NYC police dispatcher,
> senior pastor of Liberation in Truth Unity Fellowship Church.

The tendentious relationship between the police and queer teenagers came to a head at Sakia's funeral. With help from NPA, Liberation in Truth Unity Fellowship Church (LIT) made an effort to "bring down the tensions." The teenagers' hurt was intensified by the heavy policy presence at the funeral. Fifty uniformed police officers stood outside the church to provide "security" to young people who were often harassed by and left unprotected by law enforcement. For young people who knew Sakia, the police were as much to blame for their loss as was Richard McCullough. After all, McCollough's deadly assault took place less than a 100 feet from a vacant "24-hour" police kiosk. As a result, in the early days after Sakia's death LIT's activism involved serving as a mediating zone between the traumatized young people and Newark's power structure. At the funeral, many young people were enraged enough to physically lash out at the cops—who they viewed as being partially responsible for Sakia's demise. However, according to Janyce, LIT used their bodies and relationships to keep them "safe and out of jail, or worse."

According to the esteemed clergywoman, one reason that queer youth had to "hang out on street corners or travel into New York City to hang out in bars" was because they did not "have a place in Newark to simply be." Often confined to what Talmadge Wright has referred to as "refuse spaces"—spaces in which poor people (often visible but *unattended to*) are refused services, refused dignity, and refused human rights, young queer black folks on the street forged a visible, but socially maligned social geography in order to interact and *be* with each other on their own terms.[8] In the Central Ward, refuse spaces were often dangerous and negatively stigmatized public locales. Queer youth socialized in certain parks, street corners, popular bus stops, and the storefronts of queer friendly businesses—including tattoo parlors and hair salons on the Broad Street corridor. While inexpensive and assessable, these spaces were often shared with addicts, street peddlers, homeless people, homophobic passerbys, and hostile cops working their beats. From Janyce's perspective, the streets were simply not sufficient to meet the social and development needs of queer young people—especially teenagers from poor, Central Ward neighborhoods.

In light of this perspective, the creation of what Janyce called a "safe space" was seen as an important way to alleviate the alienation of queer teens by members of the NPA, including LIT. Founded in 1995, LIT is a member of the National Unity Fellowship Church, a religious organization committed to serving lesbian, gay, bisexual and transgender communities. Initiated by an out African–American lesbian minister, Jacqueline Holland, LIT sought to be a "beacon of light in the city of Newark" by addressing the issues of homelessness, poverty, and HIV/AIDS. The Social Justice Center, a Central Ward drop-in center, provided showers, laundry services, needle-exchange, and condoms to homeless people, drug addicts, and sex-workers to reduce the spread of HIV/AIDS and other sexually transmitted diseases in Newark. At Sakia's memorial service Mayor Sharpe made a shocking open promise to build a "counseling center" for LGBTQ youth. Given this seemingly heartfelt pledge, NPA activists naively assumed that the city would include young people who wanted to play a role in the planning of such a center. Such was not the case. NPA could not even get city hall to schedule meeting space downtown. Efforts to follow up with the mayor's office were met with active indifference. It was clear that Newark's newly politicized queer community was on its own. Although initially reluctant to engage in the formal political process, LIT staunchly backed NPA, and directly petitioned Sharpe James to keep his easily given promise. LIT also assisted NPA in their efforts to informally lobby city council members and bureaucrats, to requisition the city for a room that youth could use to meet to flesh out their ideas about how to proceed with the Ags and Femmes Sakia Gunn Memorial Fund, and other community initiatives for queer teenagers. The city, however, simply refused to act. Janyce explained:

> We followed up with Cathy Cuomo-Cacere as we were directed to at City Hall. I don't remember what her particular title was. But she was the woman designated as the person to talk to for helping us find place for these young people...it never happened. We wrote a letter, we wrote a proposal. We tried. They city has not helped to provide anything for those young people.

NPA needed to find a suitable place to hold community gatherings. Their efforts to secure meeting places at local high schools and other publicly funded places in the city proved futile. LIT stepped in to offer their assistance to what they hoped would be a temporary problem. Janyce recalled, "We offered our center as a space for everyone to come together and express their feelings. What we did was allow them to talk." While catering to some of the more socially despised residents of Newark on the tightest of budgets, LIT decided to donate the physical space of the Social Justice Center (SJC). Under Janyce's leadership, SJC became both a formal and informal gathering for NPA activists as well as students and other "young people" who had been traumatized by Sakia's death. In Reverend Jackson's view, the SJC was a refuge from the open hostility that queer teenagers faced in Newark's blighted, drug-infested neighborhoods, and unruly public schools. In the year following Sakia's death, SJC became the premier social space in which queer teens could receive affirmation, encouragement, and mentoring by queer adults. For Janyce, simply being able to offer a space to these teenagers and supporting any leadership efforts that girls proposed, was the most basic "political" act that LIT could engage in.

Meanwhile "the city", meaning bureaucrats and public officials, emerged as a homophobic force that marginalized and manipulated the black queer community. For example, while ignoring requests from activists to meet, Cathy Cuomo-Cacere made public statements in the New Jersey *Star-Ledger* claiming to have met with "members of the gay community." This duplicitous behavior incensed NPA activists and heightened their sense of outrage. The Janus-faced administration intensified the injury of Sakia's death for many activists, driving home the lack of respect and recognition that many felt everyday as they went about their lives. Unusually pessimistic in the context of our initial two-hour interview in 2005, Reverend Jackson remarked,

> They don't care. The whole issue of gays and lesbians is…number one; people just think it's wrong. How do you fix it? Don't be gay or lesbian. Even though those people are in office and don't say these things out loud, they bring all those feelings with them. They don't care. They didn't do anything—I mean they could have done something small.

In the black community, Sakia's death politicized black homophobia, but this was not enough. LIT and NPA insisted that the contributions of gays and lesbians in Newark be made visible by showing up at council meetings and making their sexual politics known. LIT played a major role in this effort. Janyce explained,

> The first thing that came out was that there were gays and lesbian people in Newark. You know, we had been having church since 1995, but you would think that no such thing was in Newark. After people came out in the streets after her death, that was when the dialogue opened around the fact that they have young people who identify as gays and lesbians. Before then, none of these kinds of conversations were being had.

Although black lesbians and gays were active in mainstream city politics, they were politically invisible to the establishment—meaning that their politics were actively subsumed under more mainstream agendas. While it was well-known that black gays and lesbians, like

Laquetta, were deeply involved in civic affairs, their sexual identities were ignored—basically a non-issue. The political establishment wanted to maintain the heteronormative status quo. When activists like Janyce and Laquetta tried to introduce "gay issues" into city council meetings, council members tabled them or relegated them to "talking points" to be used at some later, unspecified date.

While this political climate was untenable for queer adults, it must have been downright harrowing for queer high school students. Teachers and administrators made openly homophobic remarks, blaming queer teens for the difficulties that beset them. The principal of West Side High School, Fernand Williams, told the students, "If some choose to live a certain lifestyle, they must pay a certain price."[9] Mr. Williams then refused a student request to have a moment of silence for Sakia until over a year after she died. It was not until late 2004 that then Newark Superintendent Marion Bolden confessed: "I didn't know I had 30 to 35 kids living on the street because their parents kicked them out when they came out of the closet. It was a learning curve for me because I didn't know we had such a struggle."[10]

The attitudes of most of Newark's black clergy were no better. NPA activist June Dowell, a 37-year-old returning Rutgers University student, sent more than a hundred invitations to black churches in Newark to attend a community meeting to address homophobia. Only five churches agreed to attend, and only three showed up. June, a busty brown-skinned queer activist with an auburn, dreadlocked mohawk, surmised that the physical presentation of her queerness could have been an enormous barrier in galvanizing support from institutions that may have otherwise advocated on behalf of young African–Americans. In her opinion, it was one thing to express solidarity after a brutal act of black on black violence; it was another altogether to stand shoulder to shoulder and organize with people who repudiated the politics of respectability and openly claimed queer identities. Predictably, in spite of the initial displays of support in front of the cameras from those that showed up for Sakia's funeral and a few of the subsequent vigils, black clergymen kept their distance from NPA. Even fewer were willing to come to the Social Justice Center to talk about homophobia and HIV/AIDS with NPA and their young constituents. June stated,

> When people won't even acknowledge letters that you send them or return phone calls when you've left messages for them. It is like them treating you like you don't exist. This is how the black church looks

upon gay and lesbian folks. They act like we don't exist and we do exist.

June, who organized movie nights for queer youth at SJC in conjunction with local high schools, reported that queer students' day-to-day aesthetic sensibilities often drew negative attention from police officers, security guards, and school teachers who assumed they were engaged in some kind of criminal activity. The social confinement of queer black youth to refuse spaces in Newark's streets visibly troubled Sue "SuSu" Stewart, a self-proclaimed "aggressive" youth activist and NPA member. Not surprisingly, she attributed blamed to Newark's political establishment. She lamented,

> It hurts. It's painful to drive down the street and walk down the street and see the hopelessness on people's faces. It's like up there on the corner, or over there in the park. To see that on their faces and see young people trying to forge their identities there—and they're trying to do that, [when] people in fear, not wanting to know who they are, what they are. And I'm talking about people in high places.

At age 42, SuSu conducted weekly technology seminars and photography workshops for teens at a Central Ward Boys and Girls Club. As a part of her political work, she also organized music production classes for teenagers interested in rap, spoken word, and singing. In her opinion, all young black people in Newark suffered equally from lack of resources or lack of knowledge about how to utilize existing community resources. From her perspective, they were vulnerable to all kinds of social problems that contributed to what she called, "that blank look of despair...they don't look happy. They look depressed. What's worse is that nobody really seems to care." Her dismal interpretation of the plight of visible teen black bodies in Newark may not be completely unfounded considering that within a year of Sakia's death, West High School—a school with a majority African–American student population—banned queer students from wearing the gay pride rainbow insignia. School administrators justified this decision by arguing that the rainbow was a form of "gang paraphernalia."[11] However, the administration's decision to criminalize out gay and lesbian students who probably wore the rainbow in schools to express solidarity and support for each other—a form of queer body politics—speaks volumes about the inability of opinion leaders to grasp how homophobia intersects with class and racially discriminatory attitudes, practices, and policies. The tendency, which

permeated the local political landscape, results in further stigmatiz-
ing and alienating *all* young black bodies, but especially queer black
bodies, in Newark's inner city.

SCALING THE BODY IN A "PERFECT MURDER"

In a very basic way power operates and expresses itself through the
politics of scale, shaping how we interpret and make sense of discourses of identity, group membership, and social change (Harvey
2005). Activists and opinion leaders often make issues political
by designating them to a particular level of scale (neighborhood,
local, urban, national, international, or global). In the twentieth
century, key civil rights issues were made legible by framing these
issues within *national* discourses. Women's rights, gay rights, and
citizenship rights for African–Americans were made by making
identity-based claims to the federal (national) government. As a
result, our understanding of gender, race, and sexuality have often
been understood as "single issue" politics that are based upon
groups that are often wrongly imagined as homogenous and mutually exclusive. Under neoliberalism of the twenty-first century,
struggles around identity and against marginality are also always
contestations about scale.

Queer activists who challenged local politicians investments in heteropatriarchy also railed against construction of gender and sexuality
that reduced LGBT politics to the scale of the individual, neglecting
to attend to how the state itself produced vulnerable queer black bodies in Newark. The framing of Sakia's murder by various community members reveals how scalar politics operate in and across urban
spaces, and demonstrates how rigid scalar politics can restrict possibilities for redress and meaningful social change. As the political
establishment became involved, many opinion leaders pathologized
queer teenagers, proposing the building of a counseling center rather
than a community center for queer teenagers that could challenge
black homophobia, and provide support for teens alienated by school
administrators, politicians, and churches. As national lesbian and
gay activists became involved, they erased the reality of geographic
domination.

In the final section of this chapter, I analyze how contending identity-based frames were used by various actors to make sense of Sakia's
death. Frame analysis allows us to identify how disparate political
communities interpreted her death, and to identify which elements
of Sakia's social identity were acknowledged and how others were

denied. "Frames" can be understood as the tacit theories or unstated presumptions held by opinion leaders that provide meaning, determine what is relevant or irrelevant when considering a particular issue or event, and, as a result, implicitly suggest an appropriate response.[12] I am analyzing the framing strategies that were used by journalists, activist-journalists, and community organizers alike to define "the problem" and thereby imply a rational response to Sakia's death.[13] Understanding *how* Sakia's slain body was framed by political actors is crucial to understanding how and why her death produced such an outcry, and how and why the local political establishment ultimately refused to respond. I apply the analytics of black feminist intersectional analysis into my frame analysis of competing discourses to illustrate how closely tied identity politicking claims are imbricated with the politics of scale. In the remaining pages, I argue that NPA activists had to destabilize the competing frames of Sakia's death by destabilizing the scalar politics that precluded an intersectional framing of her death that could account for how *multiple* aspects of her social identity made her vulnerable to premature death. In Table 1, I compare the reflection of national LGBTQ activists and local black activists.

In the statements made by national organizations, Sakia's death becomes politically charged by reducing the injury to violence exacted

Table 1   Frame Analysis: Public Discourse Surrounding the Causes of Sakia Gunn's Death

National LGBTQ Activists Reflections	Local LGBTQ Activists Reflections
1a. "Sakia Gunn was murdered because of her sexual preference."[1] (Context: Hate Crimes Against Lesbians and Gays)	2a. "We have dealt with gay and lesbian issues during the anti-violence concerns over Sakia Gunn, who was [killed] downtown. They (local LGBTQ activists) came, and spoke to members of the anti-violence coalition and they asked for our support. And so we definitely accepted and supported." (Context: Violence Against Black Youth)[2]
1b. "If Miss Gunn said she was a lesbian, that doesn't give him (Richard McCullough) the right to do what he did."[3] (Context: Hate Crimes)	2b. "Sakia's death was symbolic, or emblematic of the psychic and emotional death of so many of our young people. She did not conform to the expectations of how she should behave. For that she was slaughtered."[4] (Context: Oppression of Black youth)

Continued

Table 1 Continued

National LGBTQ Activists Reflections	Local LGBTQ Activists Reflections
1c. "The most important thing that can be learned from this tragedy is that all gay people are vulnerable."[5] (Context: Hate Crimes)	2c. "Because of the Black church, preaching hatred from the pulpit has contributed to homophobia toward Black gays and lesbians, so they have responsibility for Sakia's murder."[6] (Context: Black Patriarchy)
1d. "It was a hate crime, but it wasn't covered as [though] it was."[7] (Context: Anti Sodomy Laws)	2d. "The lesbian aspect of her death might have been enflamed. She might have been a 'goner' anyway if she had gotten into any altercation with Black men at three o'clock in the morning. Black females always have to been on the defensive." (Context: Black Patriarchy)
1e. "The media generally doesn't pay attention to hate crimes, so many go unreported. GLAAD is working very hard to get those kinds of crimes the media attention they warrant."[8] (Context: Hate Crimes Against LGBT)	2e. "When has it been a crime to be out at 3:30? That is no reason for a child to lose her life."[9] (Context: Policing Practices)
1f. "To lesbian communities, the tragic death of Sakia Gunn is a painful memory not only because the 15 year old girl was killed, but also because the media largely ignored her story."[10]	

1. Source: Youth for Socialist Action "Sakia Gunn" written by Adam Ritcher. Personal interview with Tamara Brown, September 20, 2005.
2. Personal interview with Tamara Brown, September 20, 2005.
3. Quote by Basil Lucas of the New York City Gay and Lesbian Antiviolence Project. Source: *Advocate News and Politics*. "200 attend vigil for slain New Jersey Teen" by Mark Goebel, March 15, 2003.
4. Quote by Cheryl Clarke. "Three years after her murder, few remember Sakia Gunn" by Kim Pearson. Blocher: Where the Women Are, May 12, 2006.
5. Quote by Clarence Patton, New York Gay and Lesbian Activist. Source: *Advocate News and Politics*. "200 attend vigil for slain New Jersey Teen" by Mark Goebel, March 15, 2003.
6. Personal interview with Laquetta Nelson, September 16, 2005.
7. "Where is the outrage?" by Paul Schindler. *Gay City News*, May 23, 2003.
8. Quote by Cathy Renna of Gay and Lesbian Alliance Against Defamation. Source: *Advocate News and Politics*. "200 attend vigil for slain New Jersey Teen" by Mark Goebel, March 15, 2003.
9. Quote by Newark Councilman Hector Corchado. "Marchers seek justice and answers" in *City News* (Vol. 19, No. 32), May 21-May 27, 2003.
10. "Skeleton in Newark's Closet" by Gay Mundo. *The Gully*, Online Magazine, June 19, 2003.

upon Sakia's body because of her "sexual orientation." The most reductionist accounts (reflections 1a and 1b) erase all elements of Sakia's identity—race/ethnicity, socioeconomic/class status, age, and gendered self-presentation—except her sexuality to read the tragedy of her death as a hate crime. In this liberal framing, Sakia emerges as a victim of Richard McCullough's alleged hatred and disgust toward lesbians. This normalizing register equates Sakia's injury with that of other gays and lesbians who are vulnerable to violence by homophobic individuals. Within this frame, "sexual preference" over-determines her death.

In the first three reflections by national activists (1a, 1b, and 1c) Sakia emerges solely as a victim. Her potential for political agency is completely usurped by Richard McCullough, who is portrayed as a violent perpetrator of a "hate crime." In this framing, the most objectionable aspect of her death is that it was not more widely recognized as a political injury specifically directed toward lesbians. Although the reason that more people did not understand her death as a hate crime is silently questioned (racism), very little attention is given to larger structural inequalities that would enable a more holistic representation of the social implications of both Sakia's life and death. Sakia is strategically reduced to a slain, parenthetically black, lesbian body whose agency is realized through the state recognizing her as an individual victim of hate crime. This recognition is manifest solely through ability of the state to prosecute and convict Richard McCullough as a specific kind of criminal—a slaughterer of a lesbian. The categorical interpellation of Sakia *as a slain lesbian* by state apparatus is the most triumphant outcome envisioned by national LGBTQ activists who identify the hate crime as the sole injury.

There is a conspicuous silence concerning Sakia's death among national black and national women's organizations. Nationally, Sakia mattered because she was a dead lesbian, not because she was Black, not because she was female, not because she was young, and not because she was poor. At the local level, the significance of Sakia's death is contested. Some emphasis is placed on the contextual (read structural) circumstances that contributed to her erasure as a living black youth in Newark. Sakia is mourned because she is one of many, rather than because she is an exceptional case, effectively bracketing her queerness. Reflection 2a reflects the fleeting possibility of coalition building among Black LGBTQ activists and local antiviolence activists as Sakia is constructed as a victim of Black on Black street violence—a victim of structural violence due to her race. However within this set up, there is a general denial that this racialized violence is also gendered—her femaleness is ignored, as well as her gender performativity. In reflection 2b, the city of Newark is identified as playing an important role in producing a questionable "climate" for Black LGBTQ youth, suggesting that those in power have somehow produced an attitude or general atmosphere of intolerance that magnified the vulnerability of the living. The emphasis is on change, or at least on the facilitation of a new direction that might protect the lives of young Black people. In an attempt to hold some institution accountable, reflection 2c explicitly names the black church as a culprit in her death. As Sakia becomes a symbol of gay and lesbian youth, black on black violence, and gender non-conformity, the consequences of black hyper-masculinity and the complex intersections of the black girlhood are continually eclipsed. The reluctanc or inability for actors to consider the multiple ways that Sakia's identity—made it impossible to account for the totality of ways she was made vulnerable. The lack of a truly intersectional account and necessarily multiscalar politics leaves different forms of bigotry unquestioned, and thereby reinforced by community members and activists who claimed to have cared that her life was lost.

MAKING SENSE OF MURDER: A BLACK FEMINIST ANALYSIS

Theorizing the mutual constitution of race, gender, and oppression specifically links black women's sexual oppression to Black patriarchy. As Hull and Smith (1982, xxiv) have noted: "We believe that sexual politics under patriarchy is as pervasive in Black women's lives as are the politics of class and race. We find it difficult to separate race from class from sexual oppression because in our lives they are most often experienced simultaneously." Gender-based political subordination of Black women is rooted in the historical processes and ideologies of capitalism, as well as in modes of US black racialization, including chattel slavery, Jim Crowism, *de facto* racial subjugation via segregation, white supremacy, and what Patricia Hill Collins (2005, 7) has recently called the "the new Racism" and what Michelle Alexander (2010) has called the "New Jim Crow."[14] Contemporary Black feminist thought identifies patriarchy within African–American community politics as a major source of gender-based oppression of black lesbian women and gay men. Analyzing contemporary manifestations of integrationist and nationalist (autonomist) strategies of Black political leadership, Leith Mullings (1997, 154) concluded: "The final product of both visions is a patriarchal model of gender roles in which masculinity is defined as the subordination of women."

Despite the relevance of these early and sustained arguments about the importance of intersectional politics by black feminists, their insights have been evaded, ignored, misappropriated, and maligned in the black community, among white queer activists and social theorists, and even by "progressive" observers of contemporary black politics. The refusal to see how class inequality, race, and sexuality are co-constitutive forces should also be viewed as a refusal to acknowledge and apply 40 years of social justice theorizing produced by black women. These evasions allow Sakia Gunn's life to be understood solely in terms of black homophobia without specifically linking homophobia to black heteropatriarchy. Similarly, these evasions permit Sakia's death to be understood as a "hate crime against gays and lesbians" rather than as a characteristic example of misogynist sexual violence against a young Black female (Miller 2008). In the absence of intersectional black feminist analysis, the narratives circulating on the websites of several national and international organizations that politicized Sakia Gunn's death completely ignore the fact that poor, young, Black people's lives are grossly undervalued in American cities. The systemic neglect of Black feminist analyses helps explain why it is only when Sakia Gunn's death is framed explicitly as a hate crime against a lesbian that any attention at all is given to her death. In the absence of LGBTQ activism around hate crimes, Sakia would have remained another nameless, faceless young victim of Newark street violence. No story there. While the few national organizations that politicized Sakia's unfortunate death sought to challenge homophobia in black communities, these politicized narratives of Sakia's life stand in stark tension with the *testimony* of black queer feminist activists who organized locally to commemorate her life and to breathe life into the tragedy of her death. The racialized gender dynamics that produced homophobic street violence shaped both the sites and strategies of contestation and resistance taken up by queer black women. In the context of an ideologically "perfect murder," however, the voices and perspectives of black feminist politics and activisms, while perhaps the loudest, were the least respected in the politics of representation that emerged in the aftermath of Sakia's death. To this very day, over seven years after Sakia's death, queer teenagers are still waiting on their community center.

Transforming Horror Stories into Geographies of Resistance

The Central Ward of Newark can be characterized as what Kathryn Stockton (2006) might call a "bottom" neighborhood that has withstood generations of widespread black unemployment and underemployment, an eroded tax base, failing public schools, and disturbingly high rates of HIV/AIDS. As the densest and most highly populated ward in Newark, 41 percent of residents live at or below the poverty level. Seventy-one percent of all Central Ward residents are African–American, and 41 percent live at or below the line of poverty.

In spite of all of its problems Newark is still hailed by local activists as a place to be "cherished and not condemned." Amina Baraka, featured in the last chapter, lost her own lesbian-identified daughter to murder at the hands of a black man. In spite of this Mother Baraka, a sustained African–American cultural nationalist, devout socialist, and Newark enthusiastic, refused to be broken. Instead, she turned her horror story into the politics of resistance.

Sakia Gunn's life and death provides us with a deeply intersectional account of black female subjectivity in urban space because we are able to interrogate the boundaries through which particular identity categories are produced and deployed, and to situate our interrogation in an active social arena.[15] Black queer activists retold the story of her death to make legible the community of agents who were already intrinsic to the workings of the city. In so doing, they made possible a geography of resistance. Newark was already an uncomfortable home for queer people; however, black queer women made it clear that it was a home worth fighting for. By reaching out to friends, colleagues, and acquaintances and redefining the meaning of old relationships, women like Laquetta, June, Susu, Janyce, Amina, and countless others respatialized social capital. They transformed their own pain and vulnerability into spatial agency—activating networks of struggle and making new kinds of politics possible. Newark was transformed into a place where even if one could not always be safe, they could still belong. Black women invaded the black public sphere and made it clear just how often "horror stories" tormented queer teenagers. They made linkages between the failure of public institutions to meet the basic needs of those they are charged with serving and black homophobia. Not only did publicly paid teachers and administrators fail to educate, they also harassed, demeaned, and alienated their students. Black women in Newark remembered those who lost their lives literally and metaphorically. By refusing to be silent and invisible about their sexuality, and giving each other the courage to speak the truth to the heteronormative power structure of the city, they created a new geography of resistance in Newark.

7

KEEPIN' UP THE FIGHT: YOUNG BLACK FEMINISTS AND THE HIP HOP CONVENTION MOVEMENT

The Convention. I think brotha's—Black men, men of color, need to understand their maleness as well as they understand their ethnicity or race. I don't think they get it. A lot of brothas don't feel comfortable sitting parallel to another sister. Even the brothas who are a bit more cognizant of the gender dynamic than most. They don't quite get it!

Keisha Simpson, 26-year-old hip hop activist

The Hip Hop Convention, in my opinion, was another significant event, because it was an attempt by the younger generation to reach out to the older generation to help us. We realized very quickly that we still had to make our own mistakes to accomplish that.

Melanie Hendricks, 26-year-old hip hop activist

Hip hop feminists aggressively claim hip hop as a unique space for women to come to voice using the aesthetics of hip hop, incorporating the lyrics, linguistics, rhythms, body language, and attitude that has come to be associated with hip hop in mainstream culture in their writing, teaching, and performance styles (Brown 2012, Brown 2008, Perry 2004, Pough 2004, Rose 1994). Twenty-six-year-old Newark based hip hop activist Keisha Simpson, describes hip hop feminism this way: "A woman in hip hop has one of two options: she can fall off or she can fight. It's our position of struggle. For women that fight—by definition—they have to subscribe to some level of hip hop feminism to keep that fight up." Working in Newark as a community economic development activist, for Keisha, hip hop feminism encompasses women's struggles for recognition, respect, and credibility within the cultural space of hip hop. Scholars, writers, journalists, performance artists, and social critics have identified

hip hop as a source of empowerment for women of color. Through
hip hop women are able to boldly and unapologetically lay claim to
the male dominated public sphere through the four elements of hip
hop—being a female emcee, poet, b-boy/b-girl, dj, or graffiti artist—
rocking the mike and moving the crowd (Perry 2004, Keyes 2000,
Rose 1994). Whitney Peoples (2008) suggests that hip hop feminism
be best understood as a means of "reconciliation and reclamation on
the part of young black women in the U.S. trying to create a space for
themselves between the whiteness of university-based feminism and
the maleness of the hip-hop culture that most grew up on" (26). Hip
hop feminists also express a willingness to read mainstream hip hop
culture as symptomatic of the pain, trauma, distrust, and self-hatred
that plague black interpersonal relationships. Through close analysis
of hip hop icons like Tupac Shakur, Lil Kim, Foxy Brown, and many
others, hip hop feminist writers illuminate a gendered politics of pain
within inner city communities (Perry 2004, Pough 2004, Morgan
1999, Hampton 1998, Jones 1994).

In its contemporary incarnations, what is now called "hip hop"
far exceeds the four fundamental elements initially associated with
it. As hip hop has both engaged and transgressed professional, disciplinary, and socioeconomic boundaries, it has encompassed phenomena as diverse as hip hop theatre, hip hop pedagogy, hip hop
homos, hip hop politicians, hip hop fiction, and hip hop as a *bono
fide* transnational social movement.[1] Political scientist Lester Spence
(2011) surmises, "Almost forty years ago, a group of black and Latino
youths created what we now recognize as hip hop. They did so never
imagining that decades later MC's, b-boys, b-girls, taggers and DJs
the world over would use hip hop to speak to their own political,
economic, and social needs" (17). Hip hop has also produced a cultural space in which notions of racial sincerity and authenticity have
been ruptured as elements of its aesthetics have been transformed
through its spatial, transnational, transcultural, translocal, and tran-
sracial social, economic, and/or temporal political mutations.[2] The
aesthetically "pure" expressions of hip hop's earlier political edge,
manifested through the original four elements, are now as common
among Palestinian, Cuban, and South African hip hop artists whose
work circulates transnationally through social media as what now circulates in predominantly black and brown US urban communities.
In contemporary practice, hip hop can be thought of as a complex
and frequently contested artistic, cultural, and political terrain that
reflects more about the political, economic, and social location of
its producers and practitioners than it does adherence to any unitary

philosophical or ideological standpoint. If there is a core substantive appeal or "flava" that makes hip hop discernible as a unique cultural signifier (or set of signifiers) then that difference would certainly have to do with the particular ways that hip hop historically laid claim to the public sphere and how it historically shattered conventional (especially white and middle class) cultural expectations about how the Black/brown body and voice can be heard, seen, felt, and interpreted in the public sphere (Chang 2004, Perry 2004, Rose 1998). There is something unique about hip hop's ability to infuse space/place that its practitioners temporarily seize with the irony, despair, relative deprivation, marginality, and political alienation of the "hood." William Jelani Cobb 2007 explains, "The hood, the barrio the broken precincts of the city breathed life into hip hop. At it's core, hip hop's aesthetics contains three components: "beats," lyrics, and "flow" (14). These basic aesthetics have also shaped the way hip hop has sprouted globally as a translocal political movement.

Veronica Osorio, a 23-year-old substitute teacher in Newark Public Schools who mentored a group of 12–17 year old girls identified through HUD and the Newark Chapter of the Girl Scouts, became an organizer for the New Jersey Local Organizing Committee for the 2004 National Hip Hop Political Convention (NHHPC). As an outreach coordinator for a performance-based black and Latino youth organization called "All Stars" that encouraged the professional development of young people who wanted to perform, Veronica was keenly aware of the rich potential the arts held for inner city youth. "We didn't want just the best and brightest from Newark, we wanted *any* young person in the community who wanted to work to be on stage—whether singing, acting, or dancing. We helped them do resumes, auditions, interviews and do mandatory performance workshops." Veronica initially learned about the NHHPC on a website constructed by the entertainment industry whistleblower, hip hop journalist, and Convention organizer, Davey-D. She then contacted the New Jersey Local Organizing Chair, Hashim Shomari, and began attending meetings three months prior to the Convention. Her commitment to a sustained level of involvement with the NHHPC was due in part to her strong sense of identification with the "hip hop generation" as it was defined by local organizers.

> It was more than just the music, it was the generation, and knowing that the eighteen to twenty somethings, like myself, *are* interested in the grassroots issues that affect their communities, as a whole. The war was a prominent issue ... education and poverty ... What prompted

me to get involved was knowing that there were all these other people coming together for something, that we were going to dialogue, and build something off of what we think as young people.

Veronica quickly registered 50 voters within the Central Ward of Newark where she lived with her parents, fulfilling the requirement to become a Convention delegate for the New Jersey Local Organizing Committee. She also served as a volunteer during the four days of the Convention. "I was like a little errand girl. I did whatever was needed from me." Veronica did not get involved with the internal politics of the Convention, nor did she serve in any official leadership or decision-making capacity at the local organizing committee level. But this limited role did not deter her participation. Inspired by other organizers involved in the Convention, Veronica viewed it as an important learning opportunity to sharpen her own skills in community-based activism. Indeed, Veronica identified the 2004 NHHPC as one of the most "significant political events that took place in Newark within the last ten years."

DISCIPLINING HIP HOP IN GEOGRAPHY

In the last decade, theoretical innovations in the field of political geography have enabled researchers to rethink the scalar division of labor that has characterized approaches of "politics" in several disciplinary subfields including political geography, political sociology, international relations, political psychology, and even political science per se (Marston 2000, Cox 1998, Jones 1998, Delaney 1997). Typically, conventional scholars of politics have relied upon the discrete, ontological categories of scale (local, regional, national, global, etc.) that presume that politics always happen within the nested hierarchies of enclosed jurisdictions (i.e., local politics=local centers of governance). This approach has made case studies of local "politics" in their myriad forms less than desirable due to the peculiarity of local governance structures that inhibit the generalizability of observed phenomenon, including the theoretical constructs produced to make sense of politics at the local level. The ontological status of scale as a fixed category of analysis for scholars of political studies has been heavily contested on many levels. As Kevin R. Cox (1998) argues, local political agents and governing institutions actively shape how and whether or not issues will be understood as "local," "national," or even "global" by framing discourse to meet the political exigencies that exist in particular moments in time and space. While geographers with social theory interests have managed to situate the phenomenon of urbanization with capitalist production and consumption from a global perspective, most case studies of local politics have generally failed to make similar connections across scale due to the preestablished desire to fixate on agents attempts to influence local governing institutions (city council, state legislators, county commissions, etc.) (Marston 2000, Taylor 1999).

Some political geographers have responded to these critiques by denying the ontological status of scale, which prescribes a rather blunt delimitation on the kind of questions that observers can ask and methodologically pursue within a bounded arena (town-city-neighborhood-state) in favor of "spaces of dependence" and "spaces of engagement." These new ways of thinking about scale need not make an a priori assumption that "politics" emerge and are resolved at the same scale (neighborhood, city, local, state, national, or global), but that local political actors who emerge from spaces of dependence may need to strategically pursue their politics in "spaces of engagement" that may or may not be confined to local governance arenas. Greater insight may be produced then by studying how "networks of association" traverse spaces of dependence and spaces of engagement.

Conceptualizing hip hop as a translocal political space enables scholars to witness the deployment of identity across scalar structures, as well as an opportunity to witness how intersectionality influences the ways that power gets distributed within and across political space. Arjun Appadurai (1995) defines translocality as a situation in which the relations of power that produce locality are fundamentally imbricated in extra-local, national, and international relationships. These relations are typically created through ongoing interactions between locally based and circulating populations. Halifu Osumare (2007) describes hip hop as a "technologically-mediated global youth culture" that extends the trajectory of an "Africanist aesthetic that facilitates the dissemination of American popular culture globally" (22). My usage of the term "translocal hip hop" attends specifically to the ways in which the strategic deployment of hip hop can reproduce hegemonic interpretations of blackness and black politics that circulate among local and national black political "leaders." As Oakes and Schein (2006) argue, "Translocality draws attention to multiplying forms of mobility without loosing site of the importance of localities in people's lives" (23). The political space of hip hop then can then be grasped through tracing the representational strategies of local "networks of association" and linking the local circumstances in which these political spaces emerge and wane with the overlapping local, regional, national, and even global political economies. Cultural geographers' recent nod toward the importance of networks of association provide a useful theoretical framework in which to make sense of the "political" agency of US black women in the twentieth century, especially in the context of hip hop politics and activism (McMaster & Sheppard 2004, Leitner 1999, Taylor 1999, Cox 1998).

Some of the most innovative feminist studies of the politics of women of color have been conducted within the framework of "transnational" or "global" feminist politics. This literature has sought to link women's local "politics" with inter- and transnational political and economic institutions that extend their reach globally (Labaten & Martin 2004, Nagar 2004, Hernandez & Rehman 2002, Naples & Desai, 2002). This body of research has done an excellent job of identifying how interactions between local women's organizations, transnational NGOs, and local and international configurations of power enable and constrain women's agency. With this said, most studies of the politics of women of color have not specified or elaborated upon the local configurations of power that enable and constrain black women's activism, nor examined how these may be connected to larger, transnational circuits of power. Scant attention has been given to black women's effort to resist circuits of power collectively, at the grassroots level. Examination of black female agency in the context of the NHHPC provides an opportunity to witness how the convergence of power at multiple levels of scale constructs US black women as political subjects in the US urban context.

NATIONAL HIP HOP POLITICAL CONVENTION OF 2004

In the past 25 years, the eminence of hip hop has been dispersed, transfigured, and reimagined as those who have come of age in the era of hip hop have forged a spectrum of relationships in disparate communities.[3] The 2004 NHHPC was convened to increase political participation within the "hip hop generation" by 1) developing a political agenda for the "hip hop generation," 2) creating a national organizing infrastructure for the hip hop generation, and 3) hosting a Convention whereby delegates of the local organizing committees from hip hop actually vote, adopt, and endorse a "political agenda" for their generation. The idea of "hip hop generation," while controversial, was conceived by an early founding organizer of the Convention, Bakari Kitwana. He argued that the hip hop generation was closely tied to the experiences of African–American urban youth, who came of age in an unprecedented era of urban decline. This particular generation, Kitwana argued, came of age with the explosion of hip hop as a widely influential mode of Black cultural expression.[4] The effort to define the "hip hop generation" was deeply connected to resistance to the widespread vilification of African–American youth, particularly African–American male youth, by local law enforcement agencies and the criminal justice system.[5] An early version of the NHHPC Vision Statement and Platform reads, "Too many of us have experienced firsthand the trafficking of drugs and violence in our neighborhoods, rampant police violence and corruption, failing public education systems, mass imprisonment, widespread unemployment and economic decay."[6] Theoretically, this document critiqued the failures of neoliberalization to address the political and economic needs of disadvantaged youth in mostly urban communities under the rubric of hip hop politics. The convention cofounders invoked deliberative ideals of democratic participation hoping to create new spaces for more radical voices to be heard within the American public sphere.

NHHPC was the product of the efforts of more than 200 community organizers, activists, artists, professionals, and educators between the ages of 17 and 40 from 33 US states, and ten countries. This diverse body of organizers came together because they agreed that hip hop could be used as an effective organizing tool for social and political change among the hip hop generation. In fact, as a signifier, hip hop functioned ubiquitously among the major organizers, state delegates, and lay attendees of the Convention. Some were convinced that the politicization of hip hop entailed a sustained intellectual engagement with hip hop as a mode of artistic and cultural expression. Some believed that they could use hip hop as a heuristic to seduce young people broadly interested in some aspect of hip hop culture into larger discussions of systemic social inequalities concerning race and class in America. Strategic slippages between "hip hop" and "black" or "hip hop" and "black and Latino" also worked to secure the political and financial support of a variety of different potential donors and reinforced intensive coalition-building efforts among diverse leftist people of color organizations.

The Convention extended the historical trajectory of black radical social movements, including the National Black and Puerto Rican Convention Movements, which heralded close ties with urban black nationalisms, cultural nationalism, and urban-based strategies for black political empowerment vis a vis electoral politics (Woodard 2002). Some hoped that the Convention would facilitate the construction of a political apparatus that could showcase the transformative potential of hip hop by politicizing the inherent social criticisms within its artistic and cultural expression (Chang 2004, Shomari 1995, Rose 1994, Keyes 1989). Thus the creation of a national organizing infrastructure for the hip hop generation was stated as one of three major objectives of the national organizing committee for the Convention. For others, especially participants in the local organizing committees in different US cities, the signifier "hip hop" was a code for "urban," "poor and black," or "poor and brown" communities. Activists with close ties to contemporary black nationalist and black revolutionary (socialist) nationalist organizations including the Malcolm X Grassroots Movement, the People's Organization for Progress, the New Black Panther Party, the Young Comrades, and the All African People's Revolutionary Party conceptualized NHHPC as a political apparatus that could be used to liberate people of African descent from the vestiges of racism, white supremacy, and capitalism. Most activists, resisted this nationalist reading, envisioning the NHHPC as a forum in which various social issues including the criminalization of Black and Latino males, amnesty for black, Native American, and Puerto Rican political prisoners, media literacy, racial profiling, reparations for slavery, and urban educational reform could be addressed within the context of a larger progressive, youth-based social movement.[7] In the end, no specific conceptualization of hip hop or politics would achieve preeminence within the context of the Convention, or within the local politics that emerged in its aftermath.

The national steering committee was primarily composed of activists with highly respected electoral and/or issue-based grassroots political victories. Others included nationally acclaimed speakers, journalists, film-makers, public intellectuals, and those who had currency with mainstream media outlets. Making use of relatively close-knit political (and personal) relationships that predated the Convention, these activists constituted a formidable, although somewhat contentious cadre of young leaders with considerable stores of social capital in many American cities.[8] A highly organized contingent of activists who had strong electoral ambitions in cities including Chicago, Newark, Detroit, and Philadelphia made their way to the national political spotlight in the organizing leading up to and following the 2004 Convention. These young office seekers and political strategists envisioned using the Convention to flex the political muscle of an emergent generation of local, urban voters. The electoral perspective was institutionalized within the official protocols adopted to regulate the participation of delegates. To be an official delegate with the privilege of voting for the national agenda, one was required to register and submit a list of 50 potential voters in their respective communities.[9] Of more than 5,000 conference attendees, nearly 300 were registered as delegates and voted for the national agenda.

The cultivation of relationships with left-leaning democratic organizations including American Families United, the League of Pissed Off Voters, and MoveOn.Org, involved the crosspollination of internet-based political strategies, including heavy use of a national internet listserve, the Hip Hop Convention website (where more than 15,000 people registered), and heavy use of blogs from internet-based journalists/activists who functioned as media watch dogs and made explicit political linkages between hip hop, corporate media, and the exploitation and denigration of black youth culture. In addition, the inclusion of emerging scholars made possible the extensive use of university based list-serves associated with academic departments at acclaimed research institutions.

Politically astute hip hop artists including Dead Prez, Chuck D, Doug E. Fresh, Floetry, and Akon attended the convention. They functioned as living, breathing exhibits of the four original elements of hip hop, attracting young up-and-coming emcees, spoken word artists, b-boys, and b-girls, turntablists, and acclaimed graffiti artists, as well as bona fide contemporary hip hop superstars. The full participation of artists in various aspects of the Convention process created a cultural and political scene through which the most transformative elements of contemporary youth political organizing could be experienced in real time.

The city of Newark, however, viewed the overwhelming presence of black hip hop generationers in the streets as a threat to be contained, rather than a potential source of youth empowerment. Newark city officials expressed strong reservations about bringing so many young African–Americans into the city.[10] Administratively, the city of Newark was more interested in policing the hip hop concert that was scheduled to take place in Military Park to ensure that the city would not be embarrassed by predominantly Black and Latino "party-goers" than in catering to the convenience, safety, and market demands of thousands of Convention attendees. In a post-9/11 context, the local organizers were forced to have all artists scheduled to perform pre-screened by the US Department of Homeland Security. They were also required to spend nearly $80,000 for off-duty police officers and marshals, fencing, and security checkpoints, and local roof-top surveillance.[11]

THE SYMBOLIC CAPITAL OF BLACK
MASCULINITY IN THE 2004 CONVENTION

The most compelling notion cementing the radical potentiality of
hip hop with "politics" was that systematic analysis the triangular
relationship among urban youth subjectivity, hip hop culture, and
the commodified forms of rap music distributed by the entertainment industry would offer an effective critique of the enduring legacy
of racism and capitalism in which the contradictory everyday experiences of young Black folks were rooted. Within this framework, a
premier site of contestation and struggle for hip hop activists was
mainstream media.

This identification of mass media as a critical site for class struggle
and Black liberation (under a Black nationalistic ideological framework)
became the hallmark of a new politics of loosely associated networks of
young, predominantly African–American leaders. The close association
with "conscious" rap artists who articulated similar messages in their
music and with concerted efforts to educate young people politically
through a peculiar synthesis of Black (male) bourgeois and revolutionary
nationalist political agenda became the unstated, yet de facto imperative
of the 2004 Convention. These unlikely partnerships had roots in the
contradictory positionalities of the hip hop political organizers themselves, which became evident in the gender politics that unraveled during
the Convention. As a North Jersey based union organizer and convention cofounder, Hashim Shomari, admitted in a personal interview, "This
is what *we* came up with. We wanted progressive. But it *was* controlled
by Black folks." In this context "we" referred to the four Black men who
initiated the call for the Convention in 2002: Hashim Shomari, Bakari
Kitwana, Baye Adofo-Wilson, and Ras Baraka. "Progressive" indicated
a staunch ideological commitment to confront the structural forces of
capitalism, which produced the racial caste system that criminalized and
otherwise denigrated the lives of black (male) youth.[12]

From an organizational standpoint, masculinity functioned as a
powerful ideological signifier within the context of the NHHPC.
The Convention slogan "Voice, Unity, Power!" spoke volumes about
the extent to which a masculinist conception of politics permeated
the strategic imperatives of the Convention. The national logo, a
vertical microphone seized in a tightly closed fist bore an uncanny
resemblance to the erect phallus. The raised fist, heavily reminiscent
of the anger, resistance, and nationalist political determination of
the black power movement established the relationship between the
right to speak and be heard in the public sphere and Black (male)

political empowerment.[13] Although six of the 22 founding members of the Convention were women, and nine of the 22 members of the staff and Convention steering committee were women, men dominated Convention planning. At the second national organizing meeting for the Convention, the organizers verbal commitment to gender parity on various issue-based committees came to structure the national agenda committee membership.[14] Despite this liberal ideological impulse toward gender equality, the public perception of the Convention as a project led by African–American men was reinforced by the tendency of young, predominantly male office-seekers and professionals to verbally and visually dominate press conferences, podiums, and the most highly publicized panels at the Convention.

At the second national organizing meeting for NHHPC, the city of Newark was selected as a prime location for the Convention. The cities of Detroit and Chicago were bypassed because they could not offer the tactical organizing advantages of Newark. While Chicago and Detroit were home to burgeoning young African–American male office-seekers, few had the name recognition, symbolic capital, and national acclaim of the son of renowned poet and activist Amiri Baraka, Ras Baraka. Arguably, as deputy mayor in the administration of incumbent mayor Sharpe James, the younger Baraka's involvement in municipal politics and city administration would facilitate the navigation of city governance to secure venues, ensure adequate security, facilitate outreach to high school students and local community leaders, and to garner local political support and social capital. Similarly, Convention cofounder, Hashim Shomari, had also served for several years as Senator Sharpe James' Chief of Staff.[15] The rationale for selecting Newark as the Convention site is best summed in the minutes of the second national meeting, "We think it legitimizes the event."[16] The political acumen of core organizers in key leadership posts within the city would signify the hip hop generation's ability to achieve mainstream electoral victories, as well as engage in independent organizing on a national level.

Ras Baraka, the 2004 Convention Chair, embodied the political potentiality of hip hop on many levels. Not only was he a direct descendent of a strong cultural nationalist movement that emerged in the wake of the Black Power Movement, but Baraka also maintained close ties to the hip hop artists who used contemporary interpretations of black cultural nationalism and themes of Black political and economic empowerment in their artistic discourse. Ras, who by age 32, had made two notable yet ultimately unsuccessful bids for mayor and the Newark Municipal Council, represented the struggles of a new generation of aspiring black political leaders. In many ways he possessed the unique capacity to legitimize the power of the hip hop Convention. "If we can connect our organization's support to Ras Baraka being elected, our organization's profile, importance and relevancy increases."[17]

Having done extensive work as a core organizer on the "Hands Off Assata" Campaign, the "Coalition to Free Sundiata Acoli" and the Million Youth March, 27-year-old Fayemi Shakur was firmly committed to doing social justice work that carried the potential for raising awareness about the contemporary implications of the black freedom struggle, as articulated by revolutionary nationalist organizations, including the New Black Panther Party. Her rationale for involvement with such organizations, despite repeated instances of perceived sexism, stemmed from her commitment to do social justice work in predominantly African–American communities.

> I try to seek out other people who are concerned about those issues and try to figure out solutions, or at least align myself with people who are trying to make the community better. I'm of the position, if you don't like how something is going, you stay and you fight for your inclusion until you're happy. But at the same time, it should not have to be like that.

Fayemi believed that there was ample opportunity for more women to be involved in the Convention, because there was so much work to be done; however she rejected the idea that there should always be intentional gender parity on committees, something that the Convention made a deliberate effort to ensure. Indeed, she tended to reduce lack of women's presence to the individual decisions of particular women. "I think that a lot of women who could have had more influence didn't step up. But at the same time, I wasn't really around to see why those women made the decisions that they made."

Fayemi expressed a strong commitment to equal power sharing among men and women organizers. Yet she was skeptical that the deployment of power by women was necessarily respected. For example, Fayemi initially intended to be a local organizer for the New Jersey Local Organizing Committee based in Newark, but she was assigned more administrative and logistical tasks by another male organizer. Her intention to play a more central role in the local organizing for the event was thwarted by decisions made by a male organizer. While Fayemi did not speak out against her assignment, she did feel slighted, and somewhat marginalized as a decision-maker within the Convention.

Keisha Simpson remembered her first experience with Convention organizing as both intimidating and "unnecessarily contentious." Keisha, along with four or five women organizers whom she recruited to participate, attended a meeting scheduled during the evening on the campus of Rutgers University-Newark. Prepared to organize a hip hop Convention, Keisha was expecting an atmosphere that at least superficially mirrored the stereotypical aesthetics of hip hop fashion (i.e., jeans and t-shirts). Keisha was in for a surprise, however.

> All I remember seein' is these brothas rockin the suits, the satchels, the ties, the loafers. Rollin' in, like, "yeah, we here!" I remember saying to myself, I must not be at the right meeting. This is supposed to the National Hip Hop Political Convention and ain't nothing hip hop or political about these brothas right here!

Although Keisha and her female co-organizers arrived on time for this five-o'clock meeting, they ended up having to wait several minutes for the men who invited them to participate to show up. At Keisha's first meeting, the only people who spoke were the male organizers who initiated the meeting. African–American men were able to fully command the appearance of leadership in the public sphere, dwarfing the presence of the invited women activists in attendance. In short, these energetic young activists, office–seekers, and public intellectuals rarely hesitated to speak as representatives of the hip hop community, the Black community, and of urban youth, in general. Keisha explained,

> I just remember, all of them had suits, all of them were in the same age bracket, all of them had the same approach to things. It was just, the uniformity of the presentation was...really, only one of y'all had to speak, because you're all the same cat.

Keisha was initially taken aback at the homogenous physical appearance, and presentation styles of the local Convention leadership that, in her mind, also seemed to translate into a rather homogenous interpretation of what the central issues and/or strategies adopted by the local organizing committee would be. From her perspective, the women who were invited to participate were expected to more or less "fall in line" with the leadership and simply implement a predetermined plan of action. Moreover, the apparent professionalization of hip hop politics, as indicative of the "suits" that the men who occupied leadership wore, seemed to somehow intimidate the female student activists who were present, which may explain their initial silence at the first meeting.

Like Fayemi, Keisha deeply respected the efforts of male activists to organize a national hip hop politics movement and the concerted efforts to link the political edge of "conscious" hip hop artists to a larger movement. She was, however, dissatisfied by many organizers' refusal to be as self-critical about issues of misogyny in hip hop culture. She vividly explains,

> Y'all wanna do this national organizing thing. Cool. Y'all wanna talk about how the music has lost its political edge. Cool. But you define that loss of message based on the fact that they're not talking about socially conscious stuff, like defeating Bush, changing neighborhoods, but then they will stop there. They will end the critique right there. They won't talk about the misogyny. They won't talk about the sexism. They won't talk about how women are blatantly objectified. And when you call them on that, it's like it's not a big deal. "That's not really our issue. Yo, brothas are dying out there!"

The politics of scale produced a gendered division of labor that prevented Keisha from more wholeheartedly engaging in the local organizing for the Convention. From her perspective, most critical decisions were being made by men who organized at the national level, although they were implemented by women who organized at the local level. She also observed that Convention "leaders" who organized nationally, most of whom were male, assumed much of the credit for innovative organizing strategies that were being enacted in the local organizing committees.

> We got no love from national folks. No love. None! It was like, right there is when I got this bad taste in my mouth. You got all these brothas who sit around on national calls, doing all the national organizing, the national fundraising. And then you got all these sistas that are doing the local organizing, and trying to do the local fundraising.

Keisha produced one of the most successful performance-based workshops at the Convention, which combined the improvisation with the performative politics of the body: the "battleground" competition. The battleground competition was an open freestyle session in which break-dancers, emcees, and dee-jays competed for the attention, excitement, enthusiasm, and respect of audience members. When Keisha first mentioned the idea of sponsoring a battleground session, key organizers basically "brushed her off," tabling the idea in order to address more pressing, logistical issues. Only when a regionally

acclaimed promoter picked up on the marketing appeal of the battleground session and rearticulated the proposal at a later meeting,
did national organizers take the idea seriously and begin to support
Keisha's efforts to reach out to performance artists by allocating funds
to secure an appropriate venue for the event. In her own words: "We
just basically did the work for the battleground competition, but this
other dude who just came in got all the credit. It was like, we had
been saying the same thing all along, but nobody was really feelin' it;
nobody was really takin' it seriously."

Melanie Hendricks was one of the women who called the shots.
Melanie was a 27-year-old youth organizer for a Rutgers University
campus-based leadership program, Newark Student Voices. In April
of 2004, Melanie had also been recently elected as member of the
school board in the neighboring town of Hillside. Melanie did not
acknowledge feeling marginalized, tokenized, or otherwise excluded
because of her sex by the Convention, and she chalked up differences
that did emerge between men and women to differences in "personality." Melanie played a critical role in later meetings leading up
to the Convention. As the person in charge of securing classrooms
for panels and workshops, serving as a liaison between Rutgers
University, Essex County Community College, and the North Jersey
Convention leadership, Melanie routinely moderated meetings and
negotiated with warring factions within the Convention and college
administration. Melanie was also responsible for ensuring the successful registration and placement of the several hundred delegates
who would attend the Convention from the US states and around
the world.

> I came into it as the person to help out the University. So on a weekly
> basis I would help to convene meetings and make sure that all of the
> university folks, the police, the vice presidents, some of the folks from
> the Convention...that they were abreast of all the different intrica-
> cies of what was going on. I also participated in a lot of the different
> meetings, whether it had to do with the specific workshops, if it had
> to do with the performance, if it had to deal with the national vote.
> I basically would sit on each committee so I was a...I would say an
> ex-officio member of every committee except the national committee.

There was a rigid line of demarcation between local organizing work
and national decision-making power. For Keisha, this line was crossed
only by select women who contributed to substantive decision-making
at the national level. In her opinion, these women seemed to have
preexisting personal relationships with male organizers, leaving little
room for women workers who were disconnected from these personal

networks. Instead of being equal partners, local organizers were left to their own devices concerning what they could or should do to organize the Convention. Keisha noted:

> When we go to the brothas to get some help, there's not a partnership there. Its kinda like, "Look we got this thing, you got your thing. Now play your role." It's funny, the sistas had roles and the brothas didn't. There was one sista who was organizing the schedule and the agenda. There was another sista who was manning the office, and coordinating the volunteers. Another sista was doing media and outreach. I remember there were a lot of brothas there but I don't know what they did. They were there, they were contributing to the call, but in terms of what their exact role was, still to this day I have no idea.

Although Keisha, Fayemi, Melanie, and Veronica did not consider themselves "feminists," all except Veronica were sympathetic to "womanism" because they associated the term with Alice Walker and with Black women. The concept of feminism was more closely aligned in their minds with "white women" or "lesbians." During interviews most of these activists did not clearly differentiate between womanism and feminism except through these basic racial and sexual orientation stereotypes. Keisha was the only activist who explicitly mentioned the term "hip hop feminism" during an interview.

THE PROGRESSIVE WOMEN'S CAUCUS

I first learned about the Hip Hop convention from Malika Sanders, a long-time friend and mentor from the time I spent organizing with welfare moms in Selma, Alabama in the late 1990s. I was shocked to learn that she was in town, and even more shocked to learn that she was in town to help organize a national hip hop convention that my then partner had initiated the call for. At the time, I was working on my second graduate degree on the side while raising my two toddlers. In 2003, I was living as the wife of a prominent young African–American male attorney, who was widely respected as a community organizer. In the two and a half years that I lived in New Jersey, I was never invited to a single community meeting. I did not know anyone in Newark and he felt that it would be a "conflict in interest" if I were to try to be an organizer in community spaces that he had apparently staked out as his own. He wanted to "keep his personal life private," and that meant keeping me away from black community organizing in Newark. Furthermore, logistically, unless I was taking two toddlers with me alone, or paying for childcare that I could not afford, it would be too time consuming and expensive for me to attend meetings. As a result, I was more or less confined to my studies, cooking, cleaning, and raising my two daughters. It was not until after I organized the Progressive Women's Caucus that I came to be known as anything more than my then partner's, who I will call "X," "wife."

In any case, after learning about the plans for the convention, I drove Malika over to the day-long meeting, and with her encouragement, decided to stay. After all, I figured that if one of the national co-organizers from the South said it was okay for me to go then I could participate; then it must be okay. When I walked into the meeting, my hands trembled and my heart beat like a djembe. I was scared. It had been several years since I had been in the company of nationally renowned young black organizers. I was intimidated by all the egos in the room. When people introduced themselves, they did so by listing all of the organizations they belonged to. I immediately felt inadequate. I introduced myself as a graduate student at Rutgers and as a mother of two. Malika filled in some other details about my past almost as if to remind me of who I was. When we started doing work in the committees and it became apparent to others that I understood politics, black politics, and that I knew how to organize, and that I could deftly check the ideological bullshit that kept the conversations going in circles that people began to wonder who I was. They found out when X and I talked during the late lunch break. I was "X's wife." And X was one of the key organizers, X raised the money, X hosted the national meeting, and X seemed to call most of the shots, or at least tried to. To this day, I am certain that if I was not X's "wife" I would have been tossed out on my young, independent thinking, wannabe black feminist ass. But luckily I was, in people's eyes, "X's wife" and that made it much easier for the Progressive Women's Caucus of the Hip Hop Convention to happen.

Excited by the opportunity to use my dormant organizing skills, I decided I would work on gender issues since that was within my area of expertise, and no one else seemed interested in doing it. Since I had participated in the Black Radical Congress a few years earlier, and had the opportunity to see Barbara Smith, Barbara Ransby, Cathy Cohen, and a few other radical black lesbian feminists in action before I had read their works and knew that they were legends, I felt that it was important to help push forward a gender progressive agenda within the context of the Convention. I had a difficult time getting other NHHPC women organizers to work with me on the "Gender

Caucus," so I called upon other young black women organizers who you will learn about later in this section. With their moral support, commitment, follow-through, and outstanding organizing skills, we issued a call to young women of the hip hop generation to organize around gender justice. Though we worked separately from other female organizers in the convention who I later interviewed for this, *together* we mobilized hundreds of young women of color who loved hip hop and who were also in love with black freedom struggle so that they could have a central role to play in the first ever NHHPC.

In contrast to the women involved in the Convention Organizing Committees at the national and Newark levels, most participants in the Progressive Women's Caucus proudly identified as "feminist" or "Black feminist," and explicitly adopted an intersectional analysis of social oppression as a defining feature of our politics. At the time, most of us was skeptical of if not downright baffled by the term "hip hop feminism." Of course, the politicized aspect of our feminism was received with varying levels of support, indifference, and sometimes open hostility by other women organizers in the Convention who were staying home with single-axis black politics. While the female local organizers were busy ensuring the successful coordination and execution of the Convention workshops, events, venue requisition, and mobilization, members of the Progressive Women's Caucus (PWC) were involved for the sole purpose of politicizing gender-based issues that affected women of color in the context of the Convention.

The PWC functioned as an outspoken, highly organized counter-culture within the hip hop political movement. While PWC organizers were granted space to participate, some people simply did not like much of what we had to say. In 2003, PWC argued that gender was an important issue that should be addressed on its own terms. Other women in leadership positions argued that gender was a "white" thing and issues of concern to women should be incorporated into the larger slate of major issues on the national agenda. This initially seemed reasonable. Closer scrutiny, however, indicated no evidence that these "major issues" were being understood in terms of sexual, raced, and gendered specificity. Most organizers could agree that women hip hop artists should be involved in the Convention and that there should be a panel on women and media—as long as it pointed out the obvious (i.e., "hip hop is misogynist, but we can't forget the positive elements of hip hop which get little attention because of the greed of the entertainment industry"). This construction of gender and hip hop became hegemonic because, in PWC's perspective, it alleviated the responsibility of both black men and women for their own complicity in reproducing certain destructive characteristics pervasive in hip hop and in African–American culture, which had yet to receive serious attention in the black public sphere.

During our monthly meetings local PWC members shared numerous personal encounters with heartbreak, infidelity, sexual molestation, and exploitation as young girls. Drawing on our personal experiences for guidance, we agreed on the importance of politicizing the ease with which some black men patronized, deceived, emotionally abused, and neglected the emotional needs of black women and girls with whom they had sexual relations. One PWC activist who had recently ended a 20-year marriage because of the long-term infidelity of her spouse with a younger woman insisted: "There's no one to hold black men accountable for the things they do to Black women. He brought that woman around our family and friends and no one said anything—no one." PWC organizers were aware that "calling it as we see it" could come at extreme costs, including the risk of reproducing prevailing stereotypes that marked black men as dangerous, irresponsible, and prone to criminality. Nonetheless, we decided that these issues had to be seriously addressed. After nearly a year of meetings, PWC concluded that these issues needed to be addressed because black boys and black men suffered just as much if not more from some of the practices under discussion.

In 2004, the PWC strategically appropriated the core set of themes, which had come to prominence through the efforts of journalists, essayists, biographers, cultural critics, and performance artists, and used them to develop an organizing methodology that could explicitly politicize sexual violence against young women and girls in communities of color. The convention was used as a unique opportunity to generate awareness about how sexual, economic, and gender-based violence within these communities are both evidence of and exacerbated by the troubled gender ideologies spread through so much of what is called "hip hop" on the public airways. A major dilemma that PWC faced in disseminating our message stemmed from the fact that many young activists and organizers continued to cling to myths about feminism, particularly black feminisms in communities of color. Many young activists, men and women alike, still interpreted feminism as a "white woman's thing," and altogether foreign to communities of color. We reconceptualised gender-based disparities within the black communities to emphasize the positionality of poor women of color—especially how economic violence was exacerbated through state sanctioned efforts to police, regulate, and discipline Black and brown women's bodies. For example, the PWC initially discussed the importance of black women's political leadership around issues of reproductive rights, child-care, and domestic, sexual, and gender-based violence, after months of organizing, the PWC platform was reframed in terms of "gender justice" rather than "gender rights," using language that emphasized women of color's positionality vis a vis the state.

A pervasive conservatism concerning gender politics persisted among hip hop activists, and the women organizers were no exception. To confront the more subtle aspects of what we considered "regressive" gender politics that were reflected in the attitudes of some key national organizers, the PWC aggressively promoted a slate of issues under the framework of "gender justice" for inclusion in the national political agenda. The PWC also designed and organized a slate of panels that were explicitly antiracist, antisexist, and antihomophobic. These panels succeeded in reaching out to the hip hop community and in recruiting to US women of color organizations. PWC also distributed a questionnaire that challenged the respondents to identify the three most important issues facing women of the hip hop generation. Of 500 survey cards distributed, 232 were completed and returned. The cards asked respondents to "circle the three most important issues facing women of the hip hop generation." The top three issues identified were poor self-esteem, degrading images of women in hip hop, and the HIV/AIDS epidemic.

The PWC understood that the incisiveness of our language could, and most likely would, intimidate other women who did not hold what we deemed "progressive" views regarding the issue of gender. Even so, members were ill-prepared for the animosity that was directed toward those who openly claimed to be "feminist." When PWC members solicited the support of women leadership in the Convention, we were given a cold shoulder. It was rumored that although "they agreed with what the PWC was saying, it doesn't really come from the community." When PWC organizers forced the issue, we were told by the female NHHPC Co-Chair that "*Black men are the real endangered species!*"[18] Gender was somehow disengaged from other chronic social issues—"it wasn't really a 'hip hop' issue."[19] In the minds of some Convention organizers, the way black sexual politics unraveled in the context of urban crisis was secondary to the other "more important" issues facing black families in urban areas.

After the 2004 Convention, while there were very few who would dare to publicly challenge the PWC, the Convention still found ways to "table" proposals to institutionalize the PWC as part of the official body of the Convention. Although the PWC was later invoked by male organizers in public speaking engagements to boost the legitimacy of subsequent hip hop political mobilizations, PWC was never able to become a substantive decision-making body within the Convention. Keisha, Fayemi, Melanie, and Veronica and other core Newark organizers for the Convention developed enduring, working relationships with local members of the PWC, but their "political" work remained exclusively focused on "Black youth" (i.e., education, poverty, racist law enforcement practices). Although Newark activists are now more receptive to feminism and have learned not to immediately associate contemporary feminism with white women—gender as an important organizing issue remained elusive in Newark until 2007. After national radio host Don Imus attacked the Rutgers Women's basketball team, "Gender Justice" was overwhelmingly adopted as part of the agenda leading up to the NHHPC in 2008. The PWC achieved national recognition and respect for woman of color organizing in the context of the Convention, but we lacked legitimacy at the local level because few women of color had the resources, wherewithal, and political support to take up issues like reproductive justice, economic violence, and sexual violence in cities like Newark. Given such mixed results, a few members of the PWC begrudgingly agreed to continue work with NHHPC to ensure that women of color organizations that do work at the local level have some, albeit limited, access to the public stage of black politics. On the other hand, PWC managed to elicit considerable support to bring their politics to national organizing bodies, especially within organizations and associations that are interested in "gender" as a political issue.

Gender, Power, and Social Capital in the National Hip Hop Political Convention

The NHHPC was successfully used as political space by feminist and non-feminist black women activists. Not only was hip hop understood as a space that could challenge black youth marginality, and the myriad of issues that are associated with urban youth (gangs, street violence, poor education, economic disadvantage and criminalization) in ways that systematically linked art and culture with a larger movement for social justice, but it was also successfully utilized as a space through which political Black women could come to voice. Without doubt, one of the major benefits that black feminist activists enjoyed through our participation was the opportunity to use our own stores of social capital in service to a larger, predominantly African America social movement, especially the identification and cultivation of leadership among minority youth in urban communities around the nation.

While it is clear that black feminists were able to seize hip hop as a viable space for black women to enact their "politics," it is not clear that hegemonic black gender ideology within the black public sphere could be transgressed through black women's "politics," feminist or not. The ability to translate our social capital into decision-making *power* was stymied at various points and the directional flow of black women's social capital was carefully maneuvered to benefit predominantly black male political elites in the sphere of black politics, or to individually benefit select young black women activists (both feminist and non-feminist). The opportunity structures in place for young black women activists to gain access to the public stage of black politics was jointly patrolled both by nationalist, and liberal bourgeois ideologies firmly rooted in heteropatriarchal (and heteronormative) social values. While activists from the PWC managed to create an atmosphere in which the explicit intersectional political engagement with issues like rape, domestic violence, and the sexual exploitation of girls of color could be systematically addressed, we were not able to demarginalize these "gender" items, and have them addressed on their own terms. After intensive debates, the Convention adopted only two lines that had originated in the PWC agenda. These were 1) "we call for federal legislation to ensure women's reproductive health, including safe and legal access to reproductive choices, and education and awareness about reproductive issues" and 2) "we oppose all forms of economic violence," which was included as an economic justice agenda item. In the end, despite efforts by the PWC, NHHPC produced an agenda that recapitulated the political demands of the peculiarly nationalistic, racially liberal, heteropatriarchal, and ultimately *moderate* black left.

Although the talents of black women community activists and organizers were actively recruited for the larger political purposes of black solidarity and the appearance of a gender-inclusive "hip hop political agenda," support for black women's autonomous "political work" at the local level was not tolerated unless it reproduced hegemonic black cultural production, as defined and institutionalized by local black male political elites. Ideological processes embedded in patriarchal nationalism regulate interpretations of black cultural production within liberal and nationalist frames in ways that patrol black women's access to the black public sphere. Regardless of the extensiveness of transformative vision and effort, black women political activists' political work did not receive recognition, resources, and political support unless it enhanced a particular interpretation of black cultural production. Explicitly feminist antiracist, antisexist and antihomophobic politics at the local level and at the national level are particularly vulnerable to erasure. The concrete policies, platforms, and political agendas that dominate the black public sphere continue to marginalize the political interests of radical black women, while rendering their political work invisible. The issue for feminist scholarship then is not the dearth of black women's political activism, but its suppression.

In *Stand and Deliver: Political Leadership, Activism, and Hip Hop Culture*, Yvonne Bynoe attributes the lack of a contemporary, national social justice movement for black liberation and political empowerment to the apathy, individualism, and disorganization of the hip hop generation. Her complaint is quite compelling, but for reasons that she only sparsely addresses:

> A few men have claimed the leadership mantle based on their media presence and rhetorical skills. These men, unable or unwilling to examine the current state of affairs are content to use a worn-out blue print as the means of obtaining a national platform for their own advancement. Neither Black people generally, nor the mainstream media that continually spotlights these so-called leaders seem concerned that these individuals, unlike their predecessors, lack a constituency, an organization or even a plan. (2004, 27)

However, what appears to be the absence of a plan might indeed be the perpetuation of a gendered status quo. My examination of the politics of NHHPC suggests that even when "leaders" get organized, mobilize their considerable local constituencies, and develop a plan, the larger community may prefer to reject their singular, masculinist vision of progress. "Inaction" in this instance may signify dissent from the vision on offer. The contemporary national Black "social justice movement" may fail to be attractive to a new generation of activists because it simply reinforces values that are sexist, homophobic, and contrary to the needs of poor people of color who are interested in imagining and achieving an alternative conception of politics. Appeals to liberal, democratic procedures and appeals to clarity, rationality, and compromise may strengthen rather than dismantle longstanding systems of domination, especially if leaders use their power to keep certain issues off the political agenda.

Kimberly Springer (2002) has pointed out that the "wave analogy" is untenable for those who wish to understand black feminist activism. Extrapolated from the experience of an affluent cohort of white women, the notion of feminist "waves" perpetuates the exclusion of women of color from the histories of women's movements and from feminist theorizing. This research both supports and extends

Springer's insight. Many black women come to the public sphere through gendered political scripts rooted in historical struggles against gendered black racialization. Whether politicized within the Civil Rights Movement or the Black Power Movement, many black women developed political consciousness in the context of resolutely patriarchal black politics. Although these political movements made important strides against white supremacy, they failed to deliver crippling blows to the detrimental forces behind contemporary black marginality: racialized, urban poverty and gender, class, and sexual struggles *internal* to the black community.

Black women's political agency, as understood and defined by women activists within poor urban communities, is eclipsed by more than the wave metaphor, however. While the politics of white middle-class feminists have often elided the issues and struggles of women of color, so too have black heteropatriarchal politics exercised by *both* black men and women, whether in nationalist or liberal guises. Black women political activists in American cities struggle against processes both within and outside of communities that are quick to render us invisible or as mere tokens. Whether deemed invisible or apolitical, black women's autonomous political work has been largely discounted. By illuminating the context and content of black women's political activism in Newark, the research in this chapter addressed this historic oversight.

8

THE AUDACITY TO RESIST: BLACK
WOMEN, SOCIAL CAPITAL, AND
BLACK CULTURAL PRODUCTION

The 2008 Presidential election was a historic year. The Democratic Party had nominated the first African–American candidate, Barack Obama, for the coveted office of President. 2008 was also the first time that a black woman of Puerto Rican descent, Rosa Clemente, ran for the office of Vice-President alongside Cynthia McKinney, the Green Party Presidential Candidate. McKinney, who had served five terms as a US Congresswoman, serving Georgia's first district, was a long time challenger of US imperialism and war mongering in the Middle East and a champion of Palestinian statehood and the end of the Israeli occupation of the West Bank. Instead of focusing on the historic nature of the McKinney-Clemente candidacy for both women and people of color in America, millions of words and hundreds of thousands of hours were spent debating the predictable political faux pas of then Senator Hillary Clinton and the former Alaskan Governor Sarah Palin.

Instead of covering the ins and out of these two dynamic black women travelling the country to rally support for an alternative vision of American democracy, the media took Hillary to task for her "Southern Strategy." Senator Clinton's ill-fated attempt to mobilize racial resentment among poor whites in the South against then Senator Obama's presidential campaign was more important. Instead of analyzing Rosa Clemente's remarkably lucid analysis of the connection between increasing rates of poverty and homelessness in black communities and the Bush Administration's zealous pursuance of an illegal war in Iraq and the continuation of a 30-year War on Drugs in black and brown inner city neighborhoods, the media instead featured story after story about the white middle-class "hockey-mom" who boldly claimed the moniker of being a "pit-bull with lipstick". Millions of hours were spent commentating on Ms. Palin's seeming ignorance of foreign affairs, whether or not her then sixteen year old daughter had an unplanned pregnancy, and the Republican candidate's somewhat questionable daily reading practices. Very little if any airtime was designed to recognizing, discussing or even mentioning the politics of radical women of color, *black* women, trying to be heard on the national stage. Within the black public sphere, the debate centered on whether African–American voters would be loyal to Hillary Clinton or take a risk on newcomer Obama who, for many black opinion leaders, had not yet proven that he was "black enough" to get their vote (Harris 2011, Moffit and Squires 2010). When black women were mentioned, the debate settled on whether "race" would trump "gender" in their vote choice. The impoverished quality of these debates rested upon ignoring or, rather, *denying* the existence of two extraordinary political women who have consistently spoke out against the combined effects of race, gender, class, and national oppression in US politics. McKinney and Clemente have implemented resistance politics using a black feminist intersectional praxis throughout their political lives. Their political work culminated into a historic presidential campaign that was entirely ignored by mainstream media, hegemonic *liberal* white feminists *and* black political elites who functioned as mouthpieces for the so-called "black community."

Here, I think it is important to say something about the political lives of McKinney and Clemente. I will start with Clemente, because she is my peer and represents the "hip hop generation." Clemente, born and raised in the South Bronx, has long struggled for black and Puerto Rican political autonomy and self-determination. In the 1990's Clemente organized and participated in demonstrations to "Free Vieques," a territory in Puerto Rico that the US navy used to test nuclear weapons and perform military maneuvers at expense of environment and the physical health of the island's inhabitants. Rosa, a long time member of the Malcolm X Grassroots Movement, a translocal black organization that has consistently organized successful campaigns against human rights abuses perpetrated upon the African–American community in the form of police brutality/police murders of black men, was also one of the founding members of the National Hip Hop Political Convention movement of the early 2000's discussed in the previous chapter. Rosa, who identifies as both "black" and "Puerto Rican" and "hip hop" has spent the last twenty years of her life speaking out against anti-black and anti-Latino racism, misogyny, and the incarceration and exile of black political prisoners including Sundiata Acoli and Assata Shakur. In fact, she was one of the first activists who took publically took hip hop mogul and black political pundit Russell Simmons to task. She called him out for assuming the role as the spokesman of the hip hop generation, while promoting clothing labels that sold jeans and athletic wear made in sweatshops in Southeast Asia, circulating and distributing misogynist images of black women globally, and, failing to understand, acknowledge, and put into action the radical vision of hip hop activists in American cities who had long organized railed against US militarism, capitalism, and the music industry's rabid exploitation of black and Latino artists.[1]

Cynthia McKinney, on the other hand, has consistently spoken against, and introduced legislation in the Congress protesting the US occupations of Iraq and Afghanistan, and the Israeli occupation of Palestine. As a Congresswoman, McKinney also introduced articles of impeachment against former President George W. Bush for withholding intelligence that contradicted his administration's claim that Iraq possessed weapons of mass destruction. McKinney had long organized against the legality and constitutionality of the Rockefeller drug laws which mandated different sentencing requirements for the possession of powder cocaine and crack cocaine—which is now known to have had the result of criminalizing drug addiction in urban, and predominantly poor black and brown communities. While the progressive legislative stances that McKinney took were widely appreciated in urban communities across the United States, she rarely ever succeeded in garnering solid support from her peers in the Congressional Black Caucus, which has been dominated by black male politicians with more moderate political leanings. McKinney's militancy, both as a human rights and antiwar activist, has been occluded by discourses concerning her hairstyle, her attire, and other aspects of her personality that have nothing to do with her audacious and principled political stances and grassroots and translocal organizing campaigns on the most importance issues of at least two generations.

In the past decade several eminent scholars have advanced dire assessments of the contemporary state of African–American women's political activism. Patricia Hill Collins (2006), for example, examined scholarly anthologies to gauge the contemporary state of black feminisms. Conflating academic and journalistic analyses with activism, she questions whether works devoted to discursive analysis of popular culture are sufficient to challenge the dismal social conditions that face a new generation of African–Americans in the aftermath of U.S. twentieth-century social movements. When she turns directly to local activism, she poses the following questions to her readers: "In essence one might ask whether black women of the hip hop generation are beginning to make these important connections between the power of mass media and grassroots political organization, even though the connection might not be immediately apparent. Conversely, a similar question concerns how black women working within grassroots organizations are to be the beachhead of black women in popular culture" (2006, 1994). Despite the importance of such questions, in *Black Sexual Politics* Collins does little to engage the voices of non-normative black women involved in black community politics about what they think. Although she briefly discusses the murder of Sakia Gunn, she does not investigate the processes through which Sakia Gunn's life and death were politicized and made visible to larger, albeit restricted publics. Her analysis paid scant attention to the intersectional politics of identity that produced the narrative of Sakia Gunn, nor to the institutional political forces that failed to act on behalf of Newark's black LGBT youth. The black women activists who mobilized after Sakia's death remained shrouded in a cloak of anonymity. By mistaking journalists and social critics for social activists, Collins helped to render invisible the full scope of black women's political activism in Newark.

In *Further to Fly: Black Women and the Politics of Empowerment* (2000), Sheila Radford-Hill seeks to revitalize black women's political activism, calling for new alternatives to the "destructive" impact of Afrocentric nationalisms and contemporary academic feminism. Her argument for revitalization rests on the premise that there has been a significant decline in black women's community activism: "The decline of black women's empowerment is characterized by a diminution of black women's grassroots activism. Black women's abdication of community building and political action repudiates standards of black womanhood that previous generations were socialized to uphold" (2007, 23). Radford-Hill's claim that black women have retreated from the politics of "racial uplift" is curiously nostalgic. She interprets contemporary black women's political agency solely in terms of the familiar modes of social movement politics that guided the civil rights and black power movements. She defines African–American politics as highly visible, as national *demonstrations*, and does not consider that black women's political agency has emerged in alternative spaces that do not depend upon identity in the same way that earlier black women, including black feminists, imagined. Wedded to the limited notion of mass demonstration, Radford-Hill fails to recognize that the most radical manifestations of black women's political agency may lie in the direct connections and resource flows among and between non-normative identity networks, as well within and between cities, rather than through tightly bounded social ties in national membership organizations.

Many scholars have situated black women's activism within the larger civil rights movements for racial and sexual equality, especially struggles for equal access to the ballot box (Orleck 2005, Williams 2004, Hanson 2003, Collier-Thomas 2001, Springer 1999, Terbog-Penn 1999, White 1999, Terbog-Penn 1998, Robnett 1997, Guy-Sheftall 1990, Gilkes 1988, Giddings 1984). Within these works, black women's activism is tied to participation in social movements aimed at ensuring full citizenship for African–Americans, augmented by middle-class black women's associationalism aimed at racial uplift in the black community. From a strategic vantage point, these "racial uplift" programs relied upon imparting middle class values of education, poverty relief, and the cultivation of black middle-class, professional social networks that increased employment opportunities among African–Americans (Terbog-Penn 1999, White 1999). Black women's creation of and participation in these "racial uplift" programs are so central to historical accounts of black women's community activism that they have come to define it. But this conception of activism has a particular ideological cast. It is 1) largely integrationist, 2) shaped by class, yet overdetermined by racial inequality and race-loyalty, and 3) firmly situated within a liberal conception of individual self-help and community empowerment through civic voluntarism and social activism (Kukla 2005, White 1999, Terbog-Penn 1998, Giddings 1984). As this project has shown black women political activism is diverse, deeply influenced by the politics of their respective generations, and, most importantly, multivalent.

While there is little question that black women's political agency played a crucial role in organizing the highly visible demonstrations of the late nineteenth and twentieth-century civil rights politics, black women were required to play these roles behind the scenes. Thus many popular constructions of black women's political activism reinforce conventional scripts of political power, reaffirming a hegemonic black gender ideology: women work behind the scenes and black men receive credit in front of the camera. This image of "Black Politics" incorporates a highly problematic sexual politics. Failing to take gender power seriously, it overlooks the fact that the black public sphere is carefully patrolled. As political subjects, many black political women have been assigned scripts written by black male political elites.

The claim that black women have remained "silent" or have voluntarily stayed on the sidelines of black community politics, is plausible only if one accepts a masculinist conception of politics predisposed toward a certain, albeit unstated, scalar construction of politics. This conception accepts a rigid demarcation between local and national efforts that neglect translocal politics—especially oppositional politics that relies upon frequent movement within and between scalar structures and ideological stances for success (Sandoval 2000). The intensive focus of scholars and the media on a male-dominated national agenda masks black women's political work at the local level unless that work recapitulates a familiar meta-narrative of black political resistance. Such a perspective masks the intricacies of black politics at the local level. More importantly, it also masks the actual production of translocal politics that makes the illusion of a cohesive national "black politics" possible.

Some recent studies of black women's activism emphasize black women's engagement with the state, including local welfare agencies and public housing authorities. Black women have manifested their agency through the creation of formal and informal organizations that challenge state-sanctioned racial hostility toward black families headed by single, welfare-reliant mothers. This work has contested racist attitudes that have shaped official public policy and racist practices in the implementation of those policies (Orleck 2005, Williams 2004). These studies extend earlier analyses of black women's community activism, showing how ideologies of class, race, and sexuality converge in a sociopolitical environment produced by intensive policing of black women's families, personal lives, and reproductive capacities (Orleck 2005, Williams 2004, Roberts 1997). While these studies document black women's resistance to these strategies, attending to efforts to organize and mobilize within particular communities, they retain a state-centered focus that prevents us from truly understanding how black cultural production simultaneously enables and delimits black people's political agency.

In contrast to these social movement and state-centric approaches, this research suggests that black women's political activism can be found in quite different venues. Guided by conceptions of politics articulated by black women activists themselves, I have investigated translocal social networks through which black political women in Newark express their collective needs and mobilize political action to achieve tangible local program goals. The network of associations (formal and informal) that black women activists in the Central Ward of Newark have created and sustain demonstrates the permeability of the local and national networks. Local stores of social capital here translated into national visibility for specific "Black Political Issues" or "Black" or "hip hop political agendas," but this social capital also created space for the development of the leadership potential of black youth. By focusing on concrete efforts of local women activists to address pressing local concerns, my research rescues women's agency from stereotypical ideas that women's roles are necessarily scripted by black political elites. It also discloses how a narrow focus on state-centric politics serves privileged masculinist ends, excluding dimensions of political life from poor and/or working class, urban black women.

This voice-centered investigation into black women's political agency has revealed a body of political agendas that surpass the issues preferred by the black church and black elected officials. Indeed, I have shown how black women have contested the self-serving politics of local political elites and documented how they have attempted to inject issues pertaining to race, gender, and sexuality into local and national debates. These local networks have often refused to abide by the scripts accredited by the institutions of church and state. Black women have engaged myriad issues despite the fact that their oppositional politics tends to be ignored by elites, media, and academics. Indeed, my research suggests that their diverse modes of resistance politics tend to be erased from the public record unless they support hegemonic elements of black cultural production. By tracing how long traditions of black nationalism and black patriarchy continue to play out in Newark, I have identified constraints upon black women's political activism seldom acknowledged by social scientists.

PERSISTENT CONSTRAINT? MASCULINIST POLITICAL IDEOLOGY AND BLACK HETEROPATRIARCHY

Many studies have demonstrated that local black elites exercise power through established institutions such as local government, public bureaucracies, cultural and religious institutions, and community organizations. But few scholars have explored the liberal, heterosexist, and masculinist biases within these institutions. Nor do many examine the complex interrelationships between black nationalism and black patriarchy within mainstream organizations. Studies documenting black women's participation in the Black Power Movement, and other nationalist or cultural nationalist spaces, have discussed black women's agency, typically in terms of their demonstrated loyalty to the ideological missions of these nationalist organizations. As we have seen, African–American women continue to play extremely important roles in creating and maintaining educational and cultural programming for black youth, and have provided administrative and moral support and leadership through black and cultural nationalist organizations (Collier-Thomas & Franklin 2001, Kuumba 1999, Woodward 1999, Brown 1992, Wallace 1984). In these accounts, black women strongly support nationalist organizational missions designed to resist racism and racial inequality through collective black self-determination and militancy. While many women within such organizations have explicitly challenged sexist exclusionary attitudes and practices by black males, they also actively created autonomous spaces in which to cultivate their decision-making and creative capacities, especially through their community programming efforts. Organizations like the Black Women's United Front and the National Congress of Black Women emerged in the 1970s and 1980s, as well as Women in Support of the Million Man March are good examples. New historical research has also revealed the important role of black women in the Communist Party and other socialist organizations that challenged the triple jeopardy of class, race, and gender oppression (McDuffie 2011, Gore et al. 2009, Boyce Davies 2007, Springer 2005). These organizations continue to attract hundreds of progressive black activists who operate under the radar, who continue to engage in notably sustained levels of local, translocal, national, and transnational activisms.

These new women's political formations were initially positioned more or less amicably in relation to larger nationalist and Pan-Africanist organizations. Within these spaces black women were lauded primarily as formidable "cultural workers." Their labor was viewed as essential to building a strong black nation or community, particularly in urban areas like Newark. Yet these women's auxiliaries were specifically designed to cultivate women's leadership in their respective communities, and to foster the development of a womanist consciousness, which M. Bahati Kuumba (1999) argues forged a simultaneous analyses of nation/class/gender oppression. Within these spaces the seeds of womanism or, indeed, a specialized black feminist critical consciousness could emerge.

My research suggests that particular forms of black cultural production associated with black nationalism continue to be characterized by a gendered division of labor, which continues to operate in venues at some remove from cultural nationalism. Indeed, the testimonies of my respondents and my case studies suggest that patriarchal nationalism circulates throughout mainstream and progressive sectors in Newark, creating significant obstacles to the achievement of women activists' political objectives. Black women were and, sometimes are still expected to work behind the scenes in nationalist organizations. This legacy infiltrates and structures mainstream, electoral politics in Newark, as well as innovative initiatives like the National Hip Hop Political Convention.

Another case that illustrates this is the Women in Support of the Million Man March (WISOMMM). This example portrays the politics of this gendered division of labor and explains how black nationalism spills over into electoral politics. In 2005, WISOMMM received a $5.5 million subsidized loan from the City of Newark and Independence Bank to purchase the 65,000 square foot, First Presbyterian Church of Newark for use as a cultural center. Frederica Bey, a devout Muslim and Executive Director of WISOMMM, was an avid political supporter of Sharpe James, Ras Baraka, Ron Rice, Ron Rice Jr., Donald Payne, Donald Payne Jr., and other black male political elites in the city of Newark. Her close ties with Louis Farrakhan and the Nation of Islam, further cemented her formidable political and cultural clout within Newark's black community. She had demonstrated an ability to raise money, mobilize voters, and build viable institutions purchased and controlled by black people, yet she supported a decidedly masculinist conception of black cultural and political production, a conception that continues to flourish in the city of Newark to this day.

Frederica had long supported then Mayor Sharpe James' controversial redevelopment programs, which led to the decimation of public housing, even as the remaining units were overrun with crime, mismanagement, and gang violence. As a core organizer for WISOMMM, in 1995 Frederica supported the idea that African–American women refrain from attending the Million Man March so that issues that directly affected African–American men could be publicly addressed: "I got a lot of flack from women who were mad because I supported the march. But I thought they (the men) did it right. I thought that women should go some place and find their own way."

Frederica's path to politics was one that was closely tied to the urban-based social justice programs heavily influenced by revolutionary and black nationalist activisms in the 1960s and 1970s, especially the Newark-based chapter of the People's Organization for Progress (POP).[2] The POP mobilized primarily around the issue of police brutality, reparations for people of African descent, and various forms of "anti-violence work," including the routine organization of anti-war protests, gang truces, and vigils, marches, and other local direct actions aimed to both politicize and curb street, gang, and police violence in Newark.[3] Frederica viewed her own role as a woman leader as instrumental to POP's local mobilization efforts in Newark. As a result of her participation with the POP and the Nation of Islam, she was asked to form WISOMMM to raise money and coordinate the mobilization of over 50,000 black men in the Northeastern seaboard. As she recounted: "Well, Larry Hamm asked if we would be the support arm of WISOMMM in 1995, because they needed somebody to help them raise money. They always came to the women, so they asked me whether I would chair. Of course, I loved the idea and did it." Under Frederica's guidance, after the March, WISOMMM incorporated and began to develop autonomous community-based programming, including sponsoring after-school care, African dance classes, Kwanzaa and black history month programs, community health screenings, annual trips to Africa, and quarterly forums with guest lecturers who spoke on a variety of social, cultural, and political issues deemed relevant to the black community.

Frederica's political work focused on the creation of institutions to foster self-esteem and promote self-determination and self-reliance of black people, especially black youth. She was particularly concerned about the need to pass on a political, economic, and cultural "inheritance" to the emerging generation of black political leadership and saw institutionalization as key to this transmission of values.

> With us being able to purchase property so we can have the programs that we want to have in these buildings. I think that it's been pretty effective. I mean, teaching the three and four year olds like going right to the cradle, and teaching the babies, and giving them a strong sense of self. And that's what you see, when you see our children when they get up and perform. They have a very strong sense of self, because they are taught by teachers who love them. And so, that's been great. We've been able to bring street organizations and gang members in and talk them as mothers and grandmothers. We have dinners and we bring them and have Ras, DeLacey, Baye, and the other young brothers you know, talk with them.

> It's important to have a piece of land and have your property that you don't have nobody ringing bells, telling you when you got to leave (sic) or what you got to do or telling you can't have the kind of program here. That's very key. I think that's been the best when working with this organization that they are not afraid to venture out and to reach.

Frederica did not make appeals to white folks for "cultural citizenship." Rather, she used the resources she had available to her to *practice self-determination* and to *practice freedom*. She appropriated spaces in the cities to build institutions in which to practice resistance. Homemaking was a part of this political work. Beginning with the Million Man March in 1995 and continuing well into the twenty-first century with the founding of the first African–American Cultural Center in the state of New Jersey, WISOMMM under the direction of Frederica Bey, expertly cultivates social capital, enabling the flow of communication, resources, and trust within and between scalar structures. Frederica construed this powerful political work in gendered terms, indeed in terms of the ideology of motherhood. Within this mothering frame, social capital is fostered through mechanisms like talking and having dinner, nurtured by the "love" of "mothers and grandmothers."

Frederica's relationship with Sharpe James and other black male political elites in the city did not go unnoticed or uncriticized, especially in light of the numerous accusations and investigations of corruption within the James Administration. Today, Frederica is dealing with an investigation fueled by intense local partisanship. Yet Frederica understood her role in relation to the city's notorious autocrat in a rather peculiar manner:

> I know everybody calls me a Sharpe James operative. You know, they said that in the paper last week and everybody was so upset. I wasn't really upset. I know they meant it in a very derogatory way. What I do know is that he's done a lot for this town. Could he have done more? Sure, he could have. But he's done a lot. You can't say the man ain't did nothing. Nobody can't say that, Cory [Booker] can't say that.

In Frederica's view, supporting and encouraging black political leadership that contributed to the development of independent black economic, cultural, and political institutions that could impart "strong African values" in black youth was tantamount. Black women were idealized as mothers, supporters, nurturers, and as vehicles of sacrifice for the larger black community. When I asked whether or not she had ever felt marginalized at all when going about her political work, Frederica responded, "Never. I have always been thrust into leadership positions." Although Frederica understood patriarchal nationalism to be empowering, other black women who were less willing to endorse male priorities chafed against these unrelenting constraints.

In September of 2005, Frederica called a huge meeting of activists in the city of Newark to organize a Newark-based relief effort for survivors of Hurricane Katrina. We met in the main hall of the African–American Cultural Center. About a hundred African–Americans sat in pews, men, women, and gender non-conforming folks gathered to hear about the scope of the crisis from the perspective of survivors who made to Newark and that of other black community based organizations who were connected to the relief efforts. By the end of the meeting at least a hundred organizations had donated several thousands of dollars, equipment, clothes, appliances, toiletries, and countless other items. Frederica herself had helped to host a family of fourteen who had lost their homes and livelihoods. Somehow she got the Robert Treat Hotel to sponsor these displaced families. The people in emergency meetings were diverse, in terms of age, class, and gender presentation—black queer folks were present and participating and shaping the discussion. However, there was no "identity" politics, ideological posturing, or political policing in this space. Black folks were there to help black folks. And they did.

Over the next few months, several black organizations in Newark and the larger New York metropolitan area coordinated relief. The focus of most organizations over the next few months was providing food, clothing, toiletries, and supplies to Katrina victims. Most of the relief efforts I was involved in did not happen within the stereotypic black public sphere—meaning churches and black Greek organizations—rather the relief efforts I was exposed to happened in radical black counterpublics that easily connected the abandonment of the hurricane survivors by the Bush Administration to a long and deep history of intentional racial subjugation of black people. This was to be expected. What was remarkable about the work that was done across organizational and ideological perspectives was that activists like Frederica turned the crisis into an opportunity to lead—leveraging her relationships, resources, and leadership skills to enable for black people to help themselves. And across the country, from places like Saint Louis, Chicago, Detroit, Atlanta, Selma, and Jackson (Mississippi) there were activists—many of whom were nationalists who had come up through black nationalism into positions that could ensure that the resources could get where they needed to be. Women like Frederica Bey activated a social geography of resistance. They turned a horror story into a living history lesson about how to lead effectively, how to work across differences for the cause of racial justice for black people in the United States. This was very different from the victim narrative that emerged in the mainstream media's coverage of the "black public sphere" at that point in time—which consisted of sermons by the usual suspects of black punditry, images of black people in misery, young black people looting and being hunted by the police, and the rest pleading for recognition by a guilty, sickly fascinated white viewing audience.

BLACK CULTURAL PRODUCTION AND SOCIAL TRANSFORMATION

The form and content of black women's political networks in Newark reveal how identity and agency intersect to create the possibilities for social transformation and for the perpetuation of the status quo. In the case studies investigated in this research, black women create and appropriate political space with markedly different outcomes depending on whether they support or contest male initiatives. In many respects, women's ability to use social capital operates within fairly narrow parameters and is tied to black cultural production. When black women's political agency contributes to black cultural production endorsed by patriarchal nationalism, they receive political support and their projects flourish, especially at the local level. Conversely, when black women challenge hegemonic elements of black cultural production—particularly when they challenge masculinist conceptions that conflate blackness and community—their social capital tends to be stifled, thwarting efforts at social transformation at the local level.

In this book, I have investigated black women's politics, as understood, enacted, and defined in practice in the *habitus* of Newark. The cityscapes of Newark, a visual economy of urban blight, urban revitalization, and cultural production of blackness, structure the political terrain of the Central Ward, shaping women's perceptions of political need and political action. Local black women's politics entails the creation and transformation of political spaces to develop the political leadership of marginalized black youth.

In the case of Sakia Gunn, poor black youth in the Central Ward transgressed conventional sexual and gender scripts, and directly challenged the heteronormativity of public school teachers and administrators, clergy, and elected officials. Black women activists sought not only to create safe spaces for these contestations, but to politicize issues of heterosexism and homophobia within the black community, as well as black-on-black violence among youth. Black women activists mobilized in Newark's Central Ward in the aftermath of Sakia Gunn's death, building a formidable coalition of local activists who sought to empower a population marginalized by class, age, sexuality, *and* blackness. Enormous stores of social capital were expended by the Newark Pride Alliance to politicize HIV/AIDS as a crosscutting issue to solicit the support of predominantly black intervening institutions to confront the deadly social and personal implications of hatred and heterosexism. Transformative efforts to create youth-based programming and to secure political support for a center that incorporated an intersectional critique of urban power and hegemony failed to materialize. The only palpable result to emerge in the aftermath of Sakia's death addressed a generic form of street violence. Despite the arduous efforts of LGBT activists, the token transformation involved an "anti-bullying ordinance" passed by the city council. While the antibullying ordinance was an important step forward in a public school system racked by various forms of violence, this political–juridical response completely erased the intersectional critique of power articulated by the Newark Pride Alliance activists—a critique that intentionally and systematically linked the vulnerability of black LGBT youth to a racist political economy reinforced by heterosexist cultural norms.

In the case of the NHHPC, youth who expressed a nominal interest in some aspect of "hip hop" were mobilized by both established black elites and a new generation of feminist activists. Although the networking and coalition building among feminist activists throughout the Convention generated a strong and concise collective statement linking gender, sexual, and reproductive oppression with economic violence, this radical feminist agenda was reduced merely to "health and wellness" and a national stance supporting women's reproductive "choice" in the agenda approved by the Convention delegates. When the language of economic violence was detached from gender and sex-specific issues, the transformative potential of intersectional politics was reduced to its more liberal form.

Despite their inability to persuade "voters" to adopt their feminist agenda, activists at the NHHPC did succeed in transforming political spaces. An artistic and cultural terrain that is renowned for its reliance on hypersexualized, destructive deployment of black and female bodies was publicly challenged by black women who called attention to the sexism and misogyny of hip hop as well as in black (and white) communities more generally. While black feminist politics was without doubt marginalized within the context of the convention, women did succeed in contesting hegemonic interpretations of blackness.

It is worth noting that the radical interpretation of social justice politics embedded in the structural intersectionality of hip hop feminism was defeated by the adaptation of "democratic decision-making" on the convention floor. Economic justice for the women present was collectively rejected for a more convenient liberal articulation of women's "individual choice," and this terminology was defined as a "progressive" stance in black community politics. Moreover, black male activists used this de facto deradicalization of the feminism of young women of color to legitimate their own sexual politics. Adopting the unrealized norm of gender parity, black men effectively erased the more transformative elements of feminist organizing within the convention. In the process they reproduced an old pattern, reducing black women to passive supporters of black men who held political ambitions to win votes in urban communities. With this reassertion of patriarchal power, attention to sexuality was erased as homophobic and heterosexist tendencies in the black community withstood a momentary challenge.

Despite the fact that feminism flourished in the Progressive Women's Caucus at the Convention, many black women activists articulated a preference for the concept of "womanism," a view that afforded more familiar roles for black women in the empowerment of black communities. Despite the presence of a cohort of articulate black feminists at the Convention, "womanists" rejected feminism because it purportedly made the struggle of privileged white women and lesbians more important than black women's. But more was at issue in this rejection than the politics of white supremacy. Those who rejected feminism were the same political women who declined to mention sexuality, homophobia, or heterosexism in their discussions of pressing political issues in the black community. Only those activists who explicitly identified with "feminism" or "black feminism" concretely engaged issues concerning sexual and other forms of gender-based violence in their political work, or articulated an antiheterosexist political stance. Not surprisingly, then, issues of homophobia and heterosexism were politicized within the convention only by those who identified themselves as feminist.[4]

The talents of black women community activists and organizers were actively recruited for the larger political purposes of black solidarity and to achieve the appearance of a gender-inclusive "hip hop political agenda." But support for their autonomous "political work" at the local level was not tolerated unless it reproduced hegemonic black cultural production, as defined and institutionalized by local black male political elites. The more ideological processes embedded in patriarchal nationalism regulated an interpretation of black cultural production within liberal and nationalist frames in ways that constrained black women's access to the black public sphere. Black women political activists' political work did not receive recognition, resources, or political support despite the depth of its transformative vision, unless it enhanced the particular interpretation of black cultural production defined by black male political elites.

Explicitly feminist antiracist, antisexist, and antihomophobic politics articulated and acted at the local level and at the national level were particularly vulnerable to erasure. The concrete policies, platforms, and political agendas that dominate the black public sphere continue to marginalize the political interests of radical black women, while rendering their political work invisible. The issue for feminist scholarship then, is not the dearth of black women's political activism, but its suppression.

Kimberly Springer (2002) has rightly pointed out that the "wave analogy" is untenable for those who wish to understand black feminist activism. Extrapolated from the experience of an affluent cohort of white women, the notion of feminist "waves" perpetuates the exclusion of women of color from the histories of (white) women's movements and from feminist theorizing. My research both supports and transcends Springer's insight. Many black women come to the public sphere through gendered political scripts rooted in historical struggles against black racialization. Whether politicized within the Civil Rights Movement, or the Black Power Movement many black women developed political consciousnesses in the context of resolutely patriarchal black politics. Although these political movements have made important strides against white supremacy, they have failed to deliver crippling blows to the perpetually damaging forces behind contemporary black marginality: urban neoliberalilsm, racialized urban poverty, as well as gender, class, and sexual struggles *internal* to the black community.

Black women's political agency, as understood and defined by women activists within poor urban communities, is eclipsed by more than the wave metaphor, however. While the racial politics of white middle-class feminists have often elided the issues and struggles of women of color, so too have black patriarchal politics, whether in nationalist or liberal guises. Black women political activists in inner cities struggle against processes within and outside the community that render them invisible. Neither objective social science research, nor GOTV efforts have attended carefully to the autonomous agendas of black women's social networks. Although black elites have appropriated black women's abilities to mobilize funds and voters for mainstream purposes, they have not acquired black feminists' critiques of the status quo. Whether deemed invisible or apolitical, black women's autonomous political work has been largely discounted. I have sought to redress this historic oversight by illuminating the context and content of black women's political activism in Newark.

FINAL THOUGHTS ON IDENTITY, EXPERIENCE, AND BLACK WOMEN'S POLITICAL AGENCY

This book is inherently a sustained reflection on structure and agency, and on how specific identities themselves get constituted in the ubiquitous and ever continuing interplay between structure and agency. This book is grounded in a topic that was close to my heart and my own politics. Feminists with a psychoanalytic persuasion might suggest that my preoccupation with identity, and with black women as both subjects and objects of truth and meaning-making, is the result of a sufferance, of injury, and a lack. Given US black women's extenuated history of sexual, social, political, and epistemic violence, this might very well be true. However, in this research, I have defined my subjects to be the "black political women in the Central Ward of Newark" and thus, by definition, I included myself. The 29 activists interviewed for this research were nominated by community members who had stakes in Newark's political system. My informants also understood they had a stake in playing a role in the selection of black female activists in Newark as subjects.

In this research, I granted epistemic authority to my subjects. Indeed, the principle source of evidence was "knowledgeable experience," as recounted through semi-structured interviews and participant observation. The testimony of these activists was held against the empirical socioeconomic and demographic data of the Central Ward. This situated black women's agency and subjectivity within the discursive space of the Central Ward. Activists' stories were also juxtaposed against the visual economy of blackness that permeates Newark's cityscapes, as well as the larger historical processes of *gendered* racialization, deindustrialization, neoliberalization, and urban insurgencies that shaped the political economy of Newark's Central Ward. While the initial interests driving this project was a reconceptualization of politics, this focus was broadened and complicated by the growing relevance of scale as these subjects related to "politics". Here, scale itself shaped political actions of the black women's political agency. The adoption of an urban anthropological framework "demarginalized the intersection" (to use Kimberly Crenshaw's phrase) of identity and space as these related to the constitution of political subjects. In the end, this project evolved into a deeper ethnographic inquiry into the political spaces that black women created in the city as they mobilized after the murder of Sakia Gunn, and in the preparation for the NHHPC of 2004.

Sustained inquiry into the "politics" of my subjects entailed a foray into how black women activists' own narrations and actualizations of political agency were both spatially and temporally constituted. I also assessed how their statements were ideologically positioned. Specifically, the cultural production of blackness by black women activists was compared with black nationalism and black racial liberalism. The reclamation of the Newark's cityscapes as a beloved home, although mired in racialized poverty, alienation, despair, and blight, emerged as one of the most prominent themes shaping their subjectivity. Their widespread participation in a variety of community-based organizations and institutions far exceeded the purview of what political scientists like Sidney Verba (2005), Theda Skocpol and Morris Fiorina (1999) have termed "civic volunteerism" and "civic engagement." Much of their agency did *not* rest on the sole assumption that the local apparatuses of the state were "democratic" and *could be* accountable to and responsive to the needs of their communities. Even as my many subjects sought and won elected offices, much of their political efficacy was realized outside of the confines of traditional definitions of political participation.

This research illustrates the sheer ineptitude of predominantly black intervening institutions at the local level to address the claims making of black women activists—especially activists who aimed to subvert structural hierarchies based upon sexuality, age, class, and gender with the development of the "leadership capacity" of black youth by deploying identity. Ironically, I suggest that although black cultural production provides spaces of acceptance and affirmation for black women, especially their willingness to cultivate the leadership of black youth, these same spaces also constrain black women's agency by stifling their use of hard-won social capital for gender progressive political outcomes. This is true despite the reality that these women produced this social capital themselves, during their own leadership development efforts.

I have selected "experience" in this project as the primary lens to show how intersecting structures of domination shape the political identities and affect the lived experiences of black women. This choice was a result of my commitment to make use of the theoretical insights produced by black feminist thinkers Patricia Hill Collins, Barbara Smith, and bell hooks, among others. Their scholarship has laid out an emancipatory blue print from which to portray the lives, perspectives, dilemmas, agencies, oppressions, joys, pains, and lived experiences of black womanhood. Their works are largely ignored or dismissed as essentialist, dated, or worse, in most graduate courses in women's and gender classrooms today, thus inhibiting the production of knowledge about black women's lives and politics. The widespread denial of insights based on racialist and sometime racist intellectualism does not go unnoticed. In fact, in this work I have "reclaimed" identity (to use Paula Moya's phrase) in order to fulfill a larger social justice goal in black community politics. The goal is the eradication of the widespread misogyny that continues to smother the opportunities and life chances of millions of black and brown women in the United States. The sophisticated treatments and theoretical suppositions of Chicana feminists including Chela Sandoval and Gloria Anzaldua have been invaluable in producing an account of black women's agency rooted in empirical assessment of oppression, yet overdetermined by the interiority of experiences of survival, talking back, living, and being agentic in places that routinely deny the legitimacy of their existence.

This book was also informed by a black feminist standpoint epistemology. My invocation of experience was not utilized uncritically or without problems. In fact, using the deployment of black women as an identity required me to be attentive to complex ideological systems that produce black female political subjectivity and the ways in which black female political agency is made visible. In fact, ideology itself was most clearly observed in the multiplicity of "spaces" in which black women's political activism was allowed to flourish. Insights from black feminist geographers provided the methodological leverage to situate black female subjectivity in place and space. I also had to account for the impact of historical processes of racialization that required an analysis of intersectional politics on the ground, and which have made certain identities seem so real for so long.

Following Joan Wallach Scott's critique of "experience," I have tried to not only attend to the historical processes and discursive mechanisms that position black women as subjects, I have also tried to show that the project of making black women's political experiences visible does not preclude analyses of categories of representation (i.e., young, black, gay, female, and "political"). I have also tried to describe how analyses of categories of representation operate to produce both subjects of study and create valid accounts of their political agency and subjectivity. Black feminist methods were used to constitute knowledge about the lived experience of black women's politics in Newark, but I have not presumed an unmediated, direct relationship between black women's identities and their politics. In fact, the politics of identity practiced by black political women seems to be more closely tied to space than to any essentialist invocation of one or more aspect of their personal identity.

Ultimately, this project has been an exploration of how identity creates, negotiates, and reproduces complex interplays, iterations, and tensions between structure and agency. In this project, differences rather than similarities between black female activists were showcased. The heterogeneity of social locations and subject positions of black political women was privileged in my retellings rather than their homogeneity. When patterns of sameness emerged in the testimonials of my subjects, it was most pronounced in their evaluations of the larger political system in which they had to operate. These statements were marked as "non-democratic," "hostile," "cutthroat," and "despotic." When these evaluative comments are correlated with the actual persons that wielded official power in the city of Newark and within the Central Ward, specifically, this is where the politics of identity, as retold by the narrator (myself) becomes relevant. This is when it became important for me, as "knower," to evaluate the relevance of identity-based claims made by my subjects, and to specify the power relationships that actually existed in the city and, most importantly, to specify how black "political" women, including myself, were situated within them.

I have explored the myriad ways in which the personal interests of the researcher have emerged as scholarly questions to be investigated. For example, my analysis of black LGBT activism in Newark after the tragic death of Sakia Gunn revealed not only the painful ways in which Sakia became constituted as "political" but the ways in which the efforts to politicize her death were systematically foreclosed by political elites who objected to the very presence of Sakia as an interpellated, poor, black, teenaged, murdered lesbian and those who purported a positive affinity with her pariah identities.

In 1998, Barbara Smith lamented, "There is no political movement to give power or support to those who want to examine black women's experience through studying our history, literature and culture. There is no political presence that demands a minimal level of consciousness and respect for those who write or talk about our lives. Finally, there is not a developed body of black feminist politics whose assumptions could be used in the study of black women's art" (1998, 6). To a large extent this project was an attempt to answer Barbara Smith's challenge, and to develop a political theory of intersectionality that would enable the further development of these themes, and thus, to make meaning of the lives of black women in urban America. Further work needs to be done to recover black women's agency in different parts of the United States and in different parts of the world. More specifically, we need to explore how the territorialisation of blackness in different locales has shaped how black women mobilize and deploy identity, as well the diverse and complex and that black women have enacted resistance against local, national and transnational constellations of power. More work needs to be done on how black women have participated in diverse social movements including the Occupy movement, the anti-war movement, and movements for food and environmental justice in the United States and other parts of the world. Finally, more work needs to be done on how "blackness" get constituted in places where there are many diverse forms of blackness present and diverse black actors vie for political and economic power, visibility and recognition. This book, I hope, will inspire such projects to take a deeply intersectional approach that illuminates the efforts of marginalized and minoritized black people to enact transformative modes resistance in their everyday lives.

APPENDIX

APPENDIX A
Newark Cityscapes

Figure A.1 Hamidah's Café and Body Shop is a black Muslim business located on Halsey Street in the Central Ward of Newark. Photo credit: Zenzele Isoke.

Figure A.2 The Afrique Hall mural is located on Halsey Street in the central downtown district of the Central Ward. Photo credit: Zenzele Isoke.

Figure A.3 Dr. Jay's Clothing Store located near the corner of Market and Mulberry Street. Photo Credit: Zenzele Isoke.

Figure A.4 Neighborhood of the Central Ward. Photo credit: Zenzele Isoke.

Figure A.5 All Brothers Liquors #1 is a liquor store located on West Inney Street and Washington Avenue. Photo credit: Zenzele Isoke.

Appendix B

Education, Age, and Occupation
of Selected "Political" Women

Name	Educational Attainment	Age	Occupation
Tamara Brown	College Graduate	45	Property Manager
Fayemi Shakur*	Community College	29	Office Manager
Janyce Jacskon*	Post-Grad, Seminary School	54	Executive Director of Social Justice Center
June Dowell*	College Student	37	Student
Charlie Ann Grant	College Graduate	67	Retired/Volunteer
Amina Baraka*	High School Graduate	64	Poet/Organizer
Frederica Bey*	Community College-Real Estate License	62	Executive Director of African–American Cultural Center
Laquetta Nelson*	College Graduate	51	Retired Bus Driver
Dana Rone*	Community College	40	Newark School Board
Kim Gaddy*	College Graduate	39	Executive Director of Environmental Organization
Keisha Simpson	Post-Grad, Public Policy	27	Organizer for Community Economic Development Corporation
Melanie Hendricks*	Post-Grad, Public Administration	28	Director, Youth Organization
Olivia Taylor	Post-Grad, Social Work	53	New Jersey State Legislator
Marilyn Wilson	Post Grad, Law School	45	Policy Director, Hospital Adm.
SuSu Stewart*	College Graduate	42	Youth Activist, Boys and Girls Club
Henrietta Parsons	College Graduate	78	Retired Union Organizer
Ama Mdupe*	Post-Grad, Education	59	Executive Director, Social Service Agency
Yvonne Warren	Community College	39	Newark Municipal Council
Veronica Osorio*	College Graduate	22	Outreach Coordinator, Community Center

Note: *Activists who decided to go on record.

APPENDIX C

Active Organizational Membership/Civic Participation of Black Women Activists in Newark

Name[1]	Names of Organizations
Ama Mdupe	President of Newark Public Library
	First Vice President for National Congress of Black Women
	Women's Board Association of the New Jersey Performing Arts Center
	Chairperson for Commission on the Status of Women in Newark
	Member of Alpha Kappa Alpha Sorority
	Vice Chairperson for National Congress of Black Women
Fayemi Shakur	Black Student Union—"Black Freedom Society"
	The Sundiata Acoli Freedom Campaign
	Member of Malcolm X Grassroots Movement
	Minister of Education for the New Black Panther Party
	Alumni of New Leadership of the Eagleton Institute
	Member of Young Men's Christian Association
	Newark Student Voices
	National Hip Hop Political Convention
	Hands Off Assata Campaign
Veronica Osorio	The All-Star Program-Mentor
	The Leadership Institute-Mentor
	Hip Hop Convention Delegate and Volunteer
	Ebony Club Co-Founder
	Universal Zulu Nation
	Cadet Program—Alumni Program
	T & T Teens Networking for Today
	Newark Public School District-Substitute Teacher
Gayle Chaneyfield-Jenkins	Volunteer for the Integrity House
	Jon Corzine's Women's Committee
	National Association for the Advancement of Colored People
	Member of Delta Sigma Theta Sorority, Inc.
	Member of Bethany Baptist Church
	Board member for the Boys and Girls Club
	Board member for the Independence Family of Services
	Founder of the Newark Women's Conference
	Founder of 100 Black women
	Founder of the International Congress of Black women
	New Jersey State Opera Guild
Amina Baraka	Community For a Unified Newark
	African Free School
	Black Women United Front
	The National Black Political Assembly

Continued

Name	Names of Organizations
Janyce Jackson	Advisory Board of She-Project—African–American Women
	Newark Pride Alliance
	Liberation in Truth Unity Fellowship Church
	Lambda Legal Defense Fund
	Women Wear Hats
	Marriage Equality Organization
	Parent-Teacher Association Member—unspecified
Kim Gaddy	Black Voice/Carta Boricua
	International Black Women's National Congress
	First Baptist Church of Nutley
	Metropolitan Bowling Center
	"Above the Rim" Basketball Program
	National Association for the Advancement of Colored People
	Parent-Teacher Association: Harriet Tubman Elementary School and Weequahic High School
	Co-founder and President of the Weequahic Alumni Association
	Essex County Environmental Commission
	New Jersey Professional Women
Keisha Simpson	National Association for the Advancement of Colored People,
	National Hip Hop Political Convention,
	Indian Education Initiative,
	Near Eastside
	Neighborhood Association,
	Historic James Street Commons Association,
	Beyond Campus.
June Dowell	Gay Men's Health Crisis
	Mashood in Brooklyn
	Newark Pride Alliance
	Newark Episcopal Church
	Gay and Lesbian Student Network
	Project Wow!
	Gay Straight Alliance
	North Jersey Community Research Initiative/New Jersey's Aid Alliance
Frederica Bey	Jihad Health Network
	Anti-Lynching Campaign
	Concerned Citizens of Essex County
	The Legal Women Voters Great
	Women In Support of the Million Man March
	People's Organization for Progress
	Black Cops Against Police Brutality
	President of the Carmel Towers
	Parent-Teacher Association Springfield Avenue Community School

Continued

Appendix C Continued

Name	Names of Organizations
Melanie Hendricks	Leadership Newark
	Congressional Black Caucus Leadership Institute
	Member for the Hillside Board of Education
	Leadership Newark Graduate Organization
	National Hip Hop Political Convention
	Eagleton Institute of Politics
	Rutgers-Newark Urban Studies
	Rutgers-Newark Public Administration Department
	American Society for Public Administrators
	Northern New Jersey American Society for Public Administration Chapter
	Pi Alpha Honors Society
	Student Voices
	Empowerment Civics
Olivia Taylor	Member of New-Ark
	Participant of the Black Topological Library
	Newark Coalition for Neighborhoods
	Newark Coalition for Low-Income Housing
	Board Member, Institute of New Jersey
	Member for the East Orange Board of Education
	New Jersey School Board Association
	National Council of Negro Women
	Lincoln University Alumni
	National Association for the Advancement of Colored People
	Urban League
	Sierra Club
	Member of the Young Mens Christian Association
	Trustee for Prevent Child Abuse New Jersey
	Board Member of Babyland Family Services
Laquetta Nelson	United States Army (E-5)
	District Leader- 28th district in the Central Ward
	Newark Pride Alliance
	New Jersey Stonewall Democrats
	Unity Fellowship Church in New Brunswick
	Executive Board of the New Jersey Gay and Lesbian Coalition
Dana Rone	New Black Panther Party
	Court Appointed Special Advocates
	Newark Tenants Council
	Recreation Program
	General Educational Development Program (GED)
	Million Man March
Tamara Brown	Pillars of Peace Youth Ministry
	Ministry Advisors Council for the New Jersey Performing Arts Center
	Volunteer of CASA

Continued

Appendix C Continued

Name	Names of Organizations
	Newark Cycle Club, Public Relations Officer
	Churches in Cooperation (CIC)
	The Leaguers, Inc.
	Essex County Antiviolence Coalition
SuSu Stewart	National Hip Hop Political Convention
	Newark Boys and Girls Club
	Newark Pride Alliance
Yvonne Warren	The Angel's Project
	Women With Hats for Cure
	Babyland Family Services
	New Community Corporation

NOTES

1 INTRODUCTION

1. In this book the term "black women" refers to black-identified women of color, which includes Puerto Ricans and others who either identify as "black," or those whom community members themselves referred to as "black political women."

2. I define black heteropatriarchy as the localized convergence of black racialization, heterosexualization, and patriarchy that forge what is usually unproblematically deemed "black politics" by scholars of urban politics (see for instance, Walters 2005, 1988, Walton 1984). The term heteropatriarchy was originally coined by Linda Hart in *Fatal Women: Lesbian Sexuality and the Mark of Aggression*, but has since been vigorously used by women of color activists who actively link processes of racism, sexism, colonialism, and imperialism in their writings. For more extended discussions on heteropatriarchy see *The Color of Violence: The Incite! Anthology* (Incite! Women of Color Against Violence, 2005) and *Colonize This! Young Women of Color on Today's Feminism* (2002) edited by Daisy Hernandez and Bushra Rehman, and *Pedagogies of Crossing* (2005) by M. Jacqui Alexander.

3. Laura Pulido (2006) defines differential racialization as the process through which particular sets of racial meanings are attached to different racial/ethnic groups that affect and are a function of class position and racial standing.

4. M. Jacqui Alexander (2005) has called this process spiritual work, or the process through which knowledge comes to be embodied and inscribed in the daily lives of women. Alternatively, Gwendolyn Pough has theorized this process as "bringing wreck" or disrupting dominant discourses in the public sphere, and thereby reshaping the United States imaginarily. For the purpose of this book, these are theorized as "resistance politics" as it is these forms of praxis that enables political mobilizations to take place within predominantly African–American urban communities like the Central Ward of Newark.

5. Following Patricia Hill Collins (2005), I argue that black women's resistance politics operates within the logic of "the new racism." "The new racism," Collins explains, "relies more heavily on the manipulation of ideas in mass media. These new techniques present hegemonic

ideologies that claim that racism is over. They work to obscure the racism that does exist, and they undercut antiracist struggle. Globalization, transnationalism, and the growth of hegemonic ideologies within mass media provide the context for the new racism" (54).

3   MAKING PLACE IN NEWARK: NEOLIBERALIZATION AND GENDERED RACIALIZATION IN A US CITY

1. For more discussion on this usage of cityscapes, see *Feminist (Re)visions of the Subject: Landscapes, Ethnoscapes and Theoryscapes* (2001), edited by Gail Curry and Celia Rothenberg, and "Global Ethnoscapes: Notes and Queries for a Transnational Anthropology" by Arjon Appadurai in *Recapturing Anthropology* (1991), edited by Richard Fox. Also see "How Built Spaces Mean: A Semiotics of Space" by Dvora Yanow in *Interpretation and Method: Empirical Research Methods and the Interpretative Turn* (2006) edited by Dvora Yanow and Peregrine Schwartz-Shea.

2. *The Negro in New Jersey a report of a Survey by the Interracial Committee of the New Jersey Conference of Social Work in Cooperation with the State Department of Institutions and Agencies* (1932).

3. Ibid.

4. Ibid.

5. "Freedom Papers: The Manumission of Slaves in Burlington County New Jersey, 1776–1781" with an introduction by Clement Alexander Price (Burlington County, NJ: Burlington County Historical Society, 1984).

6. Joseph Atkinson, *The History of Newark, New Jersey: Being a Narrative of its Rise and Progress, from the Settlement in May, 1666, by Emigrants from Connecticut to the Present Time, Including a Sketch of the Press of Newark, from 1791 to 1878* (Newark: William Guild Press, 1878): 143.

7. In 1844, following the era of Jacksonian reform, New Jersey revised its constitution to include the words "white" and "males" to formally exclude Blacks and women from voting. For further discussion see *Reclaiming Lost Ground: The Struggle for Woman Suffrage in New Jersey* by Neale McGoldrick and Margaret Crocco (1993) and "Negro Suffrage in New Jersey in 1776–1875" by Marion Thompson Wright in *Journal of Negro History* Vol. 33, No. 2 (1948).

8. *Proceedings of a Meeting Held at Princeton, New Jersey, July 14, 1824, To Form a Society in the State of New-Jersey, to Cooperate with the American Colonization Society* (Princeton, NJ, 1824) reprinted in *Freedom Not Far Distant: A Documentary History of Afro Americans in New Jersey* (Clement 1980): 12–20.

9. For further discussion see *The Negro in New Jersey* published by the Interracial Committee of the New Jersey Conference of Social Work (1932), *Freedom Not Far Distant: A Documentary History of*

Afro-Americans in New Jersey by Clement Price (1980), "Negro Suffrage in New Jersey in 1776–1875" by Marion Thompson Wright in *Journal of Negro History* 33 (1948) and *The History of Newark, New Jersey* by Joseph Atkinson (1848).

10. Atkinson, *The History of Newark, New Jersey.*

11. For further discussion see "The Black Experience in Newark" by Kenneth T. and Barbara B. Jackson in *New Jersey Since 1860: New Findings and Interpretations* edited by William C. Wright. Trenton: New Jersey Historical Commission, 1971.

12. Ibid.

13. Ibid., 49.

14. Ibid.

15. See for instance *Newark News*, February 11, 1964; *Newark News*, December 19, 1967; *Newark News*, June 18, 1966; *The Star-Ledger*, August 1, 1962; *Newark News*, December 12, 1967; and *Newark News*, February 26, 1967.

16. Ibid.

17. *Newark News*, September 28, 1936.

18. *Public Housing in Newark's Central Ward: A Report by the New Jersey State Advisory Committee to the U.S. Commission on Civil Rights*, April 1968.

19. Now the Central Ward.

20. In July of 1954, Newark's politically districts were redrawn into a five ward system. 100% of the Third Ward was redistributed into the Central Ward, preserving the predominantly African-American demographic in this area; source: John T. Cunningham, *Newark* (3rd ed.) (Newark, NJ: New Jersey Historical Society, 2002).

21. *Public Housing in Newark's Central Ward: A Report by the New Jersey State Advisory Committee to the U.S. Commission on Civil Rights*, April 1968.,4.

22. Ibid., 7.

23. Tom Hayden, *Rebellion in Newark: Official Violence and Ghetto Response* (New York: Random House, 1967).

24. Interview aired on September 24, 2010 on the Oprah Winfrey Show. Video clip can be downloaded at www.oprah.com/oprahshow/Mark-Zuckerbergs-Big-Announcement-Video.

25. Calefati Jessica and Kelly Heyboar, "$100M Grant from Mark Zuckerberg begins to have effect on Newark School," *The Star-Ledger*, September 25, 2011.

26. Aliyah Shahid, "Facebook's Mark Zuckerberg to donate $100M to Newark's Public School on Oprah Winfrey," *New York Daily News*, September 23, 2010.

27. Calefati Jessica and Kelly Heyboar. "$100M Grant from Mark Zuckerberg begins to have effect on Newark School." *The Star-Ledger*, September 25, 2011.

28. Department of Health and Senior Services (2005), *New Jersey HIV/AIDS Report* compiled by the Division of HIV/AIDS Services.

29. James Queally, "Report: Newark's Level of Gang-Related Murders Among Highest in the Nation," *The Star -edger*, January 26, 2012.
30. Source: 2000 US Census Bureau, American Fact Finder. The Central Ward consist of census tracts 9, 10, 11, 26, 27, 28, 29, 30, 31, 34, 38, 39, 62, 64, 66, 67, 81, 82, 85, 86, 87, 88, 90, 227, 228 in Essex County, New Jersey. In some census tracts there is some overlap between the South, North, and East Wards of Newark.
31. See for instance *When Death Come Stealing, Devil's Gonna Get Him (1994), No Hiding Place (1995),* and *Dying in the Dark (2004),* and *Of Blood and Sorrow (2008).*

4   (Re)Imagining Home: Black Women and the Cultural Production of Blackness in Newark

1. Shaterra is a pseudonym created to protect the identity of the cashier.

5   The Politics of Homemaking: Black Feminist Transformations of a Cityscape

1. I would like to extend a note of thanks to Ruth Nicole Brown, Mary Hawkesworth, Richa Nagar, Eden Torres, Dara Strolovich, Jigna Desai, and the women of Newark for their support project in all of its various stages. I also wish to extend a note of thanks to the anonymous reviewers and series editors, Dana-Ain Davis and Aimee Cox, for their helpful suggestions and comments on multiple drafts.
2. Spatial stories refer to stories that black women tell about Newark that emphasise the dynamic and shifting elements of Newark's physical, symbolic, and relational space. It illuminates how activist's stories on women repudiate stable, bounded, and strictly physical understanding of Newark's geography. For example, many black women's understanding of "Newark" is based upon their experiences in organizing and living in the city's predominantly African–American and Latino Central Ward.
3. The term homeplace, as I am using it, was coined by bell hooks (1990, 42). She writes, "Historically Black women have resisted white supremacist domination by working to establish a homeplace." Homeplaces are sites of resistance to white supremacist, capitalist patriarchy.
4. Political spaces are complex social spaces that black women must engage and negotiate in order to do their political work of resisting the overlapping effects of race, gender, and class domination. The concept of political space also helps to describe the spatial–temporal configurations of power and become apparent and legible with black women's efforts to transform their neighborhoods and communities.
5. Most interviews took between two and a half to four hours to complete, and all took place in a single session.

6. Michel de Certeau argues that spatial stories transform places into spaces. He writes, "space exists when one takes into consideration directional velocity and time. Space occurs as the effect produces by the operations that orient it, situate it, and temporalize it, and allows space to function."

7. See for instance the film *Street Fight* (2005) directed and produced by Marshall Curry, and Season 1 of the documentary series *Brick City* (2009) directed by Mark Benjamin and Marc Levin.

8. Amiri Baraka and his wife, Amina Baraka's, organization, Committee for a United Newark (CFUN) was instrumental in installing the city's first black mayor, Kenneth Gibson. Using this uniquely successful model of multiracial, electoral solidarity as a rallying cry, CFUN spearheaded the first Black and Puerto Rican Political Convention in 1969, and the subsequent, National Black Political Convention in 1972 (Mumford 2007, Woodard 1999).

6   Mobilizing after Murder: Black Women Queering Politics and Black Feminism Newark

1. I use the term "queer black women" to refer to self-identified "black women" who transgress norms of heteronormativity in one or more of the following ways: (1) they love and stand in solidarity with black lesbians, gays, transsexual, and transgender people, (2) they take open political stances against sexism, homophobia, and gender violence (rape, gay-bashing, domestic violence, and/or street harassment) that is perpetrated within the African–American community in Newark, and (3) they openly reject hegemonic gender norms that require black people to perform respectability in public spaces.

2. Social capital typically refers to those features of social organization that enhance the possibility of cooperation and collective social action (Putnam 2000). Looking beyond the resources and capacities of individuals, social capital directs attention toward the common resources and capacities of communities made up of complex networks of human relationships. Some basic features of social capital include trust, rapport, and reliable means to interact and demonstrate positive norms of reciprocity with other community members.

3. Building off of Linda Hart's infamous formulation, I define black heteropatriarchy as the local convergence of processes of black racialization, heterosexualization, and patriarchy.

4. The term "aggressive" is a self-acclaimed gender category of women of color in the northeastern United States who often self-identify as "black" and who have a androgynous, often marked masculine, self-presentations rooted in urban African–American vernacular culture. Interestingly, many "aggressive" or "ag" black women reject the label of lesbian as it does not adequately represent their distinctively racialized

gender performances of sexual identity. In 2005, director Daniel Peddle produced a documentary entitled *The Aggressives* that explores the experiences of aggressive women in New York City.

5. To tap into black women's spatial resistance, I interviewed 29 activists—black women who have been or continue to be engaged in political activism and who were selected through the process of community nomination. I consulted with informants from each community of practice to identify potential interviewees. The activists who participated in this project are diverse in terms of their socioeconomic status, levels of educational attainment, and age. Six (21%) of the women interviewed were under 40 years of age, with the youngest being 24 years old. Twelve women (41%) were between 40 and 50 years of age. The remaining 11 women (38%) were 50 years or older; the oldest being 79. All of the women interviewed had completed high school, and 16 (55%) had completed an undergraduate college degree. Of those who had completed college, five had gone on to pursue professional graduate degrees. In this chapter, we hear from five gender transgressive black female activists who organized in the aftermath of Sakia Gunn's death.

6. It should be noted that Mayor James was convicted of only five counts of fraud, and later served a 27 month sentence in a federal prison.

7. Newark Pride Alliance website.

8. For more discussion about refuse spaces see Talmadge Wright, *Out of Place: Homelessness, Mobilizations, Subcities and Contested Landscapes* (New York: State University Press of New York, 1997).

9. "From loss, a lesson. District mourns loss with a day of tolerance," *The Star-Ledger*, May 9, 2004.

10. This comment was made after Bolden made a public apology for blacking out a yearbook photo of two male students kissing at East Side High School in 2007. Source: Newark AP. Staffwritter, Jeffrey Gold. Bolden's comments were also featured in the editorial pages of the *New York Times*, the *New Jersey Star Ledger*, and the online newsletter of the Trenton Gay and Lesbian Civic Association. See for instance, "Newark needs a safe place for gay youth" in *New Jersey Star Ledger*, March 24, 2009.

11. Crowley, Peggy. "Student Orientation: More Teenage Girls are Testing Gender Boundaries," in *The Star--Ledger*, May 26, 2004.

12. For a comprehensive analysis of "frame analysis," please see Rens Vliegenthart and Leisbet van Zoonen, "Power to the Frame: Bringing Sociology Back to Frame Analysis" *European Journal of Communication* 26 (2011): 101.

13. Developed by Erving Goffman, frame analysis is a strategy of making sense of the meaning that social actors attribute to often taken-for-granted actions, interactions, and larger social phenomenon. Goffman writes, "I assume that definitions of a situation are built up in accordance with principles of organization which govern events—at least social ones—and our subjective involvement in them: frame is the word I use to refer to such basic elements as I am able to identify" (1974, 11).

14. This "new racism" includes contemporary manifestations of age-old racial ideologies facilitated by contemporary processes of globalization, transnational corporate hegemony, and the global proliferation of racial ideologies via mass media.
15. For more general discussion on the deployment of identity, politics, and discursive practices see Fernandes (2003) and Rodriguez (2003).

7   Keepin' Up the Fight: Young Black Feminists and the Hip Hop Convention Movement

1. See for instance, Chang (2007) and Forman and Neale (2004).
2. See for instance, Greg Tate (2003), Kitwana (2006).
3. See for instance, Terkourafi (2010), Osumare (2007), and Nilan and Fiexa (2006).
4. For more discussion, see Forman (2002), Rose (1994), Abdullah (2006), Kitwana (2003), Pough (2004) and Watkins (2005).
5. For extended discussions about the impact of how the conservative social and economic policies of the 1980s (i.e., "Reaganomics") impacted inner urban youth culture and hip hop cultural production see also Forman (2002), Rose (1994), and Shomari (1995).
6. Organizing Manual of the 2004 National Hip Hop Political Convention.
7. These organizations include, Critical Resistance, Zulu Nation, United for Peace and Justice, Sister to Sister, Peace in the Hood, National Urban Alliance, League of Young Voters, Prison Moratorium Project, National Black United Front, Young Democratic Socialists, Sister II Sister, Prolibertad, New Black Panther Party, Audre Lorde Project, Black Cops Against Police Brutality, Fannie Lou Hamer Project, Marijuana Policy Project, Hip Hop Odyssey International Film Festival (H_2O), Right to Vote, Rainforest Foundation, New York City Environmental Justice Project, Third Wave Foundation and Refuse and Resist, among many others. *Source: National Hip Hop Political Convention 2004 Program.*
8. Ibid. Also, for instance, national organizers initiated contact with very highly respected African–American political leaders and entertainers including Cynthia McKinney, Kwame Kilpatrick, Jesse Jackson Jr., Al Sharpton, Russell Simmons, Chuck D, Mos Def, David Muhammad, Queen Latifah, and Sista Souljah among many others.
9. Organizing Manual of the 2004 National Hip Hop Political Convention.
10. Personal interview with early convention Newark-based co-founder, Baye Adofo-Wilson.
11. Personal interview with early convention founder who preferred to remain anonymous.
12. Personal interview with Newark-based convention co-founder Hashim Shomari.
13. In defining the inherent phallanthrocentrism of this cohort's under-standing of black political activism, Kitwana writes, "Undoubtedly part

of the status that Ras Baraka and Jesse Jackson, Jr. have achieved as activists/politicians comes from their familial connections. This generation represents a new age in Black America's activism, Baraka's and Jackson's comments above reflect both a new level of political sophistication and a new political reality" (2002, 147).

14. Personal interviews with Hashim Shomari. Also included in the minutes from the second national organizing meeting for the Convention.
15. From 1999 to 2006 Sharpe James served in both capacity as Mayor of Newark and Senator of the 29th Legislative District of New Jersey.
16. Personal interview with Hashim Shomari.
17. Ibid.
18. Personal copy of email exchange from January 28, 2004.
19. Ibid.

8 THE AUDACITY TO RESIST: BLACK WOMEN, SOCIAL CAPITAL, AND BLACK CULTURAL PRODUCTION

1. Personal interview with Rosa Clemente (July 12, 2012). Also see "Russell Simmons, You Are Not Hip Hop" an open letter published in the *Village Voice* on April 24, 2001. Clemente's open letter was featured in "Hip Hop War" by Peter Noel, staff-writer for the *Village Voice*.
2. The People's Organization for Progress grew out of the leadership of the Black Student Movement in New Jersey, which facilitated the development of Black Student Unions on high school and college campuses in Northern New Jersey. The organization was instrumental in the anti-apartheid movement, in which a number of the political women identified in this study took part.
3. Personal interview with People's Organization for Progress national chair, Larry Hamm.
4. It should be noted that the few gay men who attended the convention, also identified with and participated in the final proposals of PWC.

APPENDIX

1. Many, but not all, subjects names have been changed to preserve confidentiality. SuSu Stewart, Frederica Bey, Fayemi Shakur, Dana Rone, LaQuetta Nelson, June Dowell, Kim Gaddy, Veronica Osorio, and Gayle Chaneyfield Jenkins have all preferred to go on record.

Bibliography

Abdullah, Medina. "Hip-Hop as Political Expression: Potentialities for the Power of Voice in Urban America." In *The Black Urban Community: From Dusk Till Dawn*, edited by Gayle Tate and Lewis A. Randolph, 465–76. New York: Palgrave MacMillian, 2006.

Abdullah, Medina and Regina Freer. "Bass to Bass: Relative Freedom and Womanist Leadership in Black Los Angeles." In *Black Los Angeles: American Dreams and Racial Realities*, edited by Darnell Hunt and Ana-Christina Ramon, 323–42. New York: New York University Press, 2010.

Alexander, Jacqui M. *Pedagogies of Crossing: Meditations on Feminism, Sexual Politics, Memory and the Sacred*. Durham: Duke Univesity Press, 2005.

Alexander, Michelle. *The New Jim Crow: Mass Incarceration in the Age of Colorblindness*. New York: The New Press, 2010.

Alexander-Floyd, Nikol. *Gender, Race, and Nationalism in Contemporary Black Politics*. New York: Palgrave Macmillan, 2007.

Anyon, Jean. *Ghetto Schooling: A Political Economy of Urban Educational Reform*. New York: Columbia University Press, 1997.

Appadurai, Arjon. "Global Ethnoscapes: Notes and Queries for a Transnational Anthropology." In *Recapturing Anthropology*, edited by R. Fox. Santa Fe: School of American Research Press distributed by the University of Washington, 1991.

———. "The Production of Locality." In *Counterworks: Managing the Diversity of Knowledge*, edited by Richard Fardon, 204–225. New York: Routledge Press, 1995.

Arrastia, Lisa. "Capital's Daisy Chain: Exposing Chicago's Corporate Coalition" in *Journal for Critical Education Policy Studies*. 5, no. 1, 2007.

Atwater, Deborah. *African American Women's Rhetoric: The Search for Dignity, Personhood, and Honor*. Lanham: Lexington Books, 2009.

Baca Zinn, Maxine and Bonnie Thornton Dill. "Theorizing Difference from Multiracial Feminism." *Feminist Studies* 22, no. 2 (1996): 321–331.

Bates, Aryana. *Religious Despite Religion: Lesbian Agency, Identity and Spirituality At Liberation in Truth, Unity Fellowship Church*. PhD dissertaion, Rutgers University, Newark, NJ, 2002.

Beauboeuf-Lafontant, Tamara. *Behind the Mask of the Strong Black Woman: Voice and the Embodiment of a Costly Performance*. Philadelphia: Temple University Press, 2009.

Beemyn, Brett, ed. *Creating a Place for Ourselves: Lesbian, Gay and Bisexual Community Histories.* New York: Routledge, 1997.

Berger, Michele Tracy and Kathleen Guidroz. *The Intersectional Approach: Transforming the Academy Through Race, Class and Gender.* Chapel Hill: The University of North Carolina Press, 2009.

Bernard, Ian. *Queer Race: Cultural Interventions in the Racial Politics of Queer Theory.* New York: Peter Lang, 2003.

Blackwell, Maylei. *Chicana Power! Contested Histories of Feminism in the Chicano Movement.* Austin: University of Texas Press, 2011.

Bookman, Ann and Sandra Morgen. *Women and the Politics of Empowerment.* Philadelphia: Temple University Press, 1988.

Bourdieu, Pierre. "Le capital social: Notes provisoires. Actes de la Recherche." *Sciences Sociales* 31 (1980): 2–3.

———. *The Logic of Practice.* Stanford, CA: Stanford University Press, 1980.

Bourque, Susan C. and Jean Grossholtz. "Politics an Unnatural Practice: Political Science Looks at Female Participation" *Politics and Society* 4, no. 2 (1974): 255–65.

Boyce Davies, Carole. *Black Women, Writing and Identity.* New York: Routledge Press, 1994.

———. *Left of Karl Marx: The Political Life of Black Communist Claudia Jones.* Durham: Duke University Press, 2007.

Bracer, Earnest N. *Fannie Lou Hamer : The Life of a Civil Rights Icon.* Jefferson and London: MacFarland Press, 2011.

Brah, Avtar and Ann Phoenix. "Ain't I a Woman? Revisiting Intersectionality." *Journal of International Women's Studies.* 5, no. 3 (May 2004): 75–86.

Brandt, Eric. "Beyond State-Centrism? Space, Territoriality and Geographic Scale in Globalization Studies." *Theory and Society* 28, no. 1 (1999): 39–78.

Brandt, Eric, ed. *Dangerous Liasons: Blacks, Gays and the Struggle for Equality.* New York: The New Press, 1999.

Brenner, Neil. "The Limits to Scale? Methodological Reflections on Scalar Structuration." *Progress in Human Geography* 25, no. 4 (2001): 591–614.

Brenner, Neil and Theodore Nicholas. *Spaces of Neoliberalism: Urban Restructuring in North America and Western Europe.* Oxford: Blackwell 2002.

Brooks, Maegan Parker and Davis W. Houck. *The Speeches of Fannie Lou Hamer: To Tell It Like It Is.* Jackson: University Press of Mississippi, 2011.

Brown, Elsa Barkely. "'What Has Happened Here': The Politics of Difference in Women's History and Feminist Politics." In *The Feminist History Reader,* edited by Sue Morgan, 300–08. New York and London: Routledge Press, 2006.

Butler, Judith. *Gender Trouble: Feminism and the Subversion of Identity.* New York: Routledge Press, 1999.

Bynoe, Yvonne. *Stand and Deliver : Political Leadership, Activism and Hip-hop Culture.* Brooklyn: Soft Skull Press, 2004.

Caldwell, Kia Lily. *Negras in Brazil: Re-envisioning Black Women, Citizenship and the Politics of Identity*. New Brunswick: Rutgers University Press, 2007.

Cazenave, Noel A. *The Urban Racial State: Managing Race Relations in American Cities*. New York: Rowman and Littlefield Publishers, 2011.

Certeau, Michel de. *The Practice of Everyday Life*. Translated by Steven Rendall. Berkeley: University of California Press, 1984.

Chang, Jeff. *Can't Stop, Won't Stop: A History of the Hip-Hip Generation*. New York: St. Martins Press, 2005.

———. *Total Chaos: The Art and Aesthetics of Hip-Hop*. New York: Basic Books, 2006.

Chong, Dennis. *Collective Action and the Civil Rights Movement*. Chicago, IL: The University of Chicago Press, 1991.

Chow, Rey. *The Protestant Ethic and the Spirit of Capitalism*. New York: Columbia University Press, 2002.

Clarke, Cheryl. "Lesbianism 2000." In *This Bridge We Call Home: Radical Visions for Transformation*, edited by Gloria Anzaldua and AnaLouise Keating, 232–38. New York: Routledge, 2002.

Cobb, William Jelani. *To the Break of Dawn: A Freestyle on the Hip Hop Aesthetic*. New York and London: New York University Press, 2007.

Cohen, Cathy. "Punks, Bulldaggers, and Welfare Queens: The Radical Potential of Queer Politics?" *GLQ* 3 (1997): 437–65.

———. *The Boundaries of Blackness: Aids and the Breakdown of Black Politics*. Chicago: University of Chicago Press, 1999.

———. "Social Capital, Intervening Institutions and Political Power." In *Social Capital and Poor Communities*, edited by Susan Saegart, J. Phillip Thompson, and Mark R. Warren. New York: Russell Sage Foundation, 2001.

Cohen, Cathy, Kathleen Jones, and Joan Tronto. *Women Transforming Politics: An Alternative Reader*. New York and London: New York University Press, 1997.

Cole, Elizabeth and Zikaya T. Luna. "Making Coalitions Work: Solidarity Across Difference within US Feminism." *Feminist Studies* 36, no. 1 (Spring 2012): 71–98.

Cole, Johnnetta and Beverly Guy Sheftall. *Gender Talk: The Struggle for Women's Equality in African American Communities*. New York: Ballantine Books, 2003.

Collier-Thomas, Bettye and V. P. Franklin. *Sisters in the Struggle: African American Women in the Civil Rights-Black Power Movement*. New York and London: New York University Press, 2001.

Collins, Patricia Hill. *Black Feminist Thought: Knowledge, Consciousness and the Politics of Empowerment*. New York: Routledge Press, 1991.

———. *Fighting Words: Black Women and the Search for Justice*. Minneapolis and London: University of Minnesota Press, 1998.

———. *Black Sexual Politics: African Americans, Gender and the New Racism*. New York and London: Routledge Press, 2005.

———. *From Black Power to Hip Hop: Racism, Nationalism, and Feminism*. Philadelphia: Temple University Press, 2006.

Cox, Kevin R. "Spaces of Dependence, Spaces of Engagement and the Politics of Scale, or: Looking for Local Politics. *Political Geography* 17, no. 1 (1998): 1–23.

Craig, Maxine Leeds. *Ain't I a Beauty Queen: Black Women, Beauty and the Politics of Race*. Oxford: Oxford University Press, 2002.

Crawford Vicki. "African American Women in the Mississippi Freedom Democratic Party." In *Sister in the Struggle*, edited by Bettye Collier-Thomas and V. P. Franklin, 121–38. New York: New York University Press, 2001.

Crenshaw, Kimberle. "Mapping the Margins: Intersectionality, Identity Politics and Violence Against Women of Color." In *Critical Race Theory: The Key Writings that Formed the Movement*, edited by Kimberle Crenshaw, Neil Gotanda, Gary Peller, and Kendall Thomas, 357–83. New York: The New Press, 1995.

Cunningham, John T. *Newark*. Newark: The New Jersey Historical Society, 2002.

Currie, Gail and Celia Rothenberg. *Feminist (Re)visions of the Subject: Landscapes, Ethnoscapes and Theoryscapes*. New York: Lexington Books, 2001.

Curvin, Robert. *The Persistent Minority: The Black Political Experience in Newark. Published Dissertation*. Ann Arbor: The University of Michigan Press, 1975.

Davis, Angela. *Are Prisons Obsolete?* New York: Seven Stories Press, 2003.

Davis, Eisa and Ntozake Shange. "If we Gotta Live Underground and Everybody's got Cancer/Will Poetry Be Enuf?" In *Letters of Intent: Women Cross the Generations to Talk About Family, Work, Sex, Love and the Future of Feminism*, edited by Anna Bandoc and Meg Daly, 189–99. New York: Free Press, 1999.

Dawson, Michael C. *Behind the Mule: Race and Class in African-American Politics*. Princeton: Princeton University Press, 1994.

———. *Black Visions: The Roots of African American Political Ideology*. Chicago: University of Chicago Press, 2001.

Delaney, David and Helga Leitner. "The Political Construction of Scale." *Political Geography* 16, no. 2 (1997): 93–97.

Dhamoon, Rita Kaur. "Considerations on Mainstreaming Intersectionality." *Political Research Quarterly* 64, no. 1 (2011): 230–43.

Dowler, Lorraine and Joanne Sharp. "A Feminist Geopolitics?" *Space and Polity* 5, no. 3 (2001): 165–76.

Downs, Anthony. *An Economic Theory of Democracy*. New York: Harper, 1957.

Emerson, Robert, Rachel Fretz, and Linda Shaw. *Writing Ethnographic Fieldnotes*. Chicago: The University of Chicago Press, 1995.

Etter-Lewis, Gwendolyn. *My Soul is My Own: Oral Narratives of African American Women in the Professions*. New York: Routledge, 1993.

Etter-Lewis, Gwendolyn and Michele Foster, eds. *Unrelated Kin: Race and Gender in Women's Personal Narratives.* New York: Routledge Press, 1996.

Eves, Allison. "Queer Theory, Butch/Femme Identities and Lesbian Space." *Sexualities* 7, no. 4 (2004): 480–96.

Feldman, Martha S. *Strategies for Interpreting Qualitative Data.* Thousand Oaks, CA: Sage University Press.

Ferguson, Roderick. *Aberrations in Black: Toward a Queer of Color Critique.* Minneapolis: University of Minnesota Press, 2004.

Fernandes, Leela. *Transforming Feminist Practice: Nonviolence, Social Justice, and the Possibilities of a Spiritualized Feminism.* San Francisco: Aunt Lute Books, 2003.

Flammang, Janet. *Women's Political Voices: How Women Are Transforming the Practice and Study of Politics.* Philadelphia: Temple University Press, 1997.

Fogg-Davis, Hawley, "Theorizing Black Lesbians within Black Feminism: A Critique of Same-Race Street Harassment." *Politics & Gender* 2 (2006): 57–76.

Forman, Murray. *The Hood Comes First: Race, Space and Place in Rap and Hip-Hop.* Middletown: Weslyan University Press, 2002.

Forman, Murray and Mark Anthony Neal. *That's the Joint! The Hip Hop Studies Reader.* New York: Routledge Press, 2004.

Foucault, Michel. "Of Other Spaces." Conference paper entitled "Of Other Spaces, Heterotopias" (1967), *Journal of Architecture/Mouvement/ Continuite*, October 1984.

Frazer, Nancy. *Justice Interruptus: Critical Reflections on the Post-Socialist Condition.* New York and London: Routledge Press, 1997.

Gardiner, Judith. *Provoking Agents: Gender and Agency in Theory and Practice.* Urbana and Chicago: University of Illinois Press, 1995.

Giddings, Paula. *When and Where I Enter: The Impact of Black Women on Race and Sex in America.* New York: Bantam Books, 1984.

Gilkes, Cheryl Townsend. "Building in Many Places: Multiple Commitments and Ideologies in Black Women's Community Work." In *Women and the Politics of Empowerment*, edited by Ann Bookman and Sandra Morgen, 53–76. Philadelphia: Temple University Press, 1988.

———. *If It Wasn't for the Women: Black Women's Experience and Womanist Culture.* Maryknoll: Orbis Books, 2001.

Gilmore, Ruth Wilson. *Golden Gulag: Prisons, Surplus, Crisis, and Opposition in Globalizing California.* Berkeley and Los Angeles: The University of California Press, 2007.

———. "1997 Fatal Couplings of Power and Difference: Notes on Racism and Geography." *The Professional Geographer* 3, no. 25 (2004): 16–24, 17.

———. "Fatal Couplings of Power and Difference: Notes on Racism and Geography." *The Professional Geographer* 54, no. 1 (February 2002): 15–24.

———. "Globalisation and U.S. Prison Growth." *Race and Class* 40, no. 2/3 (1998): 171–188.

Gilroy, Paul. *Postcolonial Melancholia*. New York: Columbia University Press, 2005.

Glenn, Evelyn Nakano. "From Servitude to Servicework: Historical Continuities in the Racial Division of Paid Reproductive Labor." *Signs: Journal of Women and Culture*: 18, no. 1 (1992): 1–43.

Goffman, Erving, *Frame Analysis: An Essay on the Organization of Experience*. Cambridge, MA: Harvard University Press, 1974.

Goldberg, David Theo. *Racial Subjects: Writings on Race in America*. Cambridge: Blackwell Press, 1997.

———. *Threat of Race Reflections on Neoliberalism*. Malden: Wiley-Blackwell, 2009.

Gore, Dayo F., Jeanne Theoharis, and Komozi Woodard. *Want to Start a Revolution? Radical Women in the Black Freedom Struggle*. New York: New York University Press, 2009.

Graham, Ann and Joanna Regulska. "Expanding Political Space for Women in Poland." *Communist and Post Communist Studies* 30, no. 1 (1997): 65–82.

Grant, Judith. *Fundamental Feminism: Contesting the Core Concepts of Feminist Theory*. New York: Routledge Press, 1993.

Grayson, Deborah. "Necessity Was the Midwife of Our Politics: Black Women's Activism in the Post Civil Rights Era (1980–1996)" in *Still Lifting Still Climbing: Contemporay African American Women's Activism*. New York: New York University Press, 1999.

Gregg, Melissa and Gregory J. Seigworth. "An Inventory of Shimmers." In *The Affect Theory Reader*. Edited by Melissa Gregg and Gregory J. Seigworth. Durham: Duke University Press, 2011.

Grosz, Elizabeth. *Space, Time, and Perversion: Essays on the Politics of Bodies*. New York: Routledge Press, 1995.

Gutierrez-Jones, Carl. *Critical Race Narratives: A Study of Race, Rhetoric and Injury*. New York: New York University Press, 2001.

Guy-Sheftall, Beverly. *Daughters of Sorrow: Black Women in United States History*. Brooklyn, NY: Carlson Publishing, 1990.

———. *Words of Fire: An Anthology of African American Feminist Thought*. New York: New York Press, 1995.

Guy-Sheftall, Beverly and Evelynn M. Hammonds. "Wither Black Women's Studies. Interview." *Differences: A Journal of Feminist Cultural Studies* 9, no. 3 (1997): 61–71.

Halberstam, Judith. *In a Queer Time and Place: Transgender Bodies, Subcultural Lives*. New York: New York University Press, 2005.

Hall, Stuart. "Gramsci's Relevance for the Study of Race and Ethnicity" in *Stuart Hall: Critical Dialogues in Cultural Studies*, edited by David Morley and Kuan-Hsing Chen, 411–40. London and New York: Routledge Press, 1997.

Hancock, Ange-Marie. *The Politics of Disgust: The Public Identity of the Welfare Queen*. New York and London: New York University Press, 2004.

———. "When Multiplication Doesn't Equal Quick Addition: Examining Intersectionality as a Research Paradigm." *Perspectives on Politics* 5, no. 1 (2007): 63–69.

———. "Intersectionality, Multiple Messages, and Complex Causality: Commentary on *Black Sexual Politics* by Patricia Hill Collins." *Studies in Gender and Sexuality* 9 (2008): 14–31.

Hanson, Joyce A. *Mary McLeod Bethune and Black Women's Political Activism.* Columbia: University of Missouri Press, 2003.

Harris, Duchess. *Black Feminist Politics from Kennedy to Clinton.* New York: Palgrave-MacMillan Press, 2009.

Harris, Fred R. and Lynn A. Curtis. *Locked in the Poorhouse: Cities, Race and Poverty in the United States.* New York: Rowman and Littlefield Publishers, Inc, 1998.

Harris, Heather., Kimberly Moffitt, and Catherine Squires. *The Obama Effect: Multidisciplinary Renderings of the 2008 Campaign.* New York: SUNY Press, 2010.

Harris-Lacewell, Melissa Victoria. *Barbershop, Bibles and BET: Everyday Talk and Black Political Thought.* Princeton and Oxford: Princeton University Press, 2004.

Harris-Perry, Melissa. *Sister Citizen: Shame, Stereotypes, and Black Women in America (For Colored Girls Who've Consider Politics When Being Strong Isn't Enough).* New Haven and London: Yale University Press, 2011.

Harvey, David. *Spaces of Capital.* New York: Routledge Press, 2001.

Hawkesworth, Mary. "Congressional Enactments of Race-Gender: Toward a Theory of Raced-Gendered Institutions." *American Political Science Review* Vol 97, no. 4 (November 2003): 529–50.

———. *Globalization and Feminist Activism.* Lanham: Rowman & Littlefield, 2006.

Hayden, Tom. *Rebellion in Newark: Official Violence and Ghetto Response.* New York: Random House Press, 1967.

Hernandez, Daisy and Bushra Rehman. *Colonize This! Young Women of Color on Today's Feminism.* New York: Seal Press, 2002.

Hondagneu-Sotello, Pierrette. *Domestica: Immigrant Workers Cleaning and Caring in the Shadows of Affluence.* Berkeley: University of California Press, 2001.

Hong, Grace. "The Future of Our Worlds: Black Feminism and the Politics of Knowledge Under Globalization." *Meridians: Feminisms, Race, Transnationalism* 127, no. 8 (2008): 95–115.

hooks, bell. *Ain't I a Woman: Black Women and Feminism.* Boston: South End Press, 1981.

———. *Yearning: Race, Gender, and Cultural Politics.* Boston: South End Press, 1990.

———. *Belonging: A Culture of Place.* New York and London: Routledge Press, 2009.

Hull, Gloria T., Patricia Bell Scott, and Barbara Smith. *All the Women Are White, All the Blacks Are Men, But Some of Us Are Brave: Black Women's Studies.* Old Westbury, NY: The Feminist Press, 1982.

Hyndman, Jennifer. "Minding the Gap: Bridging Feminist and Political Geography Through Geopolitics." *Political Geography* 23 (2004): 307–22.

Incite! Women of Color Against Violence. *Color of Violence: The Incite! Anthology*. Cambridge: South End Press, 2006.

Ingram, Gordan B., Anne-Marie Bouthillete, and Yolanda Retter. *Queers in Space: Communities, Public Places, Sites of Resistance*. Seattle: The Bay Press, 1997.

Jackson, John L. *Harlemworld: Doing Race and Class in Contemporary America*. Chicago, IL: Chicago University Press, 2001.

———. *Real Black: Adventures in Racial Sincerity*. Chicago: University of Chicago Press, 2005.

Jackson, Kenneth T. *Crabgrass Frontier: The Suburbanization of the United States*. New York: Oxford University Press, 1985.

Jacobson, Matthew. *Whiteness of a Different Color: European Immigrants and Alchemy of Race*. Cambridge: Harvard University Press, 1998.

James, Joy. *Shadowboxing: Representations of Black Feminist Politics*. New York: St. Martins Press, 1999.

James, Stanlie M. and Abena P. A. Busia. *Theorizing Black Feminism*. New York: Routledge Press, 1993.

Jencks, Christopher and Paul Peterson. *The Urban Underclass*. Washington, DC: The Brookings Institute, 1991.

Johnson, E. Patrick. *Appropriating Blackness: Performance and the Politics of Authenticity*. Durham and London: Duke University Press, 2003.

Jones, Lisa. *Bulletproof Diva: Tales of Race, Sex, and Hair*. New York: Double Day Press, 1994.

Kelley, Robin. *Race Rebels: Culture, Politics and the Black Working Class*. New York: Free Press, 1994.

Keyes, Cheryl. "Empowering Self, Making Choices, Creating Spaces: Black Female Identity via Rap Music Performance." *Journal of American Folklore* 113, no. 449 (2000): 259–69.

Kitwana, Bakari. *The Hip-hop Generation: Young Black and the Crisis of African American Culture*. New York: Basic Civitas Books, 2002.

———. *Why White Kids Love Hip-hop: Wangstas, Wiggers, Wannabe and the New Reality of Race in America*. New York: Basic Civitas Books, 2005.

Kukla, Barbara. *Defying the Odds: Triumphant Black Women of Newark*. West Orange, NJ: Swing City Press, 2005.

Kunkel, Jenny and Margit Mayer. *Neoliberal Urbanism and Its Contestations: Crossing Theoretical Borders*. New York: Palgrave-MacMillan Press, 2012.

Kuumba, M. Bahati. "Engendering the Pan-African Movement: Field Notes from the All-African Women's Revolutionary Union," in *Still Lifting, Still Climbing: African American Women's Contemporary Activism*, edited by Kimberly Springer. NY: New York University Press, 1999.

Labaten, Vivian and Dawn Lundy Martin. *The Fire This Time: Young Activists and the New Feminism*. New York: Seal Books, 2004.

Lee, Alston. *Southern Paternalism and the American Welfare State: Economics, Politics, and Institutions in the South (1865–1965)*. New York: Cambridge University Press, 1999.

Lee, Chana Kai. *For Freedom's Sake: The Life of Fannie Lou Hamer.* Urbana and Chicago: University of Illinois Press, 1999.

Lefebvre, Henri. *The Production of Space* translated by Donald Nicholson-Smith. New York: Blackwell Press, 1991.

Leitner, Helga, Jamie Peck, and Eric S. Sheppard. *Contesting Neoliberalism: Urban Frontiers.* New York: The Guilford Press, 2007.

Lorde, Audre. *Sister Outsider: Essays and Speeches.* Trumansburg: Crossings Press, 1984.

Lovenduski, Joni. "Gendering Research in Political Science." *Annual Review of Political Science* 1 (1998): 333–56.

Lowe, Lisa. "The Intimacy of Four Continents" in *Haunted by Empire: Geographies of Intimacy in North American History,* edited by Ann Laura Stoler, 191–212. Durham: Duke University Press, 2006.

Lowe, Setha M. "The Anthropologies of Cities: Imagining and Theorizing the City." *Annual Review of Anthropology* 25 (1996): 383–409.

Lubiano, Wahneema, ed. *The House That Race Built.* US: Pantheon, 1997.

Lucas, Curtis. *Third Ward, Newark.* Chicago: Ziff-Davis Publishing Company, 1946.

Lugones, Maria. *Pilgrimages/Peregrinajes: Theorizing Coalition Against Multiple Oppressions.* Oxford: Rowman & Little Field Publishers, Inc., 2003.

McBride, Dwight. *Why I Hate Abercrombie and Fitch: Essays on Race and Sexuality.* New York and London: New York University Press, 2005.

McDuffie, Erik. *Sojourning for Freedom: Black Women, American Communism and the Making of Black Left Feminism.* Durham: Duke University Press, 2011.

McGoldrick, Neale and Margaret Crocco. *Reclaiming Lost Ground in New Jersey: The Struggle for Woman Suffrage in New Jersey.* Publisher Unknown, 1993.

McKittrick, Katherine. *Demonic Grounds: Black Women and the Cartographies of Struggle.* Minneapolis: University of Minnesota Press, 2006.

McKittrick, Katherine and Clyde Woods. *Black Geographies and the Politics of Place.* Boston: South End Press, 2007.

Mandel, Jay R. *The Roots of Black Poverty: The Southern Plantation Economy.* Durham: Duke University Press, 1978.

Mansbridge, Jane. *Beyond Adversary Democracy.* Chicago: The University of Chicago Press, 1980.

Mansbridge, Jane and Aldon Morris. *Oppositional Consciousness: The Subjective Roots of Social Protest.* Chicago: The University of Chicago Press, 2001.

Marable, Manning. *Race, Reform and Rebellion: The Second Reconstruction in Black America, 1945–1990.* Jackson and London: University Press of Mississippi, 1991.

Marston, Sallie. "The Social Construction of Scale." *Progress in Human Geography* 24, no. 2 (2000).

Marston, Sallie and Neil Smith. "States, Scales and Households: Limits to Scale Thinking? A Response to Brenner in Progress." In *Human Geography* 25, no. 4 (2001): 615–19.

Massey, Douglas and Nancy A. Denton. *American Apartheid: Segregation and the Making of the Underclass.* Cambridge: Harvard University Press, 1993.

Maynes, Mary Jo, Jennifer Pierce, and Barbara Laslet. *Telling Stories: The Use of Personal Narratives in the Social Sciences and History.* Ithaca: Cornell University Press, 2008.

Moe, Terry. *The Organization of Interests.* Chicago: The University of Chicago Press, 1980.

Moghadam, Valentine. *Globalization and Social Movements: Islamism, Feminism, and the Global Justice Movement.* New York: Rowman and Littlefield, 2009.

Mohanty, Chandra. *Feminism Without Borders: Decolonizing Theory, Practicing Solidarity.* Durham and London: Duke University Press, 2003.

Moore, Mignon. "Lipstick or Timberlands? The Meaning of Gender Presentation in Black Lesbian Communities." *Signs: Journal of Women in Culture and Society,* 32, no. 1 (2006):113–39.

Moraga, Cherríe and Gloria Anzuldúa. *This Bridge Called My Back: Writings by Radical Women of Color.* New York: Kitchen Table Press, 1983.

Morgan, Joan. *When Chickenheads Come Home to Roost: A Hip-Hop Feminist Breaks It Down.* New York and London: Simon and Schuster, 1999.

Morris, Aldon. *The Origins of the Civil Rights Movement: Black Communities Organizing for Change.* New York: Free Press. 1984.

Moya, Paula. "Reclaiming Identity." In *Reclaiming Identity: Realist Theory and the Predicament of the Postmodern,* edited by Paula M. L. Moya and Michael R. Hames-Garcia, 67–101. Berkeley: University of California Press, 2000.

Mullings, Leith. *Cities of the United States: Studies in Urban Anthropology.* New York: Columbia University Press, 1987.

———. *On Our Own Terms: Race, Gender and Class in the Lives of African American Women.* New York: Routledge, 1997.

Mumford, Kevin. *Newark: A History of Race, Rights, and Riots in America.* New York: New York University Press, 2007.

Nagar, Richa. "Communal Discourses, Marriage and the Politics of Gendered Social Boundaries among South Asian Immigrants in Tanzania." *Gender, Place and Culture,* 5, no. 2 (2004): 117–40.

Naples, Nancy. *Grassroots Warriors: Activist Mothering, Community Work and the War on Poverty.* New York: Routledge, 1998.

———. "Changing the Terms: Community Activism, Globalization, and the Dilemmas of Transnational Feminist Praxis in *Women's Activism and Globalization: Linking Local Struggles and Transnational Politics* edited by Nancy A. Naples and Manisha Desai. New York and London: Routledge Press, 2002.

Nash, Jennifer C. "Rethinking Intersectionality." *Feminist Review,* Issue 89 (2008): 1–15.

Neal, Mark Anthony. *Soul Babies: Black Culture and The Post-Soul Aesthetic.* New York and London: Routlegdge Press, 2002.

———. *New Black Man.* New York and London: Routledge Press, 2005.

Nelson, Jennifer. *Women of Color and the Reproductive Rights Movement.* New York and London: New York University Press, 2003.

O'Conner Alice, Chris Tilly, and Lawrence Bobo. *Urban Inequality: Evidence from Four Cities.* New York: Sage Publications, 2001.

Oakes, Tim and Louisa Schein. *"Translocal China: An Introduction"* in *Translocal China, Linkages, Identities, and the Reimagining of Space.* New York and London: Routledge Press, 2006.

Olson, Mancur. *The Logic of Collective Action.* New York: Basic Books, 1965.

Omi, Michael and Howard Winant. *Racial Formation in the United States: From the 1960's to the 1980's.* New York: Routledge and Kegan Paul, 1986.

Orleck, Annelise. *Storming Caesar's Palace: How Black Mothers Fought Their Own War on Poverty.* Boston: Beacon Press, 2005.

Osumare, Halifu. *The Africanist Aesthetic in Hip Hop: Power Moves.* New York: Palgrave MacMillan Press, 2007.

Parenti, Michael. "Power and Pluralism: A View from the Bottom." *Journal of Politics* 32, no. 3 (August 1970): 501–30.

Parmar, Prathiba. "Black Feminism and the Politics of Articulation" in *Identity: Community, Culture, Difference* edited by J. Rutherford. London: Lawrence and Wishart Press, 1991.

Payne, Charles. *I've Got the Light of Freedom: The Organizing Tradition and the Mississippi Freedom Struggle.* Berkeley: The University of California Press. 1995.

Peck, Jamie and Adam Tickell. "Neoliberalizing Space" in *Antipode* 34, no. 3 (2002): 380–404.

———. "Conceptualizing Neoliberalism, Thinking Thatcherism." in *Contesting Neoliberalism: Urban Frontiers* edited by Helga Leitner, Jamie Peck, and Eric S. Sheppard. New York: Guilford Press, 2007.

Peoples, Whitney A. "Under Construction: Identifying Foundations of Hip Hop Feminism and Exploring Bridges Between Black and Hip Hop Feminism" in *Meridians: feminism, race, transnationalism* 8, no. 1 (2008): 19–52.

Portes, Alejandro. "Two Meanings of Social Capital." *Sociological Forum* 15, no. 1 (2000): 1–12.

Portes, Alejandro and Ruben Rumbaut. *Immigrant America: A Portrait.* Berkeley: University of California Press, 1990.

Pough, Gwendolyn. *Check It While I Wreck It: Black Womanhood, Hip-Hip Culture and the Public Sphere.* Boston: Northwestern University Press, 2004.

Price, Clement Alexander. *Freedom Not Far Distant: A Documentary History of Afro-Americans in New Jersey.* New Jersey: A Joint Project of the New Jersey Historical Society and the New Jersey Historical Commission, 1975.

———. *To Form a Society in the State of New-Jersey, to Cooperate with the American Colonization Society.* Newark, NJ: The New Jersey Historical Society, 1980.

Puar, Jasbir. *Terrorists Assemblages: Homonationalism in Queer Times.* Durham: Duke University Press, 2007.

Pulido, Laura. *Black, Brown, Yellow, and Left: Radical Activism in Los Angeles.* Berkeley: University of California Press, 2006.

Putnam, Robert. *Making Democracy Work: Civic Traditions in Modern Italy.* Princeton, NJ: Princeton University Press, 1993.

Radford-Hill, Sheila. *Further to Fly: Black Women and the Politics of Empowerment.* Minneapolis, MN: Minnesota Press, 2000.

Ransby, Barbara. "Behind the Scenes View of the Behind the Scenes Organizer: The Roots of Ella Baker's Political Passions." In *Sisters in the Struggle: African American Women in the Civil Rights-Black Power Movement,* edited by Bettye Collier-Thomas and V. P. Franklin, 42–58. New York: New York University Press. 2001.

———. *Ella Baker and the Black Freedom Movement: A Radical Democratic Vision.* Chapel Hill: The University of North Carolina Press, 2003.

Rich, Adrienne. "Compulsory Heterosexuality and Lesbian Existence." Denver: Antelope Publications, 1980.

Rich, Wilbur C. *Black Mayor and School Politics: The Failure of Reform in Detroit, Gary and Newark.* New York and London: Garland Publishers, Inc., 1996.

Rodgers-Rose, La Francis. *The Black Woman.* Beverly Hills: Sage Publications, 1980.

Rodriguez, Juana Maria. *Queer Latinidad: Identity Practices, Discursive Spaces.* New York: New York University Press, 2003.

Rose, Tricia. *Black Noise: Rap Music and Black Culture in Contemporary America.* Middletown: Wesleyan University Press, 1994.

Ryan, Barbara. *Identity Politics in the Women's Movement.* New York: New York University Press. 2001.

Sacks, Karen. "Gender and Grassroots Leadership." In *Women and the Politics of Empowerment,* edited by Ann Bookman and Sandra Morgen, 77–96. Philadelphia: Temple University Press, 1988.

Sandoval, Chela. *Methodology of the Oppressed: Theory Out of Bounds.* Minneapolis: University of Minnesota Press, 2000.

Sassen, Saskia. *Global Networks, Linked Cities.* New York: Routledge 2002.

Scott, Joan W. "Experience." In *Feminists Theorize the Political* edited by Judith Butler and Joan W. Scott. New York and London: Routledge Press, 1992.

Seigworth, Gregory J. and Melissa Gregg. "An Inventory of Shimmers" in *The Affect Theory Reader,* 1–28. Durham: Duke University Press, 2011.

Sheppard, Eric and McMaster, Robert B. "Introduction: Scale and Geographic Inquiry." In *Scale and Geographic Inquiry: Nature, Society and Method* edited by Eric Sheppard and Robert B. McMaster, 1–22. Oxford: Blackwell Publishers, 2004.

Shukla, Sandhya. "Feminism of the Diaspora Both Local and Global: The Politics of South Asian Women Against Domestic Violence." In *Women Transforming Politics,* edited by Cathy Cohen, Kathleen B. Jones and Joan C. Tronto, 269–83. New York: New York University Press. 1997.

Simien, Evelyn M. *Black Feminist Voices in Politics.* Albany: State University of New York Press, 2006.

Simpson, Andrea. *The Tie that Binds: Identity and Political Attitudes in the Post-Civil Rights Generation.* New York and London: New York University Press, 1998.

Skocpol, Theda and Fiorina, Morris P. *Civic Engagement in American Democracy.* Washington, DC: Brookings Institution Press, 1999.

Smith, Andrea. *Sexual Violence and the American Indian Genocide.* Boston: South End Press, 2005.

Smith, Barbara. *Homegirls: A Black Feminist Anthology.* New York: Kitchen Table Press, 1983.

———. *The Truth that Never Hurts: Writings on Race, Gender and Freedom.* New Brunswick: Rutgers University Press, 1998.

Smith, Barbara Ellen. *Neither Separate nor Equal: Women, Race and Class in the South.* Philadelphia: Temple University Press, 1999.

Smith, Linda Tuhiwai. *Decolonizing Methodologies: Research and Indigenous Peoples.* Dunedin: University of Otago Press, 1999; New York: St. Martins Press, 1999.

Smith, Valerie. *Not Just Race, Not Just Gender: Black Feminist Readings.* New York and London: Routledge, 1998.

Smooth, Wendy and Tamelyn Tucker. "Behind But Not Forgotten: Women and the Behind the Scenes Organizing of the Million Man March." In *Still Lifting, Still Climbing: African American Women's Contemporary Activism*, edited by Kimberly Springer, 241–58. New York: New York University Press, 1999.

Somerville, Siobhan B. *Queering the Color Line: Race and the Invention of Homosexuality in American Culture.* Durham: Duke University Press, 2000.

Soja, Edward W. *Thirdspace: Journeys to Los Angeles and Other Real and Imagined Places.* Maldon, MA: Blackwell Publishers, 1996.

Spence, Lester. *Stare in the Darkness: The Limits of Hip Hop and Black Politics.* Minneapolis: University of Minnesota Press, 2011.

Springer, Kimberly. *Living for the Revolution: Black Feminist Organizations 1968–1980.* Durham: Duke University Press, 2005.

———. *Still Lifting, Still Climbing: Contemporary African American Women's Activism.* New York and London: New York University Press, 1999.

———. Third Wave Black Feminism? *Signs: Journal of Women in Culture and Society* 27, no. 4 (2002).

Squires, Catherine. *African Americans and the Media.* Malden: Polity Press, 2009.

Stephens, Dionne P. and Layli D. Phillips. "Freaks, Gold-diggers, Divas and Dykes: The Sociohistorical Development of Adolescent African American Women's Sexual Scripts." *Sexuality and Culture* 7, no. 1 (Winter 2003): 3–47.

Stimson, James A. *Public Opinion in America: Moods, Cycles and Swings.* Boulder, CO: Westview Press, 1999.

Stockton, Kathryn Bond. *Beautiful Bottom, Beautiful Shame: Where "Black" Meets "Queer."* Durham: Duke University Press, 2006.

Stoler, Ann Laura. "Tense and Tender Ties: The Politics of Comparison in North American History" in *Haunted by Empire: Geographies of Intimacy in North American History*, edited by Ann Laura Stoler, 23–70. Durham: Duke University Press, 2006.

Sudbury, Julia. *Other Kinds of Dreams: Black Women's Organizations and the Politics of Transformation.* New York and London: Routledge, 1998.

Sugrue, Thomas J. *The Origins of Urban Crisis: Race and Inequality in Postwar Detroit.* New Jersey: Princeton University Press, 1996.

Swyngedouw, Erik. "Scaled Geographies: Nature, Place and the Politics of Scale." In *Scale and Geographic Inquiry: Nature, Society and Method*, edited by Eric Sheppard and Robert B. MacMaster, 1–22. Oxford: Blackwell Publishers, 2004.

Tate, Gayle. *Unknown Tongues: Black Women's Political Activism in the Antebellum Era, 1830–1860.* Lansing: Michigan State University Press, 2003.

Tate, Greg. *Everything But The Burden: What White People Are Taking From Black Culture.* New York: Broadway Books, 2003.

Tate, Katherine. *From Protest to Politics: The New Black Voters in American Elections.* New York and Cambridge: Russell Sage Foundation and Harvard University Press, 1993.

Taylor, Peter J. "Places, Spaces and Macy's: Place-Space Tensions in the Political Geography of Modernities." *Progress in Human Geography* 23, no. 1 (1999): 7–26.

Terborg-Penn, Rosalyn. *African American Women in the Struggle for the Vote, 1850–1920.* Bloomington and Indianapolis: Indiana University Press, 1998.

Thornton Dill, Bonnie and Ruth Enid Zambrana (eds). *Emerging Intersections: Race, Class, and Gender in Theory, Policy, and Practice.* New Jersey: Rutgers University Press, 2009.

Torres, Eden. *Chicana Without Apology: The New Chicana Cultural Studies.* New York: Routledge Press, 2003.

Townsend-Bell, Erica. "What is Relevance? Defining Intersectional Praxis in Uruguay." *Political Research Quarterly* 64, no. 1 (2011): 187–99.

Tronto, Joan. *Moral Boundaries: Argument for An Ethic of Care.* New York: Routledge Press, 1993.

Tuttle, Brad R. *How Newark Became Newark: The Rise, Fall and Rebirth of an American City.* New Brunswick: Rutgers University Press, 2009.

Twine, Frances Winddance and Jonathan W. Warren. *Racing Research, Researching Race: Methodological Dilemmas in Critical Race Studies*, edited edition. New York: New York University Press, 2000.

Vaz, Kim Marie. *Black Women in America.* Thousand Oaks, CA, Sage Publications, 1995.

Vaz, Kim Marie. *Oral Narrative Research with Black Women.* Thousand Oaks, CA: Sage Publications, 1997.

Verba, Sidney, Kay Lehman Schlozman and Henry Brady. *Voice and Equality: Civic Voluntarism in American Politics.* Cambridge: Harvard University Press, 1995.

Vliegenthart, Rens and Leisbet van Zoonen. "Power to the Frame: Bringing Sociology Back to Frame Analysis." *European Journal of Communication* 26 (2011): 101.

Wacquant, L. J. D. "A Black City Within the White: Revisiting America's Dark Ghetto." *Black Renaissance/Renaissance Noir* 2, no. 1 (1998): 141–151.

———. "For an Analytic of Racial Domination." *Political Power and Social Theory* 11 (1997): 221–34.

Walcott, Rinaldo. "Homopoetics: Queer Space and the Black Queer Diaspora." In *Black Geographies and the Politics of Place* edited by Katherine McKittrick and Clyde Woods. Cambridge: South End Press, 2007.

Walters, Ronald W. *Black Presidential Politics in America: A Strategic Approach.* New York: State University of New York Press, 1988.

———. *Freedom is Not Enough: Black Candidates, Black Voters, and American Presidential Politics.* Lanham: Rowman and Littlefield, 2005.

Walton, Hanes. *Invisible Politics: Black Political Behavior.* Albany: State University of New York Press, 1985.

———. *Black Women at the United Nations.* San Bernardino, CA: The Borgo Press, 1995.

———. *African American Power and Politics: The Political Context Variable.* New York: Columbia University Press, 1997.

Wanzo, Rebecca. *The Suffering Will Not Be Televised: African American Women and Sentimental Political Storytelling.* New York: SUNY Press, 2009.

Ward, Brian. *Just My Soul Responding: Rhythm and Blues, Black Consciousness, and Race Relations.* Berkeley: University of California Press, 1998.

Ward, Geoff. *The Black Child-Savers: Racial Democracy and Juvenile Justice.* Chicago and London: University of Chicago Press, 2012.

Watkins, Craig S. *Hip-hop Matters: Politics, Pop Culture and the Struggle for the Soul of a Movement.* Boston: Beacon Press, 2005.

Weber, Lynn. *Understanding Race, Class, Gender, and Sexuality.* New York and Oxford: Oxford University Press, 2010.

White, Deborah Gray. *Too Heavy a Load: Black Women in Defense of Themselves.* New York and London: W. W. Norton and Company, 1999.

White, E. Frances. *The Dark Continent of Our Bodies: Black Women and the Politics of Responsibility.* Philadelphia: Temple University Press, 2001.

Wilson, James Q. *Political Organizations.* New York: Basic Books, 1973.

Williams, Rhonda Y. *The Politics of Public Housing: Black Women's Struggle Against Urban Equality.* New York: Oxford University Press, 2004.

Wilson, William Julius. *When Work Disappears: The World of the New Urban Poor.* New York: Vintage Press, 1996.

———. *More Than Just Race: Being Black and Poor in the Inner City.* New York and London: W. W. Norton and Company Press, 2009.

Wing, Adrienne Katherine. *Global Critical Race Feminism: An International Reader*. New York: New York University Press, 2000.

Winters, Stanley B. *Newark, An Assessment 1967–1977*. Newark: The New Jersey Institute of Technology, 1978.

Woodard, Komozi. *A Nation Within a Nation: Amiri Baraka (LeRoi Jones) and Black Power Politics*. Chapel Hill and London: The University of North Carolina Press, 1999.

Yanow, Dvora. "How Built Spaces Mean: A Semiotics of Space." In *Interpretation and Method: Empirical Research and the Interpretative Turn*, edited by Dvora Yanow and Peregrine Schwartz-Shea. Armonk, NY: M. E. Sharpe, 2006.

Yeatman, Anna. *Postmodern Revisionings of the Political*. New York and London: Routledge Press, 1994.

Yin, Robert K. *Case Study Research: Design and Methods*. Thousand Oaks, CA: Sage Publications, 1994.

Yuval-Davis, Nira. *The Situated Politics of Belonging*. Thousand Oaks, CA: Sage Publications, 2006.

———. "Intersectionality and Feminist Politics." In *The Intersectional Approach: Transforming the Academy Through Race, Class and Gender*, edited by Michele Tracy Berger and Kathleen Guidroz, 44–60. Chapel Hill: University of North Carolina Press, 2009.

Zaller, John R. *The Nature and Origins of Mass Opinion*. Cambridge, UK: Cambridge University Press, 1992.

Zukin, Sharon. *The Culture of Cities*. Cambridge: Blackwell Publishers, 1995.

———. "How Bad Is It? Institutions and Intentions in the Study of the American Ghetto." *International Journal of International and Regional Research* 22, no. 3 (1998): 511–21.

———. "Urban Lifestyles: Diversity and Standarization in Spaces of Consumption." *Urban Studies* 35, no. 5–6 (1998): 825–40.

INDEX